Praise for *Lessons of Lifelong Intimacy*

"*Lessons of Lifelong Intimacy* is a practical, engaging, and highly readable book that will help any couple dig deep into the sacred gift of marriage and fathom its grace, joy, love, and hope. Everyone wants a great marriage. Michael shows us how."

—Rev. Tim Wright, author of *Searching for Tom Sawyer*

"In this important book, backed up by convincing scientific evidence, therapist Michael Gurian provides a relational road map that can help any couple navigate the journey of lifelong intimacy and separateness that makes love possible. Read it yourself and give it to your friends and family and those you counsel psychologically or spiritually. Everyone will be blessed by its insights."

—William M. Watson, SJ, DMin, president/founder: Sacred Story Institute, author of *Forty Weeks* and *The Sacred Story*

"Whether you are single, newly married, or an old-timer, this book will bring light to the complex and mysterious world of love and marriage. And what's even better, it will deepen the understanding of life's most important relationship—the one we have with ourselves. Thank you, Michael Gurian, for a practical, passionate, and inspiring manual on love!"

—Dr. Shimi Kang, psychiatrist and author of *The Self-Motivated Kid*

Previous Books by Michael Gurian

PSYCHOLOGY

The Wonder of Aging

How Do I Help Him?

What Could He Be Thinking?

Love's Journey

The Invisible Presence (previously published as *Mothers, Sons, and Lovers*)

The Prince and the King

CHILD DEVELOPMENT AND PARENTING

The Purpose of Boys

The Wonder of Girls

The Wonder of Boys

Raising Boys by Design (with Gregory L. Jantz, PhD, and Ann McMurray)

A Fine Young Man

The Good Son

What Stories Does My Son Need? (with Terry Trueman)

Nurture the Nature

It's a Baby Boy! (by the Gurian Institute, with
Adrian Goldberg, ACSW, and Stacie Bering, MD)

It's a Baby Girl! (by the Gurian Institute, with
Adrian Goldberg, ACSW, and Stacie Bering, MD)

EDUCATION

The Minds of Boys (with Kathy Stevens)

Boys and Girls Learn Differently! (with Kathy
Stevens, Patricia Henley, Terry Trueman)

The Boys and Girls Learn Differently Action Guide for Teachers (with Arlette C. Ballew)

Strategies for Teaching Boys and Girls—Elementary Level (with Kathy Stevens, Kelley King)

Strategies for Teaching Boys and Girls—Secondary Level (with Kathy Stevens, Kelley King)

Successful Single-Sex Classrooms (with Kathy Stevens, Peggy Daniels)

SPIRITUALITY

The Wonder of Children (previously published as *The Soul of the Child*)

Ancient Wisdom, Modern Words: Prayers, Poems, and Readings

The Sabbath: Poems and Prayers

BUSINESS-CORPORATE

The Leading Partners Workbook (with Katherine Coles, Kathy Stevens)

Leadership and the Sexes (with Barbara Annis)

FOR YOUNG ADULT READERS

Understanding Guys

From Boys to Men

FICTION AND POETRY

The Miracle

An American Mystic

The Odyssey of Telemachus

LESSONS

OF

LIFELONG INTIMACY

Building a Stronger Marriage Without
Losing Yourself—The 9 Principles of a
Balanced and Happy Relationship

MICHAEL GURIAN

ATRIA BOOKS

New York   London   Toronto   Sydney   New Delhi

Readers should be aware that Internet websites offered as citations and/or sources for further information may have changed or disappeared between the time they were read and the time this book was published. Some of the anecdotes in this book, including some gathered from media reports, are composites of two or more comments or stories that were edited for narrative flow. In no cases have meanings been changed, and no changes involved changes in statistics. In all case studies in this book, names and identifying details have been changed.

Original pieces by Michael Gurian are copyright Michael Gurian, all rights reserved, and used with the author's permission.

ATRIA BOOKS
An Imprint of Simon & Schuster, Inc.
1230 Avenue of the Americas
New York, NY 10020

First Atria Books hardcover edition May 2015

ATRIA BOOKS and colophon are trademarks of Simon & Schuster, Inc.

For information about special discounts for bulk purchases, please contact Simon & Schuster Special Sales at 1-866-506-1949 or business@simonandschuster.com.

The Simon & Schuster Speakers Bureau can bring authors to your live event. For more information or to book an event, contact the Simon & Schuster Speakers Bureau at 1-866-248-3049 or visit our website at www.simonspeakers.com.

Designed by Kyoko Watanabe

Manufactured in the United States of America

10 9 8 7 6 5 4 3 2 1

Library of Congress Cataloging-in-Publication Data

Gurian, Michael.
 Lessons of lifelong intimacy : building a stronger marriage without losing yourself —9 principles of a balanced and happy relationship / by Michael Gurian.
    pages cm
1. Marital quality. 2. Intimacy (Psychology) 3. Married people—Psychology. 4. Interpersonal conflict. 5. Interpersonal relations. 6. Marriage—Psychological aspects. I. Title.
 HQ734.G88475 2015
 158.2—dc23
                              2014045291

ISBN 978-1-4767-5604-2
ISBN 978-1-4767-5606-6 (ebook)

For Gail, Gabrielle, and Davita

Human beings have a common nature, a set of shared
unconscious tendencies or potentialities that are encoded
in our DNA and that evolved because they were of use to our
forebears millions of years ago. We are not aware of these
predispositions, but they still motivate our actions. . . .

—HELEN FISHER, PHD, AUTHOR OF *ANATOMY OF LOVE*

In love, it would be so much easier if we could just remain self-
contained and establish an impeccable set of conditions to protect
us from risk . . . or, on the other hand, completely lose ourselves
in merging together with our partner. Yet both these alternatives
undermine love, for they destroy the tension between self and
other, known and unknown, that love actually thrives on.

—JOHN WELWOOD, PHD, AUTHOR OF *LOVE AND AWAKENING*

Contents

PART II

Practicing the Art of Intimate Separateness

The Surprising Secret of Love

The truth dazzles gradually, or else the world would be blind.

—Emily Dickinson

Ben and I walked together on a side street near my office. Some men just need to be moving around physically in order to reach deeply inward and find their voice. Ben, thirty-six, is one of those men. His marriage of seven years appears to be failing even though he and Amy, thirty-five, have just had a baby girl. As we walk, Ben says, "No matter what we do, we fight. We just may not be right for each other. What should I do?" he asks. "I don't know what to do." Over the weekend, Amy asked him to move out of their apartment, which he did. This is the second time in five years that they have separated. Amy has not kept today's counseling appointment, but Ben decided to keep it.

As we walk I respond by challenging Ben, "What do *you* think is missing in your relationship? What do *you* think you and Amy should do?" He, Amy, and I have discussed the difficulties in the marriage, and at least on the surface, both people do know what is missing and what to do. He breathes in deeply, sighs as he lets air out, then keeps silent for a while. Finally he says, "Yes, okay, I know what's going on. Amy knows. But doing something about it may be too hard. I'm not sure if we're too far gone to save us from just becoming another divorce statistic. I'm not sure if it isn't all too complicated."

I don't respond. We keep walking. He thinks things through. As we circle back to my office, he is still internally processing. When we arrive back at my office, we talk more and I give him some relationship homework, letting him know that I see hope for him and Amy. He promises to return to counseling, and he hopes Amy will return with him (which she does three weeks later). Months pass and the couple does not divorce. In the fourth month of therapy, things seem to have changed for the better. Ben moves back into their apartment. He and Amy become happier. They have conflicts, but less rancorous ones— conflicts that now involve less overreaction than before and that are more protective than before of the couple's love.

The three of us meet again on a Friday that is clement enough for another walk. We move together through the side streets and up to a park near my office. We sit on the grass, pigeons coming around looking for handouts.

I ask, "Are you glad you did these months of work?"

Amy nods. "I'm glad. It's subtle, and it's difficult, but it's good. We can see what's going on now. Hopefully we'll be on guard from now on so we don't fall back into the bad stuff." I nod and she says something that reflects how deeply she and Ben have understood a secret to remaining in love: "From now on we'll know how to avoid being too close for comfort." She and Ben have seen something about both "intimacy" and "separateness" that may well ensure a long-lasting marriage. Months ago, an attorney and a reader of popular magazines that constantly provide tips for being more intimate with a lover, she told me she found it "just plain weird" (her words) that a marriage and family counselor would tell a couple having difficulty with intimacy that they were "too close." Gradually, however, she has come to agree with the observation, as her comment today indicates.

I ask Ben if he can verbalize his understanding of what has happened in counseling and his marriage. Ben articulates his thoughts this way: "We need balance. When we take each other for granted, that's bad, but when we get too close, we get scared and just generally make mayhem." A physician's assistant, Ben is also an avid comic book and graphic novel reader. The word "mayhem" doesn't sound old-fashioned in his voice; rather, it helps him articulate how he and Amy become with one another when they do damage to their marriage.

The Counterintuitive Insight

Sigmund Freud famously mused, "Everywhere I go in psychology, the poets have been there before me." In no area of focus might his observation be more universal than in the subject of love. Every poet has touched on it, as has, perhaps, every psychologist, so that if one reads millennia of literature, from the Song of Solomon and the Bhagavad Gita to the songs of Jay-Z or Ingrid Michaelson, from the writings of Freud and Jung to the advice of columnists in *Cosmopolitan*, the complexity of love is obvious. At least on the surface, a reader of poetry, psychological literature, and popular wisdom could come to believe that being in love and staying in love happen if we make sure to remain intimate. Often unknown to us is an equally useful secret to love hidden in all our poetic history, as well as the much newer field of psychology, and this is a secret that can feel counterintuitive until it is fully realized.

Like nearly every couple does at some point in their relationship, Amy and Ben had become so intimate with one another that they were forced into a power struggle, with resulting relational damage. My work with them was very much about helping them remain married via a balance of intimacy and separateness so that they did not become, as Ben had put it, "a divorce statistic."

Facts to Ponder

While divorce is often quite necessary—it can breathe new life into our relationships, our identities, and our futures (and if we are in danger at our partner's hands, it can save our lives)—still, statistics around divorce give us a clue to something we are missing about human love in the new millennium.

- Approximately one in two American marriages ends in divorce.

- The majority of people who go through a divorce do not report increased relational happiness one year after their divorce. They have solved some problems by divorcing, but within one to two years they feel many problems unsolved, and they often feel a huge loss of love.

- Fifty percent of the recorded divorces occur between four and seven years after the wedding.

- While in just over 10 percent of cases of marital dissolution there was significant addiction, abuse, mental illness, severe personality disorder, infidelity, and/or violence in the marriage, most divorces do not involve significant danger to children, spouse, or self. The ongoing pain of "lack of emotional fulfillment" is the most commonly expressed reason for divorce—a lack of satisfying affection in the bond of love felt in the coupled relationship by one or both people and accompanied by constant fighting and/or severe distancing.

The anthropologist Margaret Mead said, "I have been married and divorced three times and not one of them was a failure." She was right. Divorce is not itself a failure, but looking at divorce gives us a lantern we can shine onto something missed in our marriage, relationships,

and romance-oriented culture today. We've searched for and sometimes found, but just as often neglected, the secret to long-lasting love.

Redefining Intimacy

This book will gradually teach the idea and process of *intimate separateness*. Intimate separateness is the daily balance of two equally
necessary components of natural human attachment, intimacy and
separateness. If either is neglected, love will fail. Our culture tends to
focus almost exclusively on closeness (what we tend to call "intimacy"
and "romance"), so much so that millions of couples lack the balance
of closeness and *psychological separateness* necessarily for long-lasting
love. On wedding days, we promise to "be one with each other from
now on," but that oneness is only a part of love; and in many months
or years of the marriage, the unbalanced search for the oneness of intimacy will actually doom the relationship.

Intimate separateness was, I believe, the age-old balanced form of
love that our ancestors discovered unconsciously. To think about this,
take a moment to recall your genetic family lines (go back at least one
hundred years): those ancestors will have stayed married for reasons
of *physical survival, religious edict, economic need,* and/or *pressure from
social norms.* While, in many cases, these marital glues encouraged
marriages in which gender power was not equal, our ancestors had an
advantage we don't have as regards long-lasting love: on their wedding
day, because of the four factors listed above, our ancestors' access to
love was somewhat protected for life. If it took them many years to
discover how to be happy together, that was fine—they had those years
to burn because they were not going to divorce. Thus, our ancestors
did not have to consciously discover and practice, within the first few
years of their marriage, the secret to marital longevity; their lack of access to divorce ensured they would discover the secret someday.

We, today, do not have this luxury. We have to discover and
practice *consciously* the secret our ancestors practiced relatively *unconsciously.* We have to *choose* intimate separateness *a million times in*

a marriage. Thankfully (painfully, it will seem, for a while, until we understand it) our love, attachment, and intimacy with our partner will provide us multiple opportunities for that choosing—in a twelve-stage cycle of love we will explore in this book. To love well—to reach the rewarding later stages of love—we need to change our paradigm for what love really is. We have to:

1. take a conscious *thinking* step forward in our marriages regarding how we love; and
2. engage in a practical process of *doing, acting,* and *practicing* intimate separateness in daily life.

To these two ends, this book has been crafted so that you can use its insights and process in whatever of the twelve love-stages your relationship, romance, partnership, or marriage is in. You can also use it if you are divorced, and even if you have decided never to marry or remarry. Because intimate separateness is a paradigm reflecting a natural part of human growth (locked into the limbic brain, as we'll see in scientific research), you can discover and use it no matter your circumstance.

Clinical Research in the Science of Love

A marriage and family counselor in my twenty-fifth year of private practice, I am also a husband of twenty-nine years and father of two grown daughters. I have practiced what I preach in this book, but the philosophy and methodology in these pages grow primarily from both scientific research and my observation of attachment needs in more than five hundred client cases. Some of these clients—with various details altered to protect privacy—will appear in this book. You'll also meet couples and individuals who have responded to our Gurian Institute surveys, focus groups, and clinical work, as we have worked in hundreds of communities to train professionals, lead workshops, and launch pilot programs. And you'll meet couples I have interviewed, as well as scientists and other experts who provide foundational information on how love works now, in the new millennium, with a specific lens on intimacy and separateness.

The secret explored in this book takes at least a few months to install in your marriage, and it represents an experiential road map for healthy, successful bonding ("resilient pair-bonding" is the clinical term) over the life span. When a couple like Amy and Ben does the work of altering its method of attachment to include equal parts intimacy *and separateness*, the couple discovers the secret to long-lasting love. Ben and Amy were able to do this over a period of six months, and it saved their marriage. They committed to doing many of the surveys, experiential work, and best practices in this book. From working with them and other couples you'll meet as this book unfolds, I have developed the teachable process that appears in each chapter. But to be clear, this is not a rigid diet for which someone tells you exactly what to do. Instead, it will constantly need *you* to modify it to fit *your* circumstance. I'll help you do that throughout our journey together.

As you explore and engage intimate separateness, the fact that the word "intimate" modifies "separateness" is important. Notice that "separateness" is the noun; "intimate" is the adjective. Without the noun where would the adjective go? What would it modify? The point is, without separateness (in all its simplicity and complexity) there will be much less love and intimacy for us past the seven-year or so mark of a relationship or marriage. Closeness is essential to love, yes. But the secret we've missed—not studied, and not mastered as individuals, couples, and a romance-oriented culture—is the secret of intimate separateness. This is the insight and process we'll unpack and activate in this book.

However, there is a caveat: if you are in the first year or two of your present relationship, this book's map of love will mainly be a map of the future, not the present. The reason is almost wholly biological: in the first weeks to about two years of a relationship with a lover (which constitutes the first of twelve stages of love we'll look at in Chapter 4), our two brains are neurologically, biochemically, and psychologically directed toward "intense passion," "you are mine, baby," "we are soul mates," and "you are more beautiful than love itself." This amazing sensorial, emotional, and sexual intimacy, without balanced separateness, is necessary for the neurochemistry of attachment and pair-bonding to get set in the limbic system and, thus, throughout the brain "for life." Not until the next eleven stages of couple attachment does *intimate separateness* become essential, and the subtle journey of psychological separateness will need to become a deep and abiding friend to our love if we want it to last.

Getting Started: Twenty Essential Questions

Before you turn to the first chapter of this book, consider taking a moment to set up a journal in a physical notebook, on your computer or tablet, or via voice recorder. This journaling—in whatever form you feel like doing it—can help you in three ways:

- It can help you become a "love-scientist," a steady, careful observer of your own and your partner's pair-bonding methodology—becoming a careful student of *your* subtle ways of love is essential to the insight and practice advocated in this book.

- Its activities can help you create a more satisfying relationship on a daily basis through experiential work during the months of this journey—those months of altered practice will then constitute a "new normal" and help you develop and maintain new habits for your relationship. Even if your relationship is in a very happy and satisfying state right now, you won't regret doing this—all relationships face hardships at some point, and you'll be ready.

- It can become a permanent artifact of your love, a personal "bible" for how *you* live out your love relationship. You and your partner can share it as the years go by, including referring back to it when you may have recurring issues in the future.

Essential Questions Survey 1: Assessing Your Present Relationship

Answer these twenty questions as you study your present relationship. If you are not in a love relationship right now, think back to your previous one.

- Do I/we get triggered by and overreact to (take personally) my/our partner's words, tones, weaknesses, personality traits, or vulnerabilities—in other words, do I/we bug each other or feel *significantly* irritated or hurt by the other person's traits? Yes ___. No ___.

- Do we criticize one another in public (and/or with friends)? Yes ___. No ___. If yes, which partner (or both partners) criticizes the other in public?

- Do I/we have "domains" in which we (not our partner) are respected as the incontrovertible expert—that is, the partner mainly does, without much argument, what the other partner wants in that domain? Yes ___. No ___.

- On the other hand, do I/we try to control one another's "domains" and/or other aspects of individual life—that is, no domain is sacred, and we are both trying to be a boss of most domains? Yes ___. No ___.

- Do we have bonding rituals in place (date nights every week, lunches together, watching TV together, sex, holding hands at the dinner table) by which to keep our bond strong? Yes ___. No ___.

- Do we talk together at least once a day, if possible (including most days when one or both are traveling away from home), to catch up on what has happened and to hear one another's voices? Yes ___. No ___.

- Do I/we say "I love you" a number of times per week to our partner, if not at least once a day? Yes ___. No ___.

- Do I/we praise one another at least a few times a week, if not at least once a day, in both private and public? Yes ___. No ___.

- In the hidden agreements that help our marriage, do we allow each of us to be right in some of our marital conflicts (as opposed to needing to always or almost always be right)? Yes ___. No ___. If one partner needs to always be right, name that partner:_____.

- Do we apologize to one another within hours or, at most, a day, after hurting the other's feelings? Yes ___. No ___. If the answer is no, which partner (or is it both partners?) does not apologize?

- Do I/we assume the best of the other and so, generally, forgive one another's stress-filled overreactions? Yes ___. No ___.

- Do I/we generally assume the best of ourselves and so, generally, forgive our own stress-filled overreactions? Yes ___. No ___.

- In heterosexual couples, do I/we fully understand and make concessions to accommodate the significant brain differences in the ways women and men practice love and intimacy? Yes ___. No ___.

- In same-sex couples, do I/we notice a natural gravitation toward different approaches to problems, including masculine and feminine, and is that okay with us? Yes ___. No ___. If no, which partner is most uncomfortable with "being different from the other"?

- Is criticism and judgment my default position with my partner—that is, rather than seeing the best intentions in my partner's actions, do I tend to see him or her as mistake-prone? Yes ___. No ___.

- Is criticism and judgment my partner's default position with me? Yes ___. No ___.

- Are we verbally fighting about something five times a week or more? ("Verbally fighting" indicates actual vehement argument rather than fun jesting, joking, teasing, bickering.) Yes ___. No ___.

- Are we having relatively satisfying sex, even if, as we age, we are not having it as frequently as before? Yes ___. No ___. If sex is not satisfying, are we able to discuss sexual needs without any rancor? Yes ___. No ___.

- Do we enjoy hearing what one another is thinking and feeling about love, children, friends, work, and other important things at least a few times per week? Yes ___. No ___. If no, does one or both of us not like the sound of the other's voice?

- Do we pay compliments to one another in public and in the company of friends? Yes ___. No ___. If not, which partner (or both partners) does not give compliments in public?

Take time to answer these questions, even the somewhat repetitive ones (repetition is important for getting at similar things in different ways); as you do so, write or tell specific memories and stories in your journal. As you move forward in this book, return at times to this first survey.

I will provide Essential Questions (EQ) surveys and other tools in each chapter of the book so that you have ample opportunity to apply what you are discovering in a sequential way as you commit to studying your own ways of love, becoming a love-scientist about the relationship you know best, and changing what needs to be changed. In following this process, you should feel new worlds of emotion and new possibilities of resilience, happiness, and love emerge in your relationship and yourself.

As you complete this survey and the others, please work hard not to make a judgment about any of your answers right away. Hold your answers in your journal (or in your mind), modify them as you have new insights about them, and discuss them with your partner, friend, mentor, counselor, and/or another person. Let these surveys function not as end statements of how things are or will be forever, but as lights you can shine in front of you during your journey.

Little Differences Have Big Consequences

One of Gail's and my closest friends, Kathy Stevens, passed away at sixty-two after a two-and-a-half-year battle with cancer. In her life, she accomplished many things, including living, even toward the end, with a great sense of humor. Married twenty-two years in her first marriage, and fifteen years in her second, she was very wise about love. As executive director of the Gurian Institute for twelve years, she guided many of our projects and provided training and classes in which she told the following story.

"A couple from Minnesota decided to go to Florida to thaw out during one particularly icy winter. They decided to stay at the very same hotel where they had spent their honeymoon two decades before.

Because of hectic work schedules, it was tough to coordinate flying down to Florida together, so the husband flew first, with his wife ticketed to come the next day. When the husband got to Florida and to the hotel, he found free Wi-Fi access in the room, so he sent his wife an email from his laptop. However, he accidentally left out one letter in her email address; without realizing his error, he sent the email.

"Meanwhile, in Houston, a widow had just returned home from her husband's funeral. He was a minister of many years who died after a sudden heart attack. The widow decided to check her email, expecting messages from relatives and friends. After reading the first email, she fainted. Her grown children rushed into the room, found their mother on the floor, and saw the computer screen which read:

To: My Loving Wife
Subject: I've Arrived
Date: February 2

I know you're surprised to hear from me. They give free Wi-Fi access in the rooms here so I am sending you an email. When I checked in, I saw that everything has been prepared for your arrival tomorrow. Looking forward to seeing you then! Hope your journey is as uneventful as mine was.

P.S. Sure is hot down here!

I love to tell this story in relationship workshops because it not only leads to some chuckles but also shows how a little thing can make a huge difference. One missing element in an email address can reconstruct a whole reality. So it is with marriage, love, and intimacy. A little change can make a big difference.

I hope you will allow the paradigm of intimate separateness to be the "little thing" that you change in your process of loving another person and being loved. As you do, that little thing will expand into a glue in your relationship that you might call, looking back on the process years later, *real love.*

PART I

The Secret to Real Love
Intimate Separateness

Some risks you cannot afford to take, but there are
some risks you cannot afford *not* to take.

—Peter Drucker

Chapter 1

The Intimate Separateness Paradigm

A BALANCE OF INTIMACY AND SEPARATENESS CREATES A HAPPY MARRIAGE

Angela, forty-five, and Harry, forty-seven, came to see me about their son Mark, twelve. As they told me about Mark's issues I found the couple to be friendly and forthright but distressed. Mark had been evaluated for ADHD and anxiety, and the specialist concluded: "I don't think he has ADD/ADHD and I don't think he has a clinical condition on the anxiety issues that needs medication right now, but let's watch this. He is definitely more anxious that his siblings." Given that Angela's father and Angela herself had both been treated for anxiety, Angela and Harry knew that this vulnerability fit with the family genetics.

My first session with the couple—which mainly involved discussions about Mark—revealed that this was a family of high performers. Angela had a master's degree in history and now worked in the software world. "As a woman and a black woman," she said, "there is a lot of pressure. I want to model to my kids how strong a black woman can be." Harry was clearly very proud of her accomplishments. He said, "Angela is a dynamo. Nothing holds her back."

Harry was an engineer in fiber optics. He traveled for his work more than Angela did, but also confessed to enjoying being home more now than before—his company had moved its headquarters to another city, but allowed him to remain in town and work remotely for most of the week. Angela complimented Harry, mentioning that Harry wouldn't admit it, but as a black man there was also a lot of pressure on him as a father and husband.

"But we're not here about either of us or our marriage," Angela said, "we're here about Mark." She reported that they had a younger son and a daughter older than Mark, and all three siblings were doing pretty well, but Mark had begun, over the last couple years, to fight with both his younger brother and, especially, with Angela. "I don't know if it's just his anxiety, or what," Harry agreed, "but something's getting worse and worse in the family. Mark's sucking everyone down into his moods. It's creating issues for me and Angie." Angela summed up the situation this way: "What's going on between Mark and his younger brother could just be sibling rivalry, you know, Mark wanting my attention, all that; but what's going on with Mark and me is crossing the line. He's screaming at me, always angry at me, and . . . well . . . sometimes . . . acting kind of like his dad."

In this comment emerged a new topic of conversation, a topic appearing as a thin seam of light under an important doorway. Harry, as one would expect, responded defensively. "Now wait a minute, I don't scream at you, I'm not a rager, don't go in that direction; I just get angry, and I get intense." Angela admitted he didn't rage, but now, as the discussion continued, his anger became a topic, so much so that Harry did ultimately admit that he had been getting more irritated over the last year at both his son Mark and his wife, Angela.

This admission meant a great deal to Angela. "Now," she suggested, "we can get to the heart of what's going on." She confessed that she was worried for the couple's marriage, worried that Harry would just keep getting angrier and make the marriage untenable. Harry said to Angela in response, "I get angry, dammit, because of what's going on with *you*. You and Mark both make me the bad guy all the time. If you're at work or not around, Mark and I are great together and there's no tension in the family. I tell him, 'Look, life's gonna knock you down harder than I ever can, so you need resilience and accountability, not overprotection.' I'm hard on him that way, but he gets it. Then *you* come home and you and Mark get all weird together, and I try to get some boundaries set again, and I'm the bad guy! You even make me the bad guy right now, saying I'm gonna ruin our marriage. It's not right!"

Angela sat silently for a minute with that comment. Then all of us remained silent, looking into the possibility that our counseling might move toward other rooms of this family's house than Mark's.

After this brief silence, Angela made a courageous admission: "Yes, Harry has become the bad guy." She agreed that she did know from talking to all three children that when she wasn't home, things were calmer. This admission, like the whole conversation thus far, raised my antennae not only regarding Mark but also the bond between Angela and Harry. I saw a pattern I see in many couples, one that creates a lead-in for the concepts and benefits of the intimate separateness paradigm.

Separateness and the Psychology of Attachment

To understand intimate separateness as a working paradigm for your relationships, it is important to begin the process (one I will support with new insights and strategies throughout this book) of "mind-expanding" about love. This new thinking is especially needed in our era because, if you read popular-culture offerings on relationships, marriage, and love, you may notice that books, programs, magazine articles, and TV shows often tend to look at the "intimacy" side of relationships with an eye toward *teaching better communication and conflict skills that directly increase intimacy*. While this is invaluable and essential work, and while the book you are reading could not have been written without all the previous work done on intimacy and attachment in the field, you do not tend to hear the word "separateness" used nearly as much as the word "intimacy." This lack is killing our marriages. "Separateness" is, as we'll show in this chapter, at least one-half or more of attachment and intimacy. In working as a culture to give people tips for feeling more intimate with one another in the short term, we have neglected to discuss the other half of attachment; this other half needs to be activated at some time before the two-year mark of a bond and kept active through the couple's life together. It is the second part of the intimate-separateness paradigm, the one we tend to know the least about.

Attachment Theory and Intimate Separateness

If you are a parent and haven't yet run across attachment theory in your exploration of your adult/relational love, you will have undoubtedly come across it in books about raising your children. Mary Ainsworth, Margaret Mahler, Louise Kaplan, John Bowlby, T. Berry Brazelton, Melanie Klein, and others have taught us that humans attach to people we love by bonding intimately with our "bonding-object" (our child) while the child goes through all the stages of the parent-child pair-bond with us (and we with him or her), including the other half of attachment—when the child compels us gradually into the separateness required for successful adult life. As attachment pioneer Louise Kaplan, author of *Oneness and Separateness,* notes, *both oneness and separateness equally,* not one or the other, collaborate to give the growing individual child "rein to discover his (her) place in the world." With oneness alone, the child will be psychologically engulfed and can't develop well; with separateness alone, the child will be neglected and also, thus, undeveloped. From the healthy experience of both oneness and separateness come the resilience and passion to be an individual in the world who can find happiness and success while retaining the family love and connection that give security and unconditional love.

Try to recall how this relates to your experiences with your own children or in your own childhood. If you do not have children, remember as far back as you can to your bond with your mother or father. If you have children, remember your infant's utter connection to you, then recall the terrible twos, when the child separated from you psychologically to explore the world and begin developing a self. Recall adolescent-parent relationships—how the child separated even further from you.

Many parents come to realize—sometimes, unfortunately, not until children are grown—that if, in a child's childhood or adolescence, one or both parents "hold on too tight" (remain too close), they may lose the child's respect, love, and attention—the child may even come to "hate" the parents. At the same time, in the parent-adolescent attachment, if parents pull too far away from the toddler or adolescent—if they don't provide adequate presence and connection with the child—that young adult may be traumatized by the neglect, get into moral and behavioral trouble, and even, perhaps, become so distant as to rarely speak to his or her parents again later in life.

The Science of Pair-Bond Attachment in a Nutshell

Contemporary science of the human brain has taken the early work of attachment theorists to new places, opening up even deeper possibilities for people in marriage and coupled relationships to understand what the heck is going on when we love as adults. Without this new science, I would not have been able to develop the intimate-separateness paradigm. Research now shows us that on both sides of the attachment equation, what happens between parents and children also happens in adult pair-bonds. If I work seventy hours a week and become much too distant from my soul mate, I will lose that mate; also (here is the hidden secret of love), if I push to be too intimate with my soul mate's psyche, I will, like a parent with a child, engulf him or her, become too entangled, lose my soul mate's unconditional love and respect, and never quite know why.

Neuroscientists Daniel Amen, Daniel Siegel, Tracey Shors, Helen Fisher, Shelley Taylor, and Allan Schore, among many others, have used brain scans and biochemical analysis to watch bonding, separation, and stress-reaction patterns in the human brain as it navigates human attachment in both childhood and adulthood. These scientists have discovered that the reason adult pair-bonds mirror parent-child attachment lies in:

1. *the limbic brain* (our midbrain, which handles our emotions and senses at their most basic, instinctive levels)
2. *our biochemical reactions*, such as the processing of dopamine in the brain
3. *the cerebral cortex* (the thinking, talking, and imaginative parts of the brain that wrap around the limbic system)
4. *the brain stem* (the control system that maintains physiological measures such as blood pressure and body temperature)

Scientists have discovered that the brain and body in love with a soul mate so mimics parent-child attachment that when a person in the pair-bond feels "impinged" (i.e., our partner is getting too psychologically close to us, trying to control us, trying to "get in our heads," trying to entangle his or her self with ours, trying to get us to talk about feelings all the time), our anxieties and angers (in blood flow in the brain, biochemical arrays, and physical and nervous sensation) get triggered in the same way a child's does when a parent will not allow healthy separateness during the terrible twos or during adolescence. Our adult brain responds to our lover's impingement by self-protecting: stimulating us to try to pull away emotionally from the impinging party and move to the periphery of emotional life and drama in order to regroup and protect the self.

Similarly, our brains mirror parent-child attachment when we feel "rejected" by our lover (i.e., our partner isn't paying healthy attention to us, devalues us through neglect and abandonment)—we feel too distant or "far away" from our lover (feeling like we are "falling out of love"). This is also tracked in the brain and bloodstream. We get emotionally triggered toward anxiety, even depression, and now we may try to get rid of this fear and pain by trying, again, to become closer and closer emotionally to our partner, trying to more constantly engage our partner, whether overtly or through passive-aggressive means. We might feel or say, "We're too far away. We need to rekindle our intimacy. I'm worried about us. I don't feel loved." The pain of not getting enough intimacy is felt acutely, and it can be insatiable.

Our limbic brain (the "paralimbic system") in the middle of our heads is triggering a replay of parent-child attachment patterns in brain and bloodstream in either case, whether we get too little closeness for psychological health or too much. Fortunately, we adults-in-love carry within us a source of power in the cerebral cortex, especially the orbito-frontal, prefrontal, and frontal lobes that we did not have when we were little children: We can take control of the attachment dynamic in modern love. We can *make the choice* to learn the balance of oneness and separateness our particular marriage needs. We can *choose* to incorporate a balanced intimate-separateness paradigm in our marriage.

We can choose to balance intimacy and separateness more quickly than parents and children often do—some children take twenty or so years after adolescence is over to discover a healthy balance of intimacy and separateness with parents, and some parent-child adult pairs never do find a balance, constantly stuck in tension with one another. We lovers need to choose to use the intimate-separateness paradigm as soon as possible in our love relationship if it is to thrive. By doing so, we will be best protecting long-term attachment. If we do the work of understanding and incorporating this quickly, we can discover and practice the secret of loving attachment before our personal issues become rancorous. We can rescue our love from both too much distance and too much closeness before the deficiencies of either one do our love irreparable harm.

THE WONDER OF SEPARATENESS

Recognizing and then mastering the pull of the self to be both intimate and separate is the most subtle kind of psychological work we do as adults. It is intriguing for me to be a part of this dance with patients because it represents the essence of the unconscious internal experience people are having while they are living their everyday lives in a relationship. This is true in all relationships, by the way. We are doing this two-sided attachment not just in the bedroom or in the home, with children, lovers, and spouses, but we are doing it also with colleagues in workplaces, with friends, with elderly parents, with leaders and other countries. We just don't realize it. We are all in a constant state of wanting to be intimately connected while also needing to be separate, self-contained, and free.

—Adie Goldberg, MEd, MSW, coauthor of
It's a Baby Girl! and *It's a Baby Boy!*

The Angry Partner and the Anxious Partner

Throughout this book, I will do with you as I do with clients—guide you in becoming a "love-scientist" who can become increasingly able to study your relationships with tracking mechanisms in place for recognizing primal, limbic brain patterns in the *emotional character* of your self-development and the *emotional mechanisms* of *your* pair-bond with your partner. As you engage in this process, you may notice that tracking the intimacy part of your marriage or love relationship is often easier than tracking the separateness part. One reason for this lies in the culture around us: our media constantly urge us to look for greater intimacy (every day a new "emotional diet plan" comes out in a magazine that promises to help us be more intimate). This popular approach can work decently in the short term, but we also need tracking mechanisms for understanding the other half of attachment. We have to become good at answering the question, "Okay, I get that intimacy is crucial to love, but now tell me: What would healthy separateness feel like for me and my mate?"

The first major tracking tool I want to share with you in this book is captured in the title of this section and in the example of Angela and Harry. While in all cases of marital distress both partners feel both anxiety and anger at various times, most couples also tend to "divide the emotional labor" into ways they *express* their distress. One partner often tends toward overtly showing more *anxiety* (rumination, worry, verbalizations/requests regarding intimacy, or the verbal or nonverbal need to be reassured that the intimacy felt in the relationship is just fine). The other partner may tend to show more *overt anger* (harsh tone, abrupt sentences, angry facial cues, harsh boundary setting that can push away the anxious partner). The more verbally inclined "worrier" may indeed be quite angry internally while the more overtly harsh or angry partner may be quite worried (anger is often a form of crying), as was the case with Angela, who ruminated and worried, and Harry, who was more harsh and set more abrupt boundaries.

Please take a moment to look into your relationship and answer these two questions:

- Is one of us *ruminating more* and thus *getting more overtly anxious* as the months and years pass (worrying more overtly, talking more about what's wrong)?
- Is one of us *getting angrier* (losing temper more or becoming more irritable)?

If you are both doing both equally, then note that observation in your journal or your mind, as well. Usually, however, you'll see at least a sixty-forty split in the behaviors and internal experiences.

The angry partner (often the male but certainly not always) is frequently easiest to spot, and so becomes the more outwardly culpable in our present marital approach to intimacy issues. In fact, because of this pattern in American relationships especially, the first half of this book mainly features couples in which the husband (male) tends to be the angry (and/or emotionally withdrawn) partner at the time of presentation (when I meet the couple). In Part II, I introduce couples who fit other patterns, including the angrier woman and the more passive or overtly ruminating and emotional man.

One reason I believe it is important to study carefully the male-is-angry-and-withdrawn/female-is-anxious-and-worrying trend is because research at the University of Washington and elsewhere has corroborated that men tend to present or be presented in therapy, by their wives, as the more angry partner. The woman in heterosexual couples and the more feminine partner in homosexual couples more often presents, initially at least, as carrying more of the overt anxiety in the relationship. We need to look at this carefully and peel back the presenting anger/anxiety pattern—a secret hides behind it. As you read this material, rest assured that I know I am generalizing based on the research; if your situation fits "angry woman" and "anxious man," please alter this material to fit your situation. But no matter which partner is predominantly angrier and which partner is predominantly more anxious, the analysis of intimacy and separateness applies.

With Angela and Harry, the man was the more obviously angry partner. Because of this, a previous therapist had focused mainly on helping Harry to curtail his anger. This therapeutic approach can make sense in the short term; especially when a man with a loud voice and somewhat scarier approach to nurturance of families is the "angry partner," a couple's therapy tends to focus on him. As John Gottman's "Love Labs" (a marriage laboratory) at the University of Washington have shown, if a man constantly and angrily criticizes his wife or partner for prolonged periods, the couple is likely to divorce. (Throughout this book we will continue to look at how to help men and women curtail their anger.)

Simultaneously, what partners often miss is that attached couples naturally tend to divide emotional labor between themselves—this happens unconsciously, in our limbic brain: one partner often shows more anxiety and one tends to show more anger—and if the marriage is under stress, this division of labor can point to a lack of the intimate-separateness paradigm. When I see the anger/anxious pattern with clients, I immediately think, "Okay, this is natural to these personalities but, also, is there a deeper reason the psychological labor is being divided—that is, is there the hidden stressor in this attachment, the lack of a balance of intimacy and separateness, that both people are reacting to, even though in their different ways?"

This questioning becomes even more specific as I try to explore the sources of the anger. In helping the couple, I am asking, "What is behind that male (or female, if the angry partner is female) anger?" Men are basically protective and caring people; they are fundamentally well-attached, empathic, compassionate, and loving, so if a man is constantly angry at and pushing away his spouse, we need to try to figure out why. In the case of Angela and Harry, *Angela's anxiety was as causative of marital distress as was Harry's anger*. Here, now, is another counterintuitive insight (especially in the context of contemporary relationship culture, which focuses so heavily on male anger): while concentrating on male (or female) anger is worthy and essential (and as you'll see below, we don't let Harry off the hook), we often miss the fact that the wife's surges of rumination and anxiety may be stimulating protective male anger and boundary-setting, which is actually quite healthy and crucial to the marriage's survival, rather than destructive. The destruction will happen in the marriage if the husband's anger is not understood and "mined" for all its potential gold.

The Clue to a Subtle Collaboration

When one person is worrying a lot and the other is angry a lot, they are actually *collaborating* to try to solve a marital problem. The way two loving people will collaborate (unconsciously) during marital distress generally depends on elements in all three selves: sources in *nature, nurture,* and *culture.* As you'll see in a moment, Angela's worrying and anxiety came from at least these three sources in herself as she collaborated with Harry in the relationship distress:

1. The anxious partner, in this case Angela, is often *genetically prone* to anxiety via an increase of brain activity in certain brain centers, such as the *cingulate gyrus* (an attention/rumination center in the brain) and left side of the *amygdala*

(a stress-response center in the brain). These genetic tendencies come with a person's genome at conception, are formatted in utero via DNA to RNA transfer, and, thus, enter the personality or "self" before birth.

2. The anxious partner may have been *nurtured* in childhood in such a way that she developed an increased tendency toward worry, rumination, and anxiety in later life. She may have been cultivated in this direction by one or more anxious parents or caregivers; and/or she suffered traumas early in life that increased anxiety functioning in the brain.

3. The anxious partner's present *culture, environment,* and *lifestyle* may create conditions that increase anxiety (alcohol, drug abuse, or another toxin) and/or she may have bought into a gender stereotype, in which a woman is supposed to be the more passive, anxious, worrying partner so that her spouse can "take care of her." This buy-in can be quite unconscious, of course, and operative even in a very "strong" personality—one in which a woman is powerful in her workplace and even her marriage and family life, yet can trigger an anxious approach to love via environment, lifestyle, or cultural imprinting.

For his part, and for similar, different, and complementary reasons in nature, nurture, and culture, the partner in Harry's position (not always the male, of course, but we will use the male pronoun here) may become more "fight or flight" in his approach, less prone to anxious, verbal rumination, and more prone to quick bursts of anger, territory or boundary setting, and paternal nurturance. (I'll explore genetically constructed male/female brain differences in more depth in Chapter 3.) He may be more overtly loud when relational boundaries are not adhered to (as Harry was with the adolescent son, Mark).

In the case of Angela and Harry, both felt anxious and both at times felt angry, and both had strong personalities, but Harry became the "bad guy" (more overt anger, more obvious boundary setting) and Angela became more anxious (more ruminating, more verbally worried), the "victim." This couple was very lucky that their son Mark's anxieties entered the couple's marriage. Mark's issues uncovered a host of conflicts in the adult world, which had gone unnoticed until Angela and Harry became entrenched in a difficult attachment pattern of anxiety/anger around their son. Because of Mark, the couple came to a critical moment in their ability to bond for life, and they decided to work deeply on reframing that ability, asserting emotional choice-making in new ways, and evolving their attachment into new stages of marriage. They decided especially to study how to use the intimate-separateness paradigm, including, initially, understanding more about the importance of emotional separateness than they ever had before.

We Are Much Too Close but Don't Realize It

The secret Angela and Harry learned was that both of them, like so many couples, were much *too close, too intimate* for their love to flourish. Their process of becoming too close had happened, they learned in therapy, in these three steps.

Step 1: While both Angela and Harry felt some marital discomfort, one partner (Angela) felt it more constantly, and in response, she kept trying to *get closer and closer emotionally* to the other partner, Harry, and to the son Mark. *More intimacy* (more talking about feelings, more emotional and sensorial connection) was her unconscious solution to issues; she pressed harder and harder for it, immersing herself in her husband's and son's ways of being, trying to alter and move both husband and son toward greater closeness with her.

Step 2: Without anyone realizing it, Harry and Mark responded by instituting *more* boundaries, *more* territorial markers, *more* distance as Angela pressed them anxiously for more closeness. These boundaries had the opposite effect of what Angela wanted. She wanted to increase intimacy and closeness, but instead, as her husband and son held their boundaries somewhat angrily, she felt even more pushed away, left out, abandoned. As she got more anger from father and son over months (even a year or more), she felt what I have come to call *intimacy anxiety*—nervousness, fear, and anxiousness about the decreasing intimacy, which creates a desperation for more closeness and intimacy.

Almost all of this happened unconsciously; remember, there was nothing "wrong" with what Angela did or felt—she was following her own nature, nurture, and culture instincts—but in her heightened state of stress and anxiety, absent an understanding of the intimate-separateness paradigm, she misread the signals of her partner and child, and she saw their separateness as a relationship killer. She did not understand how her intimacy anxiety was negatively affecting her relationships, as she constantly begged husband and son to please "open up to me," "tell me what's going on," "let me in."

This went on for Angela, Harry, and Mark for just under a year. For other couples and families, it can go on for many years. My research shows that if this goes on for a year or more, the family relationships enter at least a low-grade state of crisis in which the worrier will feel almost constantly anxious about the attachments in her life—she'll be worried they will end.

Step 3: Angela's partner and son met her constant anxiety and pleadings to be let into their emotional selves by becoming even angrier. Harry and Mark ratcheted up their boundary setting and their development of "separateness" (separated, independent selves). They both asserted to Angela (mostly unconsciously, through anger) that from now on they would *not increase emotional vulnerability and thus become enmeshed and engulfed in Mom's anxious needs.*

A key point to make here (something often missed in our popular-psychology culture) is that, just as Mom's approach was not wrong, neither was Dad's or son's. Harry (unconsciously) chose his angry course for many of his own personal permutations of the nature, nurture, and culture. He did what he had to do in order to both repair the pair-bond issues he faced with his wife and raise his son in the way he felt a father should most helpfully do. He became entrenched in pursuing separateness as much as Angela was entrenched in pushing for intimacy.

The end result was at least one marital year of a very tense situation in which Angela wanted more intimacy, Harry wanted more separateness, and they both scared each other constantly with these demands. Both partners at times switched approaches, of course—Harry becoming overtly anxious and worrying aloud and Angela becoming angry and harsh, but in general, the division of emotional labor occurred in their marital collaboration; gradually, both partners began looking for options by which to end the constant tension. Fortunately this need brought them into therapy, even though they initially thought that the only issue in their family was their son's anxiety.

YOUR INSIGHTS

What I've learned is that healthy separateness protects me from getting sucked into my partner's deepest fears. I am still sympathetic and loving, but I don't get pulled down there into that darkness with all those other demons.

I didn't used to be able to stay solid and separate. I used to think if we love each other, we should share every demon, every fear, you know, but I have my own fears to deal with. In my first marriage, I became the woman who got so wrapped up in my husband's feelings and pains that I took them into myself as my own demons. Then, I had both his and my own demons to carry. We couldn't survive that.

I'm with a new partner now, and we are very close, but we don't get sucked in. This is a second marriage for both of us, and we learned some things. We made some agreements. If I have any advice for people about this, it's to make sure to become happy and separate before your heart gets broken by your partner's fears and terrors. And I can promise you, they will break you if you let them.

—Rita Maria, 39

Part of my job as a marriage counselor was to help Angela and Harry understand their invisible marital collaboration of anger and anxiety. In that invisible tension, the natural separateness tugs of a man and a son had triggered significant anxiety in the woman and mother, but no one realized it. In showing the couple this invisible world and its tensions, I had to do something that is very difficult for anyone who provides therapy to do: I had to say, "It is very possible that Harry's anger is something of a stressor, but also that Angela's anxiety is a far greater stressor than you realize." Saying this was complex for a number of reasons, all of which show the difficulty of understanding love in our era.

Previous therapy had targeted Harry as the person who did not know how to be intimate, so it took some time to convince Angela that the "male" approach to emotion she distrusted was just as valuable as her own. In fact, Chapter 3 of this book, which compares the limbic brains of males and females, shows male and female distinct approaches to power struggles in marriage; without the gender science, PET scans, SPECT scans, and biochemical research to back me up, Angela would not initially believe that her approach to intimacy was actually a major cause of her marital distress.

Thankfully, Angela did ultimately open her awareness to it. She did come to embrace this approach, and Harry made necessary changes as well so the relationship could find a good balance going forward.

An Invisible World

In order to be both honest about and empathic with Angela's position, we looked closely at how love can't grow and evolve without understanding the paradigm behind the emotionally collaborative patterns and triggers this couple experienced. We explored how neither Angela's nor Harry's unconscious instincts toward anger and anxiety were wrong, because *they are both instinctual*—wired into the two brains. As I worked with this couple, I confessed that part of my job was to help them increase not only their emotional intelligence but also their *marital intelligence*: their ability to study the emotional and attachment instincts each brought to the marriage and to work *with* them, not *against* them, so that they could incorporate a balanced intimate-separateness paradigm in their marital work and life going forward. Indeed, we agreed in therapy that it was a *good thing* that Angela was anxious and Harry was angry. If not for these reactions, the couple might never grow, evolve, or stay married.

To go into this with the couple, I introduced them to the attachment specialists we mentioned earlier—John Bowlby, Allan Schore, Louise Kaplan, and others. We discussed how attachment cycles of "oneness" (intimacy) and "separateness" (separate self) are initially wired into our limbic systems, central nervous systems, and neocortex in utero (through genetic influences before we are born). Angela and Harry were particularly moved by a "bottom line" in this research that was captured by renowned attachment specialist John Bowlby in theory, then proven by neuroscientists such as Allan Schore, who study the brain via neural scans. In both theory and practice, scientists have discovered that adaptive attachment behavior is hardwired into our *interpersonal neurobiology*—it is wired into us. Thus, we are living in attachment patterns that both cower and revel in the midbrain areas of adaptive instinct so deeply rooted in us that we cannot turn some switch on and off (we cannot utter magic words) in order to fully survive, thrive, communicate, collaborate, grow, adapt, and love. Instead, we unconsciously collaborate with our partners in instinctive attachment patterns far more common in contemporary pair-bonds than we may realize. If we can increase our marital intelligence about them, as Angela and Harry did, we can quite literally change our own worlds of love and give us access to new (and age-old) paradigms for making love last.

Increasing Your Marital Intelligence with a New Lens

Look into your relational microscope. Do you see anger or anxiety collaboration in your marriage? Get the help you need to look at your love-relationship patterns. Look for patterns that have lasted for six months to a year or more. As you see the patterns, you will increase your marital intelligence. You'll perhaps say, "Wow, look at that: we've been doing that for a year now; it was a reflection of instinct, a pattern, and there must be wisdom in it for us. Let's see it as positive, let's plumb the depths of it, and let's come back up and out of the pain of this with a new way of relating." If you choose this course, you will most likely be ready to take a next step in your love relationship: you will need to study a root pattern of your marital relationship: *the enmeshment/abandonment cycle*.

The anger/anxiety collaboration in the marriage between Angela and Harry was a clue to this deeper way in which these two people had become "too close."

The Enmeshment/Abandonment Cycle

Angela and Harry were dangerously "close" to one another in that they were *psychologically enmeshed*. In enmeshment, two people become entangled in one another's emotions; they become so entangled psychologically that their personal boundaries become unclear, porous, and permeable. Generally, this psychological state feels uncomfortable for one person more quickly than for the other and triggers survival instincts—a "pulling away" from the emotional entanglement. Meanwhile, to the other partner, the pulling away can feel like abandonment, which is very frightening. Thus, in this cycle, the two selves are, in other words, so intertwined that they become oppressive psychologically to one another's individual growth, but when they try to pull apart, a deep fear of abandonment arises in at least one partner. Enmeshment and abandonment are, thus, two sides of the same coin.

Though it involved a woman (she unconsciously pushing toward more emotional enmeshment) and a man (he unconsciously pushing for more distancing and emotional abandonment), this "oppression" in Angela's and Harry's marriage was not "power oppression," the kind of enslavement we are most familiar with in feminist theory, academic research, and popular culture—a subjugation that is about one gender trying to make the other inferior in order to feel ascendant. The psychological oppression of too much closeness in enmeshment cycles is not generally about economic or social power per se but, rather, about psychological safety: without the feeling of safety and security in marriage, two individuals cannot have long-lasting love.

In our contemporary marriages, the loss of that safety from psychological enmeshment happens constantly, but we don't realize it. We focus on loss of romance, or angry males (or females), and on gender oppressions. These are important ideas about love, but we don't realize how much of the distress in marriages has to do with the *invisible* world, the human unconscious (limbic brain) in which enmeshment is felt by one partner and abandonment is felt acutely by the other.

In a sense, the fact that we can see and focus on this cycle—and the need for the intimate-separateness paradigm in the face of it—is a gift of cultural and marital evolution. In marriage today, we have taken most of the "culture" out of love by giving couples relative freedom from the older economic, gender, and cultural necessities for marriage; from religious pressures to stay married; from physical survival needs for marriage; and from social norms against divorce. It is logical that we now must stay together because our love is strong, not for any other reason per se. And many of us do stay together for love. But for the vast majority of us (myself included), it is not possible to stay together for love beyond four, or seven, or ten years unless we notice that along with love's primacy in long-term marriage comes the natural dark side of being in love. This dark side involves complex feelings of enmeshment at some times and of abandonment at other times. With love comes "being too close, too dependent, too much in love" and "being too distant, feeling rejected, feeling abandoned." In both enmeshment and abandonment are the hidden feeling of being devalued as a separate self; and in the majority of cases of couple therapy I have been involved in, and in nearly every case I have read about (these number in the thousands), it involves the *fear of abandonment* and the *fear of enmeshment*. These fears (two sides of the same coin) occur often in modern love.

The Fear of Abandonment

See if you sense the fear of abandonment at work in your own life; this is the *fear of losing emotional closeness with a person or system so painfully that you feel, either unconsciously or consciously, that if you lose that closeness forever, you will become somewhat worthless.* This fear is not pathological. It is normal and natural because human attachment is fragile—love is fragile. We want and need to be close, not alone; dependent, not unprotected. When we feel abandoned, we act toward increasing intimacy in order to feel better. In other books, especially those based in addiction-recovery research, you may have seen the fear of abandonment show up as "codependency," and it can be that. At the same time, the fear of abandonment that you will feel many times in your love relationship is most likely not connected to disease, though it can destroy your marriage if it remains unchecked.

In Angela's case, there was no addiction or other pathology in her fear of abandonment per se, but for many of the nature, nurture, and culture reasons noted above, she was inclined toward heightened rumination, worry, and anxiety. These both caused and were caused by her fear of emotional abandonment by husband and son. I believe that, about a year before I met her, her son's separation from her (then her husband's separation reaction to her reaction) most likely triggered her acute intimacy anxiety, compelling her to become a hovering wife and mom.

The Fear of Enmeshment

The fear of enmeshment, also natural to pair-bonding, is the fear of *being too emotionally close, boundaryless, entangled with another person's emotional and psychological structure, and impinged upon by that other person's psyche so much so that you feel that, if you remain enmeshed, you will become somewhat worthless.* For someone who is feeling a prolonged fear of enmeshment, the sense of losing oneself in an unhealthy way shows up as "If I get too close to this person, who I am (my identity as a separate person) will be lost. I will need to adhere to what this other self says I must be, and I can't do that if I am to be most helpful to others or to myself."

The person for whom a fear of enmeshment can dominate may, especially in a crisis situation, react somewhat contrary to the intimacy drive of his or her partner. Often a person who is defending himself against enmeshment will overtly or covertly be saying, "I do not do well in all that chaos. I have to stay emotionally separate from it so that I and my family will be safe." He may get so entrenched in this viewpoint that he may, indeed, risk becoming emotionally distant and build a too-separate life from his partner—for instance, by working constantly away from the partner, never coming home for dinner, living at his computer, or taking the other person for granted.

For Harry and Angela, the two instinctual fears began gradually to control the attachment in the marriage, as we described in the three steps earlier. This was immensely hurtful for the whole family, though as often happens in male/female relationships, the male hurt manifested in behaviors of harshness, masking, defensive independence, distancing, and anger while the female hurt manifested in emotional language, obvious intimacy anxiety, more rumination, and overt sadness.

No-Fault Cycles and Rumination Distress

I cannot say this enough: in the vast majority of cases, this enmeshment/abandonment cycle within a marriage is not either party's fault, nor is it mainly about cultural oppression from the outside. It is, in most cases, an attachment issue; it needs to be understood as an integral part of the couple's evolution of love, so that it does not destroy that marriage. It is often set in motion by either a gradually increasing abandonment or a gradually increasing enmeshment or both; so, as you study it, you might want to look for those features.

For instance, you might find that if you (or your mate) did not adequately separate from a parent during adolescence, you (or your mate) can feel enmeshed by a spouse who tries to get too close now. Or you might have been abandoned by a parent in childhood—in this case, you may feel abandoned by a spouse now, though that partner may not mean to reject you (as Harry did not mean to reject Angela at a deep level of love).

As we'll keep exploring in this book, there are thousands of combinations we can see in couples who display the enmeshment/abandonment cycle. There are also many layers of "becoming too close" and "becoming too distant."

To focus on whether you are gravitating toward the cycle right now, see if there has been, in your relationship, gradually increasing anxiety or anger on one or both of your parts. To focus on that, look at your relationship for a moment by answering these questions:

- Am I (or my partner) becoming increasingly anxious about our marriage?
- Am I (or my partner) becoming increasingly angry in our marriage?
- Do I (or my partner) feel that the other person is becoming too distant, is not intimate enough, is too far away?
- Do I (or my partner) feel that the other person is trying constantly to be too close, too "inside my head"?

As Angela and Harry answered these questions, and as we worked together to understand what was happening in the marriage, Angela asked, "Are you saying that Mark and Harry were doing something normal, but I am the one who is at fault for being too anxious? Are you saying that I am ruminating and worrying and trying to get into their heads, and that causes a fear of enmeshment in Harry and Mark so I'm at fault for their fear?"

I responded, "None of this is about blame—for one of you or all of you." I explained that the abandonment/enmeshment cycle in another marriage might have been triggered by a man's entering andropause and being constantly angry or by his losing his job and becoming anxious, or anything similar, or by a woman's entering menopause or losing a job, or by one partner having an affair. In Angela's marriage, however, it manifested itself after Mark's school and relational issues arose, and the couple struggled to cope. "You both were involved in 'causing' issues but neither was to blame,'" I assured Angela. "Remember, this is all a kind of *collaboration* between spouses. In your particular case, Mark's, and then Harry's, methodology got read as abandonment by your emotional system rather than as healthy separation. As you became more anxious about the abandonment, you kept trying to get closer and closer to your husband and son to resolve your anxiety. Mark and Harry both stiffened at your approach. Harry, as your husband, most likely (unconsciously) protected what he considered to be healthy emotional boundaries, but this triggered more anxiety in you, and the cycle got more and more acute. You felt increasing amounts of abandonment, and acted to feel better; Harry felt increasing amounts of enmeshment and entanglement, and acted to put up even stronger emotional boundaries."

The couple was able to see this, and that vision helped them immensely in their next steps in love, though I kept reminding them that Harry's boundary setting and anger needed to be adjusted now that the couple understood what was happening. In other words, not just Angela but also Harry had to change. I worked with Harry to be more forgiving of his wife's anxieties and to feel more sympathy and less anger toward her.

The Bottom Line

However it occurs in a marriage—whatever crisis, if any, triggers an enmeshment/abandonment cycle in a relationship (and it will get triggered at some point in yours, I promise you)—and whoever or whatever initially triggers this dynamic, recognizing it is absolutely essential to moving forward in human love. If we are to save marriages and experience the profound happiness possible in marriage in our new, free world, we will have to see through the anger of one or both partners to a hidden culprit in the marital distress: the enmeshment/abandonment cycle we are now living as we experience our distress. And remember, while Harry and Angela had been married a long time and had multiple children, half of couples experience the enmeshment/abandonment somewhere in the first seven years of marriage.

Please take a moment to answer the four questions again. See if any other or new words or memories are triggered.

- Am I (or my partner) becoming increasingly anxious in our marriage?
- Am I (or my partner) becoming increasingly angry in our marriage?
- Do I (or my partner) feel that the other person is becoming too distant, is not intimate enough, is too far away?
- Do I (or my partner) feel that the other person is trying constantly to be too close, too "inside my head"?

I want to reiterate: as you get help with the enmeshment/abandonment cycle from professionals—and throughout this book—and you disentangle yourselves from it, you will be *disengaging* (as we'll see Angela and Harry do in a moment). In disengaging, you will be doing something that each couple *must do* to move forward in the stages of a long-lasting relationship. The word "must" is important—it's not about "can" or "might," or even "should"; it is about the survival of long-term love. Here's the reason: in every stage of our lives and our love relationships, through every storm that comes at us from the outside world, we can flourish and even find lasting happiness if we feel we are living in, or at least quite near, what attachment theory calls *a secure base*.

Two relational patterns can disrupt that in any couple:

- When we become *too distant from our partner*, we become too distant from our secure base.
- When we become *too close to one another* (constantly trying to control one another, "open one another up," and/or engage in biting conflict in this enmeshment/abandonment cycle), the secure base is no longer secure.

Nervous about whether we have a secure base or not, we feel what psychological pioneer R. D. Laing called *ontological insecurity*. The longed-for healthy rhythm of love we need as a couple to survive a lifetime of difficulties from the outside world, and to thrive as mature adults, will likely not exist for very long anymore. We begin to look toward divorce. So, that is how important dealing with the enmeshment/abandonment cycle is.

Recognizing and Embracing Your Crisis in Attachment

Mining a crisis for all its worth can be crucial. Every event, crisis, or reflection in a marriage can help the couple take steps to strengthen that bond. Even if you are not seeing Angela and Harry's anxiety/anger in your own marriage, some aspect of enmeshment/abandonment will be there in your past or present relationships, somewhere. Take a moment to think about your own pair-bond (present or past) and search for a major event that may have triggered internal responses, like painful intimacy anxiety or intense boundary protection, such as we've described thus far. Some of these events might be:

- your wedding (Yes! For some people, the enmeshment/abandonment cycles start on the honeymoon.)
- pregnancy
- the birth of a first child or the coming of more children
- an addiction emerging in one or both of you
- financial troubles, loss of a job, recession, or other similar environmental stressor
- different maturity development (one person maturing quicker than the other)
- infidelity
- loss of a child or significant difficulty affecting a child
- change in a person's physical well-being (serious accident leaving one partner paralyzed)
- empty nest
- midlife passage
- aging

Sometimes the life events or crises that trigger ruminations, worries, fears, and angers are obvious; just as often, they are caused by a less obvious crisis, such as what was happening around Mark. That triggered the couple's abandonment/enmeshment cycle. And just as often, no crisis or life event triggers it—it just evolves in the relationship unnoticed until, perhaps, too late.

Early in our work together, Angela said, "You know, we didn't used to be this way. Harry didn't used to be so angry." Harry concurred from his viewpoint: "She's always been kind of high-strung, as Angela will admit, but she didn't used to be so worried and anxious, especially about me or Mark." Theirs was likely a marriage intimacy that may have been going along just fine—until the crisis occurred. The vulnerabilities in their personalities remained dormant, then a perfect storm of stressors abruptly changed the couple's emotional life.

Essential Questions Survey 2: Are You Enmeshed?

Please take a moment to look deeply at your own relationship (as always in these surveys, if you are not in a relationship now, please use a most recent long-term relationship as your template). If you are in a long-term relationship but your partner won't participate in this survey, you might find it interesting to fill out a second survey for your partner (as if you were him or her). However, watch out about sharing with your partner too much of what you've "answered" for him or her! Your partner may feel impinged, engulfed, or enmeshed by your efforts.

Please answer yes or no to each question. Feel free to write in a journal any explanations, stories, and narrative you find helpful.

1. Do I tend to play the victim in my relationship and, thus, mainly blame my partner (either consciously or unconsciously) for my/our troubles in love and marriage?

2. Do I tend to blame myself for our relationship issues, seeing myself as "the problem," and thus the victim of my own flaws, while my partner is much more "perfect" than I am?
3. Do I tend to play the rescuer in my relationships, seeing myself as the one who knows it all and must save the other person from him- or herself?
4. Do I (or my partner) often become enraged about "little things"?
5. Am I (or my partner) possessive and constantly jealous of the other?
6. Do I and my partner have a major fight (one that I fear can destroy our relationship and/or my own self-esteem) twice a week or more?
7. Do I take things my partner does or says personally (i.e., does she or he hurt my feelings) more than once a week?
8. Do I complain often to my partner (or my friends) that my partner and I are not doing enough activities together?
9. Do I complain often to my partner (or my friends) that my partner and I are not talking together enough of the time?
10. Do I feel that my partner and I are doing too much together, or trying to do too much together—that we talk too much together and that my partner "just can't be emotionally satisfied?"

Quite often (though not always), playing the victim and/or rescuer is evidence of enmeshment. If you follow this internal script, you have not developed and/or maintained a healthy, separated self with which to be an equal to your partner, and/or you have not developed a healthy self with which to be confident and secure; you want to be rescued by your partner from your own debilitating flaws.

Domestic violence is almost always a revelation of too much intimacy, yet we often think, "No, the abuser and the abused are not close or intimate at all! The abuser sees the abused as an *object of power*, not as *an intimate person*. If the abuser were intimate with the person, he or she would not abuse the victim." The opposite is often true, though. These two selves are inextricably melded together. This is why the abused person finds it so difficult to leave her or his abuser; the abused person merges with the abuser in complete intimacy, and the abuser merges with the abused person. Domestic violence almost always requires some form of emotional separation if the two people are to be saved and if both people are to remain physically safe.

Similarly, addictive personalities tend to become too close to partners at some points, too far away at others. Like the abused person, the person married to an addict will have to increase his or her separateness in order to flourish. This may not mean divorce, but it will definitely mean more emotional separateness.

Abuse and addiction create obvious ways of seeing enmeshment, and they are also extreme cases. From a statistical standpoint, most enmeshment shows up when a partner constantly wants to do things together, never separately; is possessive of a partner's time and energy; and believes her or his lover is abandoning that person because of outside interests. Often, these issues graduate into anger/anxiety as two people swing back and forth emotionally between being too close to one another and too far away for at least one of the partner's sense of a secure base. The couple will replay this pendulum-swinging love (push-pull love) for months, even years, until they feel they must pull apart as independent selves (separate/divorce) in order to survive. When they finally come to the endgame of divorce, they will often say something like, "I just can't do this anymore, I'm exhausted." Both partners have become hypervigilant, one predominantly aware of being abandoned and the other conscious of being enmeshed. It is incredibly tiring to be in this attachment crisis situation.

Returning to the Secret

If you are in any kind of difficult marriage right now, for any of the above reasons or for any other reason, and if you feel you are not emotionally fulfilled anymore, I hope you will find a therapist who can help you look at *separateness* now as much as *intimacy*. Ask him or her about enmeshment/abandonment anxieties, how they weave together, and how you and your partner can disentangle yourselves psychologically. Get help in discovering the roots of the enmeshments. Disentangling may mean one person moving into a different bedroom in the house for a period of time. It can also mean making trial-and-error attempts at less radical steps.

Here are the kinds of things Angela and Harry did at a practical level:

1. We discussed together (and they further, at home) the points made in this chapter so that both made the ideas *conscious* and developed personal and couple language dealing with the concepts of enmeshment and abandonment anxieties. They especially tracked how their anxieties emerged from the crisis with Mark—in other words, how they got so entangled after Mark began having difficulties.

2. They answered the surveys in this book, both the two presented so far and those that follow in later chapters. All the questionnaires are set up to help a couple gradually disentangle and then develop a healthy balance of intimacy and separateness in the face of the enmeshment/ abandonment cycle (and other cycles we will explore in later chapters).

3. They explored their survey results and the concepts behind them for as long as it took—until one or both of them experienced an epiphany. They made new commitments that altered the course of their love. They worked at this until they became love-scientists who could study together their own patterns in the marriage.

It was Angela who had the first major epiphany. "Dammit, yes, I see it," she said one day in session. "I become more anxious and scared, and Harry becomes more angry and distant. He thinks he's doing the right thing, but I feel like he's shoving me away. I feel more like a victim, like my mom was with my dad, and then I get even more anxious. Harry tries to fix this with all his rules and boundaries, and by the way, that makes me angry, too!"

As this kind of self-analysis became the new normal for the couple, they gradually began to say critical things to one another, such as, "I feel impinged, too controlled. I can't solve that problem for you, sorry." Or, "It's too abandoning when you don't call me from your business trip. I need to know you're okay." They built a new language that helped them develop answers to the perennial couples' question: "How do I/you feel?" with answers such as, "I feel engulfed," and "I feel abandoned." This deepened a scientific self-consciousness for both people, and assisted them in dealing with the sources of their feelings.

4. As a couple they consciously tracked—through verbal discussion, written journaling, and therapy and mentoring— the various ways that *victim/villain* has come to harm their relationship.

Angela, who was more verbally inclined than Harry, said she realized that she had internally decided she was the victim, was not "at fault" for the problems; she had decided (subconsciously) that Harry's distance, anger, and harshness were at fault: if Harry would just stop being angry, everything would be fine and she would be safe. But as the therapy continued, she realized that anxiety/anger had become the yin/yang in their partnership, each triggering and completing the other, rather than one person being a victim and the other a villain.

5. While they worked on their enmeshment/anxiety cycle, they also worked to solve the *presenting crisis*.

Angela and Harry developed two separate lists of what should be the *new rules* they each wanted Mark to follow. Once each parent had written his or her own list, they compared the two and negotiated a final list. They then proposed this list to Mark and explained the consequences of not meeting their expectations. Over the next number of weeks, as Mark failed to meet expectations, the consequences were immediately meted out by both parents. Angela agreed to "let Mark go to Harry more" (her words)—that is, spend less time with her and spend more time with Harry at soccer games, shopping, working in the yard, playing video games, hiking, and so on.

Not surprisingly, the two mother-son/father-son pattern shifts increased Angela's anxiety in the short term. She became anxious when Mark failed, made mistakes, and received consequences and punishments from Harry; she also became anxious and felt guilty ("I must be the bad parent") as she let Harry have more time with Mark and diminished her own time with her son.

In all this, however, one thing helped her immensely: Harry was hardly ever getting angry anymore and, thus, they were fighting much less. "Our marriage is definitely stronger," Angela told me. "We're happier and more peaceful as a couple. But I'm still the mom and it's very hard for me not to get worried for Mark and just want to hold my baby close."

Angela was, throughout her therapy, an immensely wise and conscious person. She understood that Mark's growing up, his new growing pains, his natural anxiety (for which, finally, this couple did see a psychiatrist and did get him on meds at thirteen) caused her increased anxiety about him and her husband. Very much because of her strengths as a mom and an individual, Angela (and Harry and Mark) persevered through the anxiety, and she ended up feeling much better about her son's and her marriage's future.

6. Make the angry partner *responsible* for his (or her) anger by helping him understand the root cause of the anger within him.

As Harry decreased his anger and harshness toward Angela, he became even "harder" on Mark. After a couple of months, this began to harm his relationship with Mark, so I worked with Harry and Mark to see how Mark's anxiety and "failures" were triggering Harry's fear of failure as a parent. We looked at *fear of failure* as a root cause. We compared how when Angela felt like a failure, she tended to become overtly anxious (and thus verbalize worry, ruminate, and make requests for more intimacy), but when Harry felt failure (e.g., when his son failed), his anxiousness (fearing the failure) led to more overt anger rather than rumination. Harry's own father had been extremely hard on him, and got angry a great deal; Harry was repeating this pattern, but he came to see that his quick bursts of anger and harshness were a personal issue that he had to claim and grow through.

YOUR WISDOM

One of our Gurian Institute surveys, to 4,109 recipients, asked for advice from people who had been married for ten or more years. In this and every other chapter, I share the wisdom in these answers. One of the most impressive things I noticed in the survey results was the natural balance that long-term married individuals tried to strike between intimacy and separateness.

Here is the first question cluster and an answer: If you were mentoring a person younger than yourself on how to succeed in couple relationships, what wisdom would you share? What tips and success-ideas have worked best for you? What are the keys in your mind to a long-lasting relationship?

• • •

Communication is critical. It is important to communicate authentically with the goal in mind to benefit the relationship. Come from a perspective of trust that your partner is not intending to hurt you with their actions or words. Be willing to be wrong. Be willing to listen and see things from their point of view.

The other important aspect for me was to be committed to something in addition to my husband, because when I am mad at him it can be too easy to let the relationship go. In difficult times, I remember I made a promise to God to love him and be with him. Or you can think of it as making a promise to the Relationship, if you are not a churchgoer. That promise kept me sane.

Date nights were crucial, especially when we were raising our children. These were literally marriage savers. Even just a lunch or meeting or a coffee is a great way to reconnect. Also marriage-saving was to treat each other the way we want to be treated. If you want more romance, be more romantic. If you want more freedom, give more freedom.

Finally, life is precious. Spend more time seeing the good and enjoying life than in finding fault. Usually, finding fault was more about my own shortcomings than his. As I stopped looking for mistakes, I felt a lot better about not only him but also myself, and I just all-in-all felt more safe and loving.

—Ally, 58, married thirty-two years

Question Cluster 2: If you were mentoring a person younger than yourself in what *not* to do in relationships, what wisdom would you share? What have you or your spouse/partner done that you know does not work? What pitfalls have you learned to avoid so that love can last?

. . .

When arguing with each other, remember that it is too easy to slip into insults and sarcasm, so it is important to tame that anger and that need to "win" and focus on the relationship and what it needs. To be able to focus on the relationship itself, you have to keep per-spective and keep some healthy emotional distance. You have to not obsess about your own feelings and his feelings all the time. Remember to be humble. The relationship is more important than either person.

Avoid refusing to compromise. In other words, compromise! My husband and I communicate openly and calmly now, and work to understand each other's perspectives. I used to want to win each battle. I learned there is compromise, there is understanding, and out of that is a deeper love and trust.

Argue all you want, but no matter what, you have to avoid low blows and mean comments. We avoid speaking poorly about each other's family. We avoid bringing up the past too much. We used to spend way too much time rehashing past wrongdoings. That was not fair to my husband or myself or our relationship.

—Ally, 58, married thirty-two years

The Freedom to Love and Be Loved

Rabbi Tamar Molino, who leads the Temple Emmanu-El Reform congregation in Spokane, Washington, told this story at a recent Yom Kippur (Day of Atonement) service:

A rabbi is talking to the class while holding a glass of water in her hand. She holds it for quite a while, until one of the students says, "Rabbi, isn't that getting pretty heavy?"

The rabbi responds, "The water itself is not very heavy, but if I hold the glass for a few minutes, I'll start to feel my fingers tingle a little; if I hold it for ten minutes or so, other parts of my hand will feel sore; if I hold it for even more time than that, my whole arm can feel numb and paralyzed. The water itself is not heavy; exhaustion and pain come in how long we hold it."

If your marriage is in any kind of distress, it is likely that one or both of you is holding on too long to something. The intention of this book is to take you to some places you have been before, yet shine a new light on them, while also taking you to some places you may not have seen quite as clearly before or not even at all. Over seven more chapters, building theory and practice step-by-step, we'll reach the ultimate place I am hoping you will go with me, where love is held together not by the stressful search for intimacy or distance (these are glasses of water that become heavy very quickly) but by the experience of intimate separateness—a balanced love that does not exhaust us or cause us constant marital pain.

As you'll see in the next chapters, we will not be any less intimate with one another because we work through the enmeshments; we still love one another intimately by working on communication skills, taking date nights, having dinner-table conversations, going on vacation together, giving and receiving flowers, sacrificing our own needs for the other. But these will become sweeter, more kind, more conscious, and more beautiful. As we back away from the drive for hyper-intimacy or hyper-separateness, we will feel free together to "be who we are" and come to feel, to a greater extent than we could before, safe and secure. We may well still argue, bicker, have conflicts—in fact, over the decades, that is a certainty—but we will also have emotionally self-disciplined and long-lasting marriages. As the decades pass, we will gradually sense that we have learned how to love.

Chapter 2

Becoming the Scientist of Your Own Marriage

MARRIAGES SUFFER WHEN WE BECOME AND REMAIN TOO CLOSE

Sarah, forty-four, and James, forty-five, both had very difficult childhoods and struggled to learn how to love. They did not want to divorce, but they worried that they would. Sarah and James were both depressed about their relationship, though for Sarah, the depression showed up as sadness; in James, it was masked in irritation. A powerful new study in the *Journal of the American Medical Association* has confirmed what therapists have suspected for a long time. For many males who are angry or irritated, like James, depression is a cause. For mainly biological reasons, but also some reasons of socialization, males tend to use anger as the go-to strategy for communicating a number of complicated emotions, including anxiety and depression. In fact, according to the new research, when male anger is factored into depression diagnoses, nearly as many men as women suffer from depression.

When I began working with Sarah and James, the couple disagreed on a lot, but they agreed that their marital stresses were passing on some "bad dynamics" (Sarah's words) and "too much tension" (James's words) to their three children (ages fourteen, twelve, and six). Their twelve-year-old daughter, especially, seemed to be suffering: the couple reported that she was having trouble in school—fighting, discipline referrals, fallen grades. The parents had been having marital stress for so long, they confessed in our first session, that they were thinking about divorcing "for the sake of our kids." Sarah was especially wondering if divorce wouldn't "heal everything—just give everyone a fresh start."

There was a great deal to unravel in this relationship, including the possibility of one or both of them getting treatment for depression. There was a great deal of enmeshment in this marriage, too—Sarah and James were both too close and too far apart, boomeranging constantly. Another descriptor for boomerang love is "push/pull intimacy." The couple would get close ("come close, come close!"), then move far apart ("go away, go away"), then try to come close again. Both Sarah and James recognized this pattern in their love once we began to study it together in therapy.

Some of what we worked through matched what you read in Chapter 1. In a particularly useful session, I asked them to study at least three other couples they knew to complete a scientific "anatomy of intimacy" (study the three couples for enmeshment/abandonment patterns), so that they could experientially understand some of the issues they themselves faced. From speaking with this couple, I could see that they were each *dangerously merged* with one another—and with personal shadows, illusions, and projections that we will delve into in this chapter. I hoped they would discover this merger, too.

Studying Conflict in the Relationships Around You

Albert Einstein said, "Science should not be left to the scientists." He meant that science is for all of us: we all should use it. I believe (though I do not know how to objectively prove this) that one of the reasons we have, as a culture, become so completely "closeness focused" is that "closeness" and "intimacy" can be studied in laboratory and academic environments more handily than separateness. I believe academic environments may not have in place right now the protocols that you can establish at home to study both your intimacy *and your separateness, or lack thereof.*

To go deeper into all this, please create three new sections in your journal:

- one for "couple"
- one for "parent-child"
- one for "workplace"

Please take a month to study some couples, parents/children, and your workplace. During this month (or more), write down, type, or dictate observations, anecdotes, and analyses of *conflicts* in these environments. These conflicts will help you uncover clues to ways in which the people around you—and perhaps you—might be dangerously *merged.*

Essential Questions Survey 3: Studying Conflicts in Your Relationship, Family, or Workplace

Sit with your journal and recall details about a recent conflict you got embroiled in. Talk with your partner, child (if old enough to answer), and/or workplace colleague about that recent conflict. If your relationship is too strained right now for this conversation, or if your workplace is not set up for this kind of vulnerability, try to talk with this other person about another couple's relational issues, another child's conflict-ridden friendship with a peer or teacher, or another colleague's workplace conflicts with someone else. Ask these questions (and any others that flow from dialogue about these):

1. Why do I think, from a psychological viewpoint, I get into conflicts?

2. How is my partner like my father?

3. How is my partner like my mother?

4. Do we get into conflicts because we feel too far away, or too enmeshed, or both?

5. Does one of us ignore or reject the other as a way of being mean, or for self-protection, or both? If both, in what circumstances does each one occur?

6. Does one or the other of us keep creating the same conflict in order to get a same result? If so, what is that result?

7. Is one of us too controlling of the other person?

8. Which of us has the flash/quick temper?

9. Is one of us cold or unfeeling? Does that create a lot of conflicts?

10. Does one of us constantly feel like she/he is drowning in too much of the other's feelings?

11. Am I too focused on what you feel for our own good?

12. How often, when I get mad at you (or anxious about you), am I mad, anxious, or sad about my own problems? And can I say the opposite of this about you?

Keep asking questions until you have answers that shed some light on many of the conflicts in your family, marriage, and workplace. Take those answers and those observations into this next section.

Studying the Danger of Merging

By answering questions and by studying themselves and other couples, Sarah and James discovered that they were a *dangerously merged* couple. They came to realize that they used conflicts to *disentangle themselves psychologically from being merged*. Both people needed psychological "space" (separateness, disentangling) from one another and from their own feelings and internal projections, but they didn't realize any of this consciously, so they overreacted to one another and grated on one another in order to ensure space and try to disentangle—to push each other away. Then, when being "far away" came to feel bad toward one another (it felt like abandonment), one or both would try to get close again. Then, when they felt too close for comfort again, they created conflicts (many times, they introduced permutations of the same four or five conflicts, over and over again) by which to disentangle themselves and push away again.

Sarah and James had become a couple that "related through conflict." This meant that they "loved" by fighting. The fights, and the silences in between (punctuated once in a while by very good make-up sex), came to actually feel "right" to the couple—like, "I guess this is how life should be." But the conflicts and the merger were wearing down the marriage and the family.

As I studied this couple and helped them study themselves, I asked them survey questions from the marriage counselor's viewpoint, and thus I helped myself and them to discover the following examples of how they were dangerously merged:

1. When Sarah was providing discipline or help to one of the kids, James would step in to disagree with her. A fight ensued. Sarah had become so tired of this she had threatened James with divorce because of it, and so James had learned to not intervene when both parents and a child were together, but then to go rescue the child (even countermand Sarah's discipline) later, when Sarah wasn't around. When Sarah found out her orders had been countermanded, she rightfully accused James of being manipulative behind her back, not supporting her, and not respecting her. More conflict ensued.

2. When James was doing a task such as cleaning out the garage (working independently), Sarah went to find him and tried to engage with him. She would say innocuous things like, "I want to help," "What should I do for you?" If he didn't invite her to help, she might ratchet up her verbalizations. This irritated the focused, independently

successful James. He would tell her he didn't understand why she had to bug him and try to talk with him right now. She would keep trying to engage with him, and she would feel hurt and then angry that he was busy. He would finally yell at her to back off and let him be.

3. When the couple entertained friends at home or went to social gatherings at other people's homes, James had a tendency to repeat stories and jokes he had already told before. Especially when he got two glasses of wine in him, he would say things like, "Sarah thinks I'm crazy, but I'm going to tell this one again." Sarah came to "hate" (her words) this joke/story-repeating quality in her husband. She would invariably roll her eyes, apologize to the group "for my husband who's still so immature," and/or say, "James, just shut up." James would generally go ahead with his joke or story, or decide not to tell it and, meanwhile, clearly resent Sarah.

4. When Sarah was talking at a social gathering, James would often interrupt her. He seemed unaware of it most of the time. Once, in therapy he suggested, "Maybe she's right that I do that, but it's probably because she's such a nag, sometimes I just have to get back at her." When I asked him for other possible reasons for the behavior, he said, "She's too strict about stuff and just makes me feel like I'm shit sometimes—so why do I have to listen to her when she won't listen to me without rolling her eyes?" James's interrupting behavior was causing significant stress in the marriage, and he wholly blamed Sarah for it.

5. When Sarah and James had a fight, James would tell Sarah she was "crazy." He emphasized that she was "insane." When he was especially angry, he would accuse Sarah of being like her "crazy mother." Sarah tried to defend herself

against this, but it cut so deeply into the fabric of her self-confidence that she felt powerless. Her mother had indeed suffered significant depression. Her mother had battled alcoholism and had been in a mental hospital for a brief time during Sarah's childhood. Sarah felt that James was, in her words, "killing me when he says that . . . just destroying me."

Sarah and James were merged like two flowers wound tightly together with snakelike tendrils. Even when winds might brush them apart so they can receive more sunlight, the tendrils' hold is too strong, and neither gets enough sun to grow straight. Soon, they do not feel like beautiful flowers anymore, but instead sense only the friction of being so close that they are always in the shadow of one another.

Another way to picture this is to hold your hands open, in front of you, facing one another. In a healthy relationship, your hands will be about six inches apart—just close enough to safely feel one another's presence and love, but not so close that the hands can't operate independently. In an unhealthy, entangled relationship, the hands will be pressed together, fingers intertwined so that the two hands make up one large fist. This is what Sarah and James had become. They fought constantly to break free, but they would get entangled again soon afterward.

In prior periods of human existence, partners who were merged in unhealthy ways could and would stay together for the reasons mentioned in the previous chapter—for physical survival, economic necessity, religious beliefs, and in keeping with social norms. In our modern era, most couples do not stay merged for more than a few years because, without these cultural glues, there is no need to stay together if two people are fighting constantly, for years on end. Sarah and James studied their five merging patterns (listed above) in order to become vigilant in avoiding or circumventing those patterns (as we'll explore further in a moment).

In addiction recovery, "codependence" is used to describe "unhealthy merging." Its use implies that merging is always a dysfunction developed in response to a disease, addiction. I don't tend to use the word (unless addiction is present) to describe enmeshment, preferring "merging" for relationships in general, because "merging" is an attachment term. In fact, to become "merged" is, initially, *a very good thing*; it is crucial to healthy bonding. Every person who falls in love *merges,* and the resulting "I will love you forever" is crucial to marital longevity. So, merging is natural and normal; it is hidden within our limbic system's initial attachment drive toward our partner.

However, if merging lasts beyond the first years of a relationship or marriage, it can damage the very love that we swore on that wedding day to protect. Sarah and James's intimacy had become an unhealthy merging for so long that they had a counterintuitive question to answer: *Are we still so merged after all these years that we can no longer be intimate?* That is a mind-bender, but one of the most important questions contemporary couples must deal with. Sarah and James, as they moved toward dissolution, had been dangerously enmeshed for so long that they felt they had to abandon one another in order to regain psychological safety, independence, and a future possibility of being intimate with another partner.

That is what divorce is, in the majority of cases, viewed from the context of the merging that we'll look at in this chapter: a forced and permanent disentanglement of two intimate people who have become so dangerously and confusingly merged (boomeranging between enmeshment and abandonment) for so long that the only way to find real intimacy is to divorce.

The Even More Subtle Merging—
with Our Projections

If you are involved in unhealthy merging, this situation will make itself apparent in obvious ways, such as in constant arguing and, in a more subtle way: you will see that you are not only too merged with your partner's self but also with *projections, shadows,* and *illusions* from your past. This kind of unhealthy merging will be discernible in the following ways:

- You will have merged with projections of your parents' selves. You will be projecting your parent or parents onto your partner—and, of course, your partner may be doing the same with you. This might show up when you get angry at your spouse for being too clingy (in exactly the way your mother got angry at your father) or for being too distant (in exactly the same way your father was with your mother).

- You will have merged with projections of your partner's early attachment self (the person you fell in love with years ago, a person somewhat different from your spouse now). When you see your partner who is thirty pounds overweight, you will judge him or her harshly because, in your mind, he or she is the partner of fifteen years ago with whom you are still merged, the partner who was once so thin, lithe, and whimsical.

- You will have merged with projections of your own early attachment self (the self your partner fell in love with). Perhaps that first self, the one your partner fell in love with, was comical, glib, always happy. You are not that now, but you remember that self, and you want to be that and that only, so you try to be constantly cheerful, and you hate yourself for it.

- You will have merged with illusions, ideas, and stereotypes of what love or a lover should be. You will project these onto your spouse without knowing it. (We will give more examples of this kind of projection and merging in a moment.)

After violence, addiction, and other obviously dangerous situations in a marriage, the most dangerous demons we often face in our marriages are projections—these shadowy figures that only our unconscious (limbic brain) sees, feels, smells, and battles. Sarah and

James got into conflicts not necessarily with "Sarah" and "James" (the real people in the room) but with projections, ghosts, mirror images, and shadows that they both had come to embody in one another and in their selves. To save their marriage, they needed to understand all these projections and move beyond them to a new stage of love. In order to do that, though, they needed to understand the who, what, where, when, how, and why of their projections.

When We Fall in Love

The projections begin the day we meet and fall in love. When we fall in love, we engage in a neural process of both *discovering* who our beautiful partner is and *projecting onto* this beautiful person the images and iconography of "lover" we want and need in order to be attached and to love. Back when you first fell in love, you did this. I did this, we all did it. We have to. Love is set up this way. Initially, we don't know our lover yet—we don't know our lover's real self, nor who she or he will be in ten years. We have to project man/woman, self/person, lover/companion, truth teller, sexual being, best-of-my-mother (or "not my mother"), best-of-my-father (or "not my father"), parent-of-my-child, marriage material, communicator, kind person, and/or breadwinner onto this other person. And even more subtle (as if all of that were not hidden enough), not only were we enthralled with this other person whose psyche was still unknown to us, and thus we projected these selves onto the person while asking that person to reveal who she or he really was, we were in a state of constant new growth and emerging self ourselves. That is, *we were not formed selves yet*, so we kept projecting images of who we were onto that new friend. How did we do this? We told lots of little psychological lies about ourselves, creating illusions about ourselves, so we would be loved. "Be honest about who you are!" our new friend or our peer mentors would implore us, and we tried to be honest, but sometimes we were too ashamed of who we are, so we projected images.

This, again, is quite normal. Humans bond in this internal and mutual ignorance (a blissful ignorance, to be sure) of our real selves because pheromones and hormones motivate our brains to figure out the thinking and feeling of bonding through images—ideas of who the other should be and will be, and the imagined iconography of who we ourselves will be in the future. Biochemistry primes us to cover up some "bad stuff" and try to lead, mainly, with our good stuff. If you think back to your months of early attachment, ask yourself when you first saw your lover's faults. Didn't you downplay them, substituting for them, in your internal imagery, all the "good stuff"? Of course, you did. If, during early attachment, your partner had the habit of inter-rupting you while you were speaking, you forgave that quickly—you projected his or her positives instead. You saw how the sex feels with him or her, how in the future you will train him or her not to inter-rupt anymore.

No matter the "fault," during early attachment we project around it so that we can love and be loved in a cellular euphoria. This is the stuff of poets, not just neuroscientists or psychologists. We are each Shakespeare, writing plays and poetry about ourselves and our mate in those early months of attachment. If you think about this, you'll notice that there is very little the human brain handles that does not involve some projecting, visioning, or imagining. No art gets made or technology gets invented without the imagination's visualizing it first. Love, beginning with early attachment, is the brain's masterpiece—a beautiful artwork created of illusions about Mom and Dad (our earli-est attachment figures) and self or partner that are neurologically wired into us via links between our limbic system (where we are *feeling* our love and infatuation, and where the neurochemistry of dopamine, pheromones, and other "love chemicals" are primarily sourced) and our cerebral cortex (the four lobes at the top of the brain that are charged with thinking, imagining, and most especially, *making love permanent via visionary, projective strategies and tactics*).

In artful collusion, our midbrain and upper brain work to re-ward our love object and, thus, ourselves by guiding our feelings and thoughts regarding the person our lover wants—projecting that person onto our lover—and our lover does the same. A number of research studies have shown this mechanism, using brain-scan technology. One study was done at the New York State Psychiatric Institute, as psychiatrist Michael Liebowitz tracked the neurons in the limbic system during early romantic bonding. He and his team saw on brain scans that the neurons were saturated with dopamine and phenylethylamine, PEA, a molecular substance, like dopamine, that stimulates feelings of elation, bliss, joy, and excitement in the brain. The team found that neurons saturated the brain with the feel-good reward chemistry *as long as the lover remained connected with the love object*—in other words, the lover has great incentive to do everything needed, including molding and projecting different selves onto the love object in order to keep the reward chemistry flowing.

Object relations psychologists such as James Masterson have called this natural method of attachment to one another, including attachment via projections, "object relations." The idea here is that we each relate to other people—especially our parents, lovers, spouses, and children (the people we are closest to) as psychological objects. In doing so, we naturally mold the object to fit what we need; simultaneously, we are ourselves objects being related to, attached with, molded by our mates. What we don't realize early in our love relationship is that, while "falling in love" with this "object," we project so much onto that object that we fall in love with illusion as much as reality. We don't realize the ghostly and false projections that come into the molding of that "object"— projections that enter the clay of the self like a million specks of dust.

What Have You Projected?

When you merged with your partner and soul mate, what did you project (and what did she or he project) to make sure that merging was successful? This question ought to be asked many times over a period of weeks so that you can keep making lists of those projections.

Here are just two examples provided by clients:

- When we first got together, Simeon talked about *everything*. He made himself seem like a girl to me, very open, very vulnerable. Now, twelve years later, he is not that at all. He has not been for years.

- When we fell in love, Grace was a thrill seeker, very free, very full of life. She pushed the limits and I knew I wanted to follow her anywhere. Now, eight years later, she hardly wants to go on a date. She is mainly about the kids and her work, which I get, but she is very little about anything thrilling between us. When I suggest something new sexually, she is not interested.

Early on, his pheromones and hormones made it possible for Simeon to "seem other than he was." Similarly, it is possible that pre-maternal biology helped Grace to project or be someone she no longer is (at least for a while now).

Here are two more analytic examples of deeper projections, one from a man and one from a woman, both in their forties:

- I learned in therapy that I made Kim Yee, my first wife, into my mother. I bonded with her like I bonded with my mother, and I didn't realize it. For instance, when I think about my mother dying, I can't sleep. I get nauseous, afraid. This is what happened when Kim Yee would go about her life, not paying attention to me. I would get nauseous. This has happened with two other women. I understand now that I have not separated psychologically from my mother. I keep projecting her onto the women I love.

- Tony was definitely my knight in shining armor. It's cliché and silly to think it now, but it's true. My father was my hero growing up, and Tony was just like my father—tall, athletic, quick-witted, a cute smile, neat, clean. He paid attention to me, cared about me, really believed in me. At least that's how it was at first. Later, he became a workaholic like my father, and I had to see that my dad was that, too, and I had to decide if Tony was really right for me. When I confronted him about not paying enough attention to me, he would say, 'I'm not your dad!' throwing what we learned in therapy in my face.

If in your notebook, journal, counseling, and marital conversations you take time to sort through your "complaints" about your spouse, you'll get a first look at projections. You'll glimpse some shadows from your first years of merging, years in which you projected your parents onto your partner and yourself. Doing this can be like going back in time—recalling that a lot of your complaints now can be therapeutically traced back to a bundle of selves you merged with but didn't *see* in early attachment. Now, you are fighting not only with your spouse but also with ten or twenty other people, images, ghosts, shadows, demons. Behind at least some of your present conflicts are broken dreams, lost expectations, unrequited illusions, and attachments to former selves. All of these (in the form of your partner) seem to constantly let you down, betray you, deny the truth of who you are.

YOUR INSIGHTS

Note: As part of their journaling practice, I ask clients to quote their own sources of wisdom in literature, film, art, and spirituality. We discuss arts and spirituality in our sessions as ways to trigger insights. It's an expressive arts tool useful for both female and male clients. It is also a tool that male clients often need more than women (just as they may need to physically move around when they talk) in order to discover hidden feelings. This is especially true of men who often cannot access as much emotional language as their wives or female partners in a fifty-minute talking session.

• • •

In Yehuda Amichai's poem "Poems for a Woman," the poet says, "Both of us are an illusion." As an Israeli and a Jew, I used to think this poem and this line was about how fleeting love really is, you know, like, "love is just an illusion and can be destroyed in a second." Okay, love is fragile like that, of course, but now I also see Amichai's line is about the projections Michael and I talked about in our session. When Carrie and I are merged, we can see the whites of each other's eyes but not the real face. We are not seeing the real person right here—we are seeing other people. She sees a passive man like her father, I see a woman who dislikes me. She sees a slob, I see a nagging Jewish mother like my mother.

   Love is ironic this way, I realize now. Being close all the time should make it such that I see my lover most clearly, but this is just not so. Closeness blinds me. I know this because when I complain about Carrie to my friend Tom, Tom just shakes his head and says, "But that isn't the Carrie I know." So who is the Carrie that I am knowing with all my closeness?

—Avi, 44

Separating and Disentangling
Ourselves from Projections

Avi's insight asked a question about closeness that may seem counter-intuitive if all we want from love is closeness. But if we want long-term healthy love, we need as much separateness as closeness, and Avi saw why: when he is close to Carrie, he is often merging with projections. He needs to detach somewhat from her and all those projections to see who she really is and who he really is. In realizing this, he is realizing that love can become a veneer covering hatred if the two people in the couple don't develop the psychological separateness to transcend their shadows and projections. For love to last, both people have to create separateness:

- From the selves the partner has projected onto them (including mom or dad projections).
- From the selves each has projected onto the other (including mom or dad ghosts).
- From the images each projected onto the other in the early stages of their lives (more on this in a moment).
- From the images each projected onto him- or herself and became so attached to that love seems impossible without them.

These four quadrants of personal scientific study involve understanding the four ventricles of the "heart" so that we can protect those four ventricles. Put a different way:

- I must courageously become a person who can love my partner without needing to remold him or her in my mind anymore.
- My partner must become a person who can love me without remolding me in his or her mind.
- I must become a person who disentangles my psyche from past projections of myself.
- My partner must become a person who disentangles him- or herself from past projections.

Sarah and James were actually trying to do all this in their conflicts, but they were unsuccessful because they didn't know what they were doing. They had become so merged and confused by love that they risked emptiness in order to survive. Later, they might have said, "We fell out of love with one another." Looking back, they might, we hope, see that they fell out of love with their early attachment–projected selves; they will have spent seven years, or even ten or twenty, loving the early attachment object and its projected selves from the past. They did not develop the healthy intimate separateness to discover who their lover (and who they themselves) really is—and in that discovery, and new stage of love, be happily satisfied.

Helping Sarah and James with Their Projections

To help Sarah and James, I looked for patterns in their behaviors that revealed projections, ghosts, and shadows. These were some of the patterns we explored:

- They were both *watchful* of one another's behaviors, both in the home and in public, not trusting one another emotionally or psychologically; they were constantly vigilant to see "who" or "what" the other lover would be that day.

- They were constantly *embarrassed by and resentful of one another*, in public and private, wanting to change the other person. They hoped, constantly, to remold the other's clay.

- They *took personally* a great deal of what the other said, did, did not say, and did or did not do.

- When one of them (usually James) said, "I don't want to talk about that," in response to an emotional or psychological query from the other (usually Sarah), the questioner became irritated, pressed harder, would not allow that space.

These patterns revealed that Sarah and James were *hypervigilant*, constantly studying one another (and themselves), judging and critiquing (within each separate mind and with the other), trying to change the "object" (the other person) who was so merged, so close, that they each "felt" every pinprick, every slight, every shadow's touch. Popular wisdom would say that these people need to get closer to one another, more intimate, so they can know who the other is and thus fully trust the other person. That popular wisdom is half of the puzzle, but in the case of Sarah and James, each needed to *detach* from one another's projections before they could both ever really be intimate. Though they had been married for many years, they were in the adolescent phase of their attachment (seeking to get free of parental control), but didn't know it.

The Family of Illusions

If you have ever been in therapy, you know that we can begin to understand our present projections by looking back at illusions from childhood and adolescence. By reflecting on our pasts, we can understand the ideas, illusions, shadows, and ghosts we carry forward regarding what "real love" is. As we hinted earlier in this chapter, the word "illusions" is an important one. These illusions can be ideas that were internalized in childhood and adolescence about what a parent (lover) should or should not be.

Sarah and James, like all couples that succeed in love, needed to go back into their histories to find some of the sources of their personal and couple projections and their hypervigilance so that they could become aware of and begin to deal with the unhealthy merging in their relationship. That unhealthy enmeshing had led, for them—as it can for all of us—to one of the killers of love: *overreactions.*

Here, now, are some of the illusions that created the hypervigilance and, thus, the overreactions in their closely merged selves, as both Sarah and James unconsciously fought with one another in the unrequited hope that their fights would heal and change their tender issues.

- James's intervention with his kids when Sarah disciplined them reflected painful physical discipline he suffered as a child at his alcoholic father's hands. As a trauma survivor, he overreacted to Sarah's disciplining his children (projecting himself, an abused boy, into those children). As he felt protective of his children, he would unconsciously project onto Sarah the role of "abuser of the children." While Sarah did not discipline her children physically, she was an authoritative parent. As she pursued good discipline from her children, unbeknownst to James and her, his childhood fears, anxieties, and angers affected his biochemistry and nervous system. The trauma stored in the limbic system of his brain (especially in memory centers in his hippocampus) flooded his amygdala and other parts of his brain. Unaware that he was projecting his father onto Sarah, he acted from his anxiety regarding being hit and intervened constantly to "rescue" his children from oppression and trauma. But this unconscious protectiveness of his children was dangerous to his marriage because he was imagining his wife as an abusive parent. Each time he did that, he damaged his relationship with Sarah.

• James took Sarah's eye rolls and other critiques personally, feeling that Sarah "nagged" at him, and that he was being "constantly cut with a million tiny knives." "Sarah wasn't critical of me in the beginning of our relationship," James said. "Whoever I was was fine with her then." Now, years later, a more critical nature showed up in Sarah, but James projected the "first" Sarah, not able to really see who Sarah was now. Sarah said, "Yes, but, you know, James was very close to me back then; he really wanted to please me—not so much anymore. In fact, now he says he's a victim. Why shouldn't I get critical of him?"

There was significant projection by James of parental disappointment in him, which created hypervigilance with Sarah and overreaction in his own psyche. His father had been, James told me, constantly disappointed in him; also, James's mother had been constantly disappointed in James's father. This created a kind of double whammy for James and Sarah: when Sarah asked James not to have a second drink, or otherwise critiqued or corrected him, or rolled her eyes, he projected his mother onto Sarah and his father onto himself. He "felt" his mother unreasonably nagging him and also felt that there was indeed something wrong with him as a man. ("Is Sarah saying I'm a pathetic alcoholic like my father?") These feelings amplified the shame and anxiety in him. He responded to Sarah by interrupting her, especially in public, and thus creating conflict with Sarah.

Sarah's psyche, for its part, was also dangerously merged with projections from her own history.

- Raised by a single mother who was distrustful of men (her parents divorced when Sarah was nine, and the divorce was a brutal one in which her father lost custody). Then, deeply affected by a date rape in high school, Sarah came to the marriage with an inherent distrust of men. As her parents' daughter, and then a victim of trauma at the hands of a violent man, she projected herself in a victim role with James, even though in reality she had smartly chosen a very nonaggressive man who wanted to please her, was not violent, and was inherently kind. Nonetheless, she projected a "bad man" onto James and overreacted to his actions and behaviors.

  I recall in one session her telling me she was a "mama bear" with her kids, but "I'm totally confused about what is happening inside me with James. I hate him and love him and hate him again." As we analyzed her projections with a scientific lens, using her journal entries as "proof," we discovered that she understood how to keep a healthy balance of intimacy and separateness with her children's developing psyches (she knew how to keep them close and let them go as needed), but she did not know how to safely feel independent of and separate from illusions and projections onto her husband. Feeling the danger of James as a bad man in her midbrain (especially the amygdala) created constant overreactions, like a person walking down a street always afraid of shadows and imaginary villains.

- An example of just how deep her negative and confusing projections went occurred as James felt a sense of happiness from doing a task on his own in the garage. Sarah felt abandoned, and thus interrupted him, trying to get him to pay closer attention to her so that she could feel rescued, loved, valued, and not abandoned by the untrustworthy, bad man. For his part, working in the garage, James felt that he was already doing a great deal to love her—by cleaning out the garage and thus making the house a better place for her and the children—but she couldn't see or value what he was doing. When I said to her, "You know, Sarah, men are basically protective and caring," she snapped, "No, they're not!" Sarah was so merged with the illusion and projection of James as victimizer, untrustworthy, and dangerous that she "saw" a bad man whenever James was not in her control; she "needed" him to become the intimate "rescuer" of her, not the brutal man. When James unconsciously felt her intimate tendrils invading his psyche, he finally yelled, "Back off!" He wanted her to pull away, give him space, let him be. But this call for integrity and trust in the relationship felt to her like psychological destruction of her core self.

Detachment at the Center of Love

Every coupled relationship will most likely evolve naturally to a point where love and intimacy may be at risk if both people don't see through their projections. As we'll explore in Chapter 4, this point in a relationship is one of the twelve stages of love. Just as freedom from projections must happen for every parent and every child, it also has to happen for every couple if an adult-adult relationship is to flourish. James and Sarah, as well as the other couples you've met thus far in this book, decided to do the subtle work of breaking through. They became observational, scientific students of their own love. They learned in therapy, in their journaling, and in their work together to identify their projections.

The couple gained tools for this work not only from therapy and the tools in Part I and Part II of this book but also through their faith. When I learned that they were practicing Buddhists, I asked them to bring in books, quotes, and arts from their life path to help with our counseling. For couples who are spiritually oriented, faith can help build and rebuild trust in marriages. One way this happens involves spiritual teachings regarding detachment. The word "detachment" is used in most religions and very much in the Upanishads and Sutras, so I asked Sarah and James to bring to our work insights from ancient texts on detachment. They brought these:

Katha Upanishad (Hindu): "The human mind is of two kinds, attached and detached: It is attached when in the grasp of things, desires, appetites, and illusions; it is detached when free from this grasping. If all people thought of love as occurring without the grasping as much as with the grasping, each would find peace."

Lama Surya Das (Buddhist): "Both yin and yang are essential for healthy, loving relationship; the one emphasizes attachment, the other detachment. Without one, the other is empty. Together, they are love."

Krishnamurti: "Have no image about your wife, your husband, your neighbor, or about another; just look, just see, directly, without the image, the symbol, the memory of yesterday, of what she said or did to you, what you said or did to her . . . stripped of these things there is a possibility of right relationship. Because then everything in that relationship is new; relationship is no longer of the dead past."

Sarah reflected, "Okay, in this context of detachment, I get what you mean about separateness and detachment from projections. I get what you mean about the illusions during attachment."

James said, "The message of Buddhism is nonattachment to outcome. Victim, rescuer, abusive father . . . these are illusions of outcome, as if I'm projecting ahead to the worst outcome."

Sarah agreed. "Me, too. I get too attached to certain images from the past."

James said, "If I take a detached point of view, I can see that most things Sarah does or says, including her tone of voice or facial expressions or eye rolls, are things to get attached to. They are not dangerous to my psyche."

Sarah agreed, "When I'm overly attached, too much yin and not enough yang, I project emotional or psychological, or maybe even moral, stuff into James working alone in the garage, as if what he's doing is dangerous to me, but it's not."

Using spiritual language, James and Sarah came to see that even though in the first months and even years of passionate romance they needed to merge constantly in a no-holds-barred, heart-open-to-the-max, image-projecting intimacy as the primary focus of the relationship, that time was past; now, they were at a tipping point of merging/enmeshment; now, they needed to gain spiritual detachment in love. While remaining intimate (yin), they needed to become detached (yang). Their love, they saw, could not survive if they did not take upper-brain control (frontal and prefrontal cortex executive control) of the shadows, projections, and illusions that plagued their biochemical, limbic, and nervous system responses to one another's projections.

The word "danger" especially helped them both. Their motto became, "Only react when I am in actual danger from my wife/husband." Applying this kind of detachment would take time and hard work, but it was exciting to them both: the idea that they were not in as much danger in their relationship as they had thought they were both intrigued and delighted them with its immense possibilities.

THE WISDOM OF SEPARATENESS

St. John of the Cross: "The soul that seeks to know God solely by attachment, even solely by intimacy, will not arrive at divine love, for the soul held only by the bonds of that human affection, however glorious the bonds might be, cannot fully make its way to God."

• • •

Rabbi Henry Glazer: "Forgiveness and gratitude are essential to human love. Both require us to be attached enough to feel our partner's open heart, and also be detached enough—as if we are in a detached state of solitude and prayer—to understand the long-view of God's plan for us with this lover."

• • •

Ibn-Arabi (Muslim): "In our attachments, when the heart weeps for the part of love it has lost, may the spirit laugh for the part of love it has found. Thus we discover union in two ways—one through touch in this world and the other through touch away from this world, in the other world without end."

Essential Questions Survey 4:
How Do I Know If I Am Too Merged?

In your journal or elsewhere, please complete this survey. Do it first for yourself, then for your partner. Ask your partner to complete it as well. This should give you four completed surveys.

1. Often, when my partner begins to talk with me about emotional stuff, I become tense. T ___ F ___

2. Often, if my partner does not initiate emotional conversation for a number of days, I become tense. T ___ F ___

3. Often, when my partner spends a lot of time doings things that don't involve me personally, I become anxious. T ___ F ___

4. There are certain tones of voice my partner uses that, as soon as I hear them, make me anxious or angry. T ___ F ___

5. Often, I ruminate about things that are going on (or not going on) with my partner for hours, even days, even when I know I should stop. T ____ F ____

6. I often overreact to small things my partner does or says, but just can't stop myself. T ____ F ____

7. I have understood from previous therapy experiences that I project my mom or dad onto my partner. T ____ F ____

8. I sense images of my parents and my partner's parents constantly circling our relationship, though I can't exactly track them. T ____ F ____

Did you generally answer True or False? If you generally answered true, you are most likely too merged. You will need to decrease your rumination and anxiety by increasing your detachment, and this is one of the most frightening steps you will ever take in your relationship. This book is a primer and companion for taking this scary step. You will have fits and starts, times when you think you've taken the step, and then relapse. This can go on for months, even years, but things gradually can get much better.

One of the most frightening aspects of this whole process is that you may learn separateness and detachment from illusions while your partner does not. You may become increasingly conscious of projections, overreactions, ways you are merged; you may assert more personal space and time, and become more independent, but your partner won't. In fact, it is possible that your partner will react to your new detachment by assuming you are rejecting him or her, which will cause even more pressure and stress in your relationship.

This kind of work is very much like grief—no two people face someone's death the same way, and both death and grief are mainly about separation. Like facing the ultimate detachment—death— your separation from dangerous enmeshment and merging needs support from others who have lived through it already and understand it. These people, often friends or counselors, can help us all create the authentic selves and relationships that await us. If you do not right now have a therapist and/or friend or friends who "get" what we've talked about so far in this book, I hope you will make it a mission during the next month to seek out those people and form bonds with them. You can do this in a group, individually, or in a combination. They can help you work on your own compulsions to ruminate, overreact, and battle shadows. While the future chapters of this book will keep providing new tools you can use individually, don't underestimate the power of one or two other human beings to help you gain the confidence to step out of the war with imaginary threats.

Instituting the Fourteen Free Passes Rule

As you gradually study and alter your relationship toward healthy separateness, there is a "cold turkey" technique you can use to speed your process. I call it the "fourteen free passes rule." The "fourteen" comes from multiplying the days of the week by two. The "free passes" will sound like this in your head:

- That's his mom talking, so I won't react. (I'll give him an emotional free pass on that one.)

- That's his dad talking, so I won't react. (I'll give him an emotional free pass on that one.)

- She's projecting her father onto me when she says
  _____. (I get that. I won't react.)

- She's projecting her mother onto me when we talk about
  _____. (I get that now. I won't overreact.)

- That's his ex that he is really talking to when he says
  _____. (I will not engage.)

- It's her ex she's mad at, not me. (I will just nod and say, "I'm sorry. Let's think that over.")

- That's trauma from _____ in her anger. (I need to step back and not engage.)

- That's stress talking, it's not about me. (I need to give him/ her space.)

If you both give each other two of these free passes per day (either because you now recognize projections and will not react or do not yet fully recognize the enmeshment and entanglement with the exact projections, but are giving the benefit of the doubt anyway), you will have twenty-eight free passes per week in your relationship. Over a period of months, even years, this powerful, daily, graceful tool for disentanglement from dangerous closeness will change your marriage away from enmeshment/abandonment, away from the cruelty of complex merging, away from pain, fear, distrust, even devastation—and toward real love.

You won't be perfect at this, you may not give exactly fourteen free passes every week, and some weeks you won't need them at all. Sometimes, you'll give a free pass when you perhaps shouldn't have. Other times, you'll grant one but your partner will not. This tool can't be perfectly applied, but if you use it even somewhat (you may go through a few weeks of being unsure of whether you should even do it—"Why should I give in, surrender, retreat, let him/her get away with that?"), a month later you'll most likely be feeling less pain and, hopefully, have enough increased happiness in your marriage that you will make this a habit going forward through the remaining stages of life. It is a form of detachment that bears a great deal of fruit over the long life of a marriage.

YOUR WISDOM

Start with making the commitment that you will stay together no matter what. Only break this commitment if you or your kids are in grave danger. When the opt-out option isn't an option, you will find the strength and courage to press on and make the relationship work, which will make it deeper and richer in the process.

Find ways to play together—hobbies, traveling, exercising, game nights, etc.

Never stop dating. Set a date night at least once a week. And enjoy a honeymoon at least once a year.

Root your relationship in a faith experience. I'm not saying this just because I'm a minister—actually there is a lot of research to support the fact that relationships in a faith community are happier and healthier.

Allow room for individual expression. You don't have to do everything together. In fact, it's healthier to have something you do that your significant other doesn't do, and vice versa.

Remain self-aware and emotionally separate enough to forgive one another freely.

Keep your relationship front and center when you become parents. Work on both its intimacy and its off-times consciously.

Love, ultimately, is a decision. Act in love, and you will stay in love.

Don't go to bed angry (even if you miss a night or two of sleep).

Don't take things personally and hold grudges.

Don't allow your significant other to fall into second or third place.

Lead separate lives as you need to, but don't drift so far that you lose touch. Keep your radar on so that when you begin to lose track of each other, you rectify the situation immediately.

—Tim, 55, Lutheran minister, married thirty-four years

The Joy of Separateness

The thirteenth-century poet Jela-leddin Rumi told a story (one that presumably came from Muslim or other traditions that predated him) of a man (it could be a woman, of course) who knocked on a beautiful door to the palace of love and heard a voice ask, "Who's there?"

The man answered, "It is I, Rumi." He expected the door to open, but it did not. This made him feel both saddened and angry. He kept knocking, kept trying the door, but he couldn't get in. "Why not?" he wondered as he walked away. "What am I doing wrong?" He went back to his life, and sometime later, he returned to the beautiful doorway. He knocked again, heard the same question, gave the same "It is I, Rumi" answer, but still he was not allowed into the palace.

This happened a number of times, until one day during a state of prayer and detachment, he had an epiphany. The next day he journeyed back to the palace, knocked on the door, and as the voice asked, "Who's there?" The man answered, "It is You." The door opened, and the man entered the palace of love.

This story has been told for centuries and has been given many interpretations, including the most obvious, that the man had to become utterly intimate with God as Self—he had to realize that he and divinity are not separate—in order to discover enlightenment. This is a powerful and accurate interpretation theologically. If we apply this story to intimate partnerships, however, we can add to that interpretation.

This man didn't understand intimacy; he had to become separate and detached for a time in order to have the insight that led to accomplishing true intimacy. In this interpretation, the story shows both the need for utter intimacy with our beloved—such beautiful intimacy that we feel like our lover and we ourselves are all of one beauty, all of one connection, "best friends," two people who complete one another from the inside out—*and* the need for separateness in the process of understanding and protecting that love.

In workshops and focus groups I have told this story as a "love story," and generous discussions have occurred. In one focus group, in order to study separateness and detachment as an essential part of love, I brought together six couples, all married or living together between twenty and sixty years. As the group began, I asked typical questions about marriage like, "Why has your marriage lasted so long?" Some of the answers involved comments like, "My parents stayed together, and that was really good role modeling for me," "When things got tough in our marriage, we fought through it," "My parents divorced, and that was really traumatic for me so I promised myself and Kate that I would never give up on our marriage."

Then I asked questions about closeness and intimacy rituals—questions like, "What strategies do you use to stay close?" Some answers were: "We make sure to have a good sex life." "We do something fun together every week." "We try to pay each other compliments as much as possible." "We talk about everything that we can talk about." "We never go to bed without saying, 'I love you.'" "We give each other a kiss every day."

Then I asked the focus groups to look at detachment and separateness. I asked, "How is 'separateness' and 'detachment' integrated into your marriage?" They knew some of the language and content of this book, so this somewhat abstract question did not come as a surprise. Some answers were:

"We give each other a lot of space, both internal and external." (This person was a therapist and explained that she meant, "I know when I need to take a time-out to figure things out myself, and so does he.")

Her husband, also a therapist, concurred: "We each take care of most of our internal psychological baggage ourselves. We don't expect our partner to heal it. Stuff about Mom and Dad and past trauma is not our lover's job to solve."

"We constantly check in with each other so we are very clear on what's happening with projections, illusions, feelings, thoughts, ideas—we don't try to read each other's minds too much anymore."

"We don't try to change one another too much—yes, okay, just a little, but not too much!"

"If there is something important, like the kids or grandkids, we talk about it, and we chat together at least once a day, but we don't mind having lots of silences together."

"I don't get in her way and she doesn't get in my way. We respect each other—we try hard not to control each other's favorite domains."

"I let him tell me what to do, and he lets me tell him what to do, but we do it to be helpful, not to be critical and judgmental. We're not perfect at this, but we're getting pretty good at it."

"We bicker or argue about gobs of stuff and somehow that works for us, don't ask me why. I think maybe it keeps us entertained. But we don't take the bickering personally."

"We're honest with each other, but we don't get bent out of shape if we're wrong. Our motto is: 'Honey, when you're right, you're right.'

"I don't expect him to make me happy, and he doesn't expect his happiness to depend on me. We each have our own projects and friends. We drive separate cars to everything so we can be free spirits and just come and go as we please."

"We used to say, 'She *should be* (fill in the blank) or 'He *should be* this way,' but we learned what that was about—the projections. We just kept projecting other people onto one another and expecting that the other person *should be* the projection. It took a long time to figure out the problem and stop doing that."

This statement came from a man and his wife who had been my clients. His wife concurred, "I tried to get him to be like me for years, but that was a mistake. He is who he is and I am who I am."

These couples possessed the wisdom of years, and just enough balance in intimacy and separateness so that the combination gave them a love that was filled, even decades after their initial attachment, with wonder and joy. Because of their intimacy, they could be in love when in each other's arms; because of their detachment and separateness, they could be in love for decades.

As we move forward in this book, I hope you'll carry with you all that you've learned so far in order to study how *you* love. If you notice that you are knocking on your lover's door and not being let in, step back and study, live, work, be psychologically separate enough to see what your shadows and illusions are, what things are triggering you to become enmeshed, how you are too merged with your partner. If your lover is constantly knocking on the door to your heart and you are not letting him or her in, get help to become psychologically separate enough to really learn what is going on. Study yourself and your lover (even if in your silent thoughts) until you discover any dangerous merging in your love.

And from this moment on, I hope you will promise to engage with your therapist or friends in as many conversations about separateness as about intimacy, as much about detachment as attachment, about rumination as anger, and about merging as love. As you do all this, you will be taking a major step toward increasing a healthy separateness: becoming a scientist not only of your own marriage but also of many other fields at once—psychology, leadership, parenting, and even faith and spirituality.

The new complexity of love in our era—the complexity in which, because the traditional marital "glues" are gone, we must make the choices that make love last—is actually a wonderful thing, not just for your relationship but also for the progress of human love. Finally in our human history we have arrived at a time when each of us can learn how to love one another—deeply and completely—through mastery of *both* attachment *and* detachment. This is some of the most sacred and freeing work we will do in our lifetimes.

Poets speak constantly of arriving at this kind of love. In the early twentieth century, the German romantic poet Rainer Maria Rilke wrote, "The trees you have planted in childhood have grown too heavy. You cannot bring them along." More recently, the American poet Alison Funk wrote, "In this ambiguous world . . . love can exceed our intentions." Like these poets, we can become very wise about love. Together we can discover a love that is less heavy than it has been, and a love that far exceeds the expectations we projected on our wedding day. It will be a love so real to us that we will know it as *our own* love, no one else's; and from it will grow wisdom in each of us that we perhaps never knew we had.

Chapter 3

Relationship Wisdom from *Both* Women and Men

UNDERSTANDING HOW WOMEN AND MEN LOVE DIFFERENTLY CAN HELP BUILD LIFELONG INTIMACY

Cindy, forty-one, and Tomaso, forty-three, have been married for fifteen years. They have two children, nine and eleven. In our first session of couple counseling, Cindy said Tomaso was, in her words, "a great father," and I learned from her that he was also the 65 percent breadwinner. She worked part time, earning about 35 percent of the family's income, and was "a devoted mother" (Tomaso's words).

The problem was, Cindy said, that Tomaso had been pulling away from her for about three years. The harder she tried to get him to connect with her, the farther away he became. She said she felt emotionally unfulfilled. The couple reported no affairs, and appeared to me trustworthy in that regard; there were no addiction or abuse issues, either.

In our first session, I asked both of them to fill out the first Essential Questions Survey (in the Introduction). We used their survey results as (1) a way for me to gauge the levels of both intimacy and separateness in their marriage, and (2) a way for them to look at elements of common focus for the therapy.

As we reviewed the results of the survey, both Cindy and Tomaso saw ways in which they were similar and different. For instance, Cindy and Tomaso discovered that they both felt a loss of emotional fulfillment but also felt it differently:

1. It was first and most comprehensively noticed by the female partner, Cindy, not so much the male.
2. It was experienced by Cindy in ways similar to the journey of grief defined by Elisabeth Kübler-Ross—denial, anger, bargaining, depression, acceptance.
3. Cindy saw the loss of fulfillment as caused mainly by the flaws of the male, Tomaso.

These male/female differences (and many others) are quite common, and very impactful, in understanding intimate separateness.

How Women and Men Love Differently

More than one thousand clinical and academic studies have explored the nature, nurture, and culture of male/female difference in the last few decades. These studies indicate a "worldwide gender spectrum"— that is, among the over 7 billion people on earth, there are around 3.5 billion ways to be female and around 3.5 billion ways to be male. You are one of the 3.5 billion. How you were nurtured, especially in early childhood, affects how you act as an adult female or male. What culture you live in affects how you live and love as a female or male. Nurture and culture profoundly affect gender. At the same time, the same research shows that there are robust brain and biochemistry differences in males and females that transcend culture and nurture; they operate in all of us, no matter what race or culture we come from. These differences enter the body and brain via the X and Y chromosomes, thus they are *nature-based* differences. Of these, here are four primary categories of difference related to how we attach and love one another.

- Neural processing: different ways male and female brains process all stimuli, including stimuli related to attachment, love, and romantic relationships

- Neural chemistry: different amounts of brain chemicals for love and attachment in the cells of body, blood, and brains of females and males

- Neural structures: differences in the actual structures or parts of the brain used in the action and meaning of love in males and females

- Brain activity: differences in blood flow in various areas in the brain depending on the stimulation, activity, including what gives joy, satisfaction, and reward to those parts of the brain that are "in love" and attach with others

While women and men both want and need love, and while both similarities and differences are born into the brain's gender regulation of that love, the understanding of the impact of brain differences on intimate separateness can profoundly change a marriage for the better, protecting intimacy quite powerfully.

One of the most important areas of difference in our brains and biochemistry is our differing needs and tempo for both intimacy and separateness. As I will show in this chapter, a psychological source of the intimate-separateness paradigm lies in the evolution of male/female brains, so these dissimilarities must be reckoned with if love is to flourish; they won't go away because they are wired in. Neuro-anthropologist Helen Fisher has noted, "Women and men are naturally different people—this has a profound effect on how they love."

A caveat: most contemporary research on the nature, nurture, and culture of gender differences focuses on heterosexual couples, leaving a relative paucity of studies in same sex and LGBT relationships. Gradually, over the next number of years, more same-sex couples will be studied; but right now, if you are in a same sex or LGBT relationship, you might read this chapter and think, "I don't need to read this because it is focusing on women and men in relationship, not gay or lesbian marriages." Please don't think that; a number of studies show that many gay and lesbian couples gravitate toward a similar "masculinized" and "feminized" division of emotional and psychological labor. Gender location on the sexual spectrum can exist in the brain even when the sexual organs are the same.

Looking at Brain-in-Love Differences

There are hundreds of differences, and we will not try to cover them all here; I'll focus on dissimilarities that relate to the intimate-separateness paradigm in love relationships. Even with all exceptions noted among the more than seven billion people on earth (and there are definitely exceptions; in fact, I'll show you brain scans of the exceptions later in this chapter), scientists find these differences run across cultures and races in regard to how we live and love.

1. A Gray Matter/White Matter
Processing Difference

Scientists such as Richard Haier, at the University of California, Irvine, and Ruben Gur, at the University of Pennsylvania, have shown that men tend to process life and love through approximately 6.5 times more gray matter activity than women, while women process life and love through nearly 10 times more white matter activity than men. "Gray matter processing" represents information-processing centers in *specific places* in the brain, and "white matter processing" represents the networking of or *connections between* processing centers.

In part because of this difference, you might see women connecting a number of emotional "dots" in a marital conversation—moving thoughts, insights, memories, and feelings back and forth through the different lobes and structures in their brains, including their verbal centers, and hoping for intimate conversations that allow them to express all the different dots, memories, feelings, and emotions. By mentally and emotionally going through the past and present to fully process all of the angles and complexities of the emotional situation, the woman might feel intense word- and conversation-based intimacy; she might seek constant emotional connection and contact to solve "a relational issue." To some extent, in some cases, talking intimately together is in itself the solution to an issue for her—as long as she is heard.

Among men, you may notice a more "gray matter" approach—a man may try to think out the problem in a particular part of the brain, and may verbalize the problem and its potential solution from only the perspective of that part of the brain; he may not connect all of the dots, emotions, memories, thoughts, and feelings that his partner is verbalizing and internally processing. For him, an intimate conversation may seem most helpful if it naturally inclines both parties toward separating themselves from intense emotions in order to help and serve the needs of the person who is hurt or confused. Getting embroiled in complex feelings and constant verbal intimacy may trigger defense responses in him, in part because his brain is following its gray-matter protocols. Especially if the man is "very male" on the gender-brain spectrum (already a fellow who doesn't talk about feelings a lot), his brain may be set up like this even more than his wife realizes.

As always, there can be exceptions to all these male/female patterns, because there are countless reasons a brain will do something. The psychologist JoAnn Deak calls the exceptions "the 20 percenters." My own research on bridge brains (see below) confirms her research. Researchers in the United States and England have confirmed this idea. Thus, we must figure that one in five people are exceptions to what we have just said. These women and men are useful "exceptions to the rule," bringing immense diversity to our gender dialogue and also pointing to the fact that gender differences ought to be taken seriously, since they do include most of humanity.

2. Brain-Chemistry Differences

Both males and females possess the same neurochemicals, but in differing amounts; and we secrete these chemicals through our blood, cells, bodies, and brains differently in different degrees in the same emotion-charged situations. So, for instance, when a couple is in a conflict—that is, their stress level rises—women's bloodstreams and brain cells fill up with more *oxytocin* than men's and men's fill up with more *testosterone* than women's.

Oxytocin is a bonding chemical—what scientists call our "tend and befriend" chemical. The neuropsychologists Shelley Taylor and Tracey Shors have done powerful work in this area, tracking how instinctual it is for women to tend and befriend (show direct empathy, get emotionally close, take care of, do what we think of as nurturing) when under stress, and how instinctual it is for most men to respond to significant stress by increasing their "fight or flight" responses (aggression/withdrawal, including nurturing others through aggression and challenge). Even given the obvious fact that men show empathy, get emotionally close, take care of a partner (tend and befriend), and women also fight or flee, the difference in stress response is so robust across cultures that Dr. Shors has called it "basic to human life."

If you think just about the two differences noted so far—white/gray matter and oxytocin/testosterone, you might look at Cindy and Tomaso this way: when life gets stressful for Cindy, she will most likely try to become verbally, physically, and emotionally *closer* to her husband's inner world—to bond more, talk more, connect more, search through her own and his mind, heart, and soul as much as possible to tend, befriend, and feel intimate. In her bloodstream, this is what has happened: her stress hormone (cortisol) rose, and that hormone stimulated a wash of Adrenalin and the bonding chemical oxytocin, which in turn stimulated her white-matter processing to look for multiple ways to tend and befriend. Thus, as a survive-and-thrive strategy, she seeks *more intimacy* rather than less. Shelley Taylor observes, "The women's tend and befriend instinct is one of the foundations of human civilization." Dr. Taylor is reflecting that, in large part because women are and do things this way (on average), our civilization, our children, our workplaces, and our relationships survive and thrive.

Simultaneously, however, Tomaso's brain, blood, and body have a somewhat different response to the stress. When Tomaso's cortisol level rises in his blood and cells, his body and brain systems experience an increase in testosterone—an increase that may make him more aggressive or territorial at one moment and more withdrawn or separate at another (fight or flight), depending on how his brain processes the threat he is facing. Thus, in a marital conflict—or in any area of stress—just as Cindy is trying to get closer, Tomaso may be trying to fight her emotional incursion and/or may move farther away. The couple may notice it in these ways:

1. Tomaso may become harsh and aggressive, pushing Cindy away emotionally (hurting her feelings significantly) by raising his voice and/or interrupting her, or by moving forcefully toward problem solving rather than prolonged listening.

2. He may withdraw from her, cutting conversations off before Cindy has fully processed, or by leaving the room once he is overstimulated, or withdrawing into himself in a way that she will feel is devaluing her emotional experience.

The normal takeaway from this research has been: "So, to solve this, men should become better listeners to women's emotions and learn to remain close and intimate throughout a woman's emotional process." While men can always become better listeners and work to feel emotionally closer to their partners, that popular interpretation does not fully take into account either the science of male/female difference or the long-term success factors that real love needs. Real love needs equal parts female and male, not more of one or the other.

You and I know this now because we've explored the intimate-separateness paradigm from the viewpoint of natural human attachment. We know that both intimacy and separateness are built into the human brain as primary needs; the brain makes the successful journey of attachment by fulfilling both edicts: to be close and to be separate. You and I know this, but most people may not. Human love is under destructive stress right now in our culture, as much because the "separateness" part of love is not understood as because the "intimacy" part is not fully realized.

YOUR INSIGHTS

I was married for fifteen years and now I've been divorced for five. For the first three years after the divorce I was very depressed. I just decided men were incapable of love and I didn't need a man. I went through the stages of grief, and what I came to call "the stages of failure."

But last year I got back into therapy and now I'm seeing things in a new way. The gender differences are profound for me. I see that Ichiro (former husband) turned away from my angry criticisms for more reasons than I realized. I used to think it was just because he was raised Japanese; "he just wants a docile wife." That's somewhat true, but now I see something else. He himself was pretty self-contained, pretty easygoing, pretty sensitive. Even when he got angry he did it in a passive-aggressive way most of the time. He was actually not the dominant Japanese male stereotype when we were alone.

For my part, I am more direct, I want to talk about things, I want to feel them and think them out and share them; he just wasn't built that way. I would constantly think he didn't love me because he was silent; I would think his passive-aggressiveness was all about him being an emotionless man. I would respond by trying to get him to change, be more emotional. I would get angry at him, criticize him. He would just pull further away.

I wish I saw this back then. It wasn't wrong to get angry at his passive-aggressiveness, but it just made things worse. I didn't understand that the separateness in him wasn't about me, against me, meant to hurt me—it was his way of trying to protect himself. And now I realize I think he was actually *trying to protect our love*. His brain was wired to pull back when we got stressed out so that things wouldn't get worse.

I misread it for years, just like he misread me for years. I wish every couple would go to therapy at five years into marriage if for nothing else than to just learn who each other really is.

—Sandra, 42

3. Brain Structure Differences

A number of structural elements in the human brain differ between males and females. As of 2014, scientists know of more than one hundred such elements. Many of these create differences in how and when the brain's reward chemical, *dopamine*, is processed. In other words, by instinct and brain chemistry, males and females experience the rewards of love, safety, comfort, and self somewhat differently.

The hippocampus, for instance, which is our primary memory center, is generally larger in women than in men, and there are usually more neural pathways between the hippocampus to emotive and sensorial centers in women's brains than in men's. While males may feel rewarded for remembering trivia—baseball scores, data for a project, and other countless areas of status-raising information, which is information that helps them compete better (testosterone)—women may feel rewarded for remembering "intimacy details," such as sensorial and emotional details that enhance tending and befriending (oxytocin). This is one way that different brain structures interact with different chemicals.

Verbal centers in the brain also differ in structure and placement in males and females. Thus, what rewards each gender verbally may be felt differently. Females have verbal centers in both hemispheres of

the brain, and they connect words to feelings and their own sensorial experiences on both sides of the brain. Males have verbal centers
mainly in the left hemisphere and connect their brains to the details
of intimacy, love, emotion, and sensorial information mainly there.
As British neuroscientist Simon Baron-Cohen has shown, women's
brains express more dopamine (feel more intrinsic reward) on average
when they remember disparate intimacy and emotional details. Men's
brains, on average, express more reward chemistry when the details
they've verbalized fit in a logical model, a "system" of logic, which aids
in status, competition, helping others through problem solving, and
keeping others safe.

Knowing these differences can help explain why so many women
go to a social gathering and remember more sensorial, emotional, and
relational details than their boyfriends or husbands, then ruminate
longer than males on those details. This brain difference may also explain some of what happens in a conflict between Cindy and Tomaso
a few days after a party. She may remember and talk about more:

- Sensorial details—the color of a tablecloth, the kind of
  flowers in the room, who was with whom.
- Verbal or conversation details—who said what to whom
  at which point and with what inflection and potential
  meaning.
- Relational or romantic details—how others in the room
  treated people during various interactions.
- Emotive or feeling details—what Cindy herself was feeling
  (and what other people may have been feeling) at various
  times during the gathering, with various people, in various
  parts of the room.

Because female brains may have more blood flow through structures at any given time, process life situations through more white-
matter neurotransmission, pick up more cues through all five senses,
store and process more sensorial and emotive information in the hippocampus and elsewhere in the brain, and verbalize on average more

of that emotive data throughout the life span, Cindy is evidencing an *intimacy imperative* in her brain. This intimacy imperative is instinctive, built in, reward based, and inchoate; it is *not* primarily "socially conditioned," though people often like to say it is.

And it is a beautiful thing to behold. To experience that kind of constant intimacy, both within the brain and in relationships, is a powerful way of connecting to many people, many hearts, many minds, in potentially constant empathy. However, it is also, as neuroscientist Louann Brizendine has put it, difficult. "Women will tend to ruminate on their intimacies to such an extent that they will become depressed." The constant "closeness" of the intimacy imperative built into the female brain is not all good for relationships or love. It may need male brains to balance in the short term and, via male separateness, to help love last in the long term (more on this in a moment).

4. Activity and Blood Flow in the Brain

Women's brains don't rest or deactivate (zone out, take a break, and separate themselves from life and from stress) the way men's brains do. One of the first scientists to show this was Dr. Ruben Gur at the University of Pennsylvania. Using PET scans of the brains of women and men, he discovered in the 1980s that women's brains are constantly working on life and intimacy, whereas the male brain almost completely shuts down a number of times per day, pulling away from intimacies and connections.

One fun example of this (which you can try at home) is to watch what a male's brain is doing while he's channel-surfing. You may notice that he is not absorbing much of the content of what he's watching—he's taking a "mental nap"; he's not connecting with the people on the TV (twenty of them can get mowed down in an action movie and the deaths will barely register on his brain). If you scan his brain at that moment, you'll see that his brain structures and areas for connection, intimacy, and love are shut down (see the graphic on the opposite page).

Males "shut down" more than females. Evolutionary biologists believe this ability in males—which shows up in males of all races, on all continents—was an evolutionary advantage in hunting. Males kept their brains activated when needed for their important tasks, then went into a state of separation from emotive, sensorial, and verbal stimuli when they were recharging or just waiting for stimulation (the deer to come onto their path).

In other words, we again see the "separateness" part of the human equation of love. When you look at brain scans of women who are trying to "rest," you'll observe that more than half of their brains are still lit up. Women sense this; they complain, "I can never shut my brain off!" Sometimes they look enviously at husbands who seem to be able to turn their brains off and separate themselves from emotional rumination, seemingly at will.

To show you this on brain scans, I asked Daniel Amen, founder of the Amen Clinics, for images of a female brain (on the left) and a male brain (on the right); he scanned these brains while both women and men were resting their brains (zoning out). On these SPECT scans, you can see that a brain like Cindy's is constantly active in centers of intimacy and relationship, even when she's trying to zone out, while a brain like Tomaso's has deactivated emotive, relational, verbal, memory, and intimacy centers during the rest state.

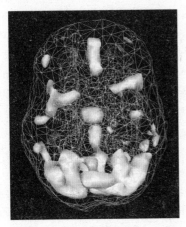 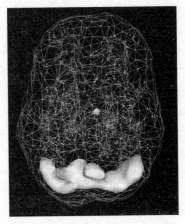

Female at rest   *Male at rest*

Dr. Amen has done more than ninety thousand brain scans over three decades, and he recently completed a twenty-one-thousand-scan study of women's and men's brains. In this most recent research, he found profound differences in seven out of the eight primary elements of male/female brain activity. He concluded, "People sometimes want to say that men and women are not different, but we have proven that they are."

Like the work of Drs. Gur, Brizendine, Haier, and others, Dr. Amen's work shows us something we must come to grips with in the new millennium if we are planning to make love last: women tend to pick the *intimacy imperative* because their nature, nurture, and culture all lean their instincts in that direction; men are quite intimate and loving, too, but they bring a *separateness imperative* to human love. And the wisdom of that separateness needs to be equal in importance to the wisdom of the intimacy imperative. Intimacy and separateness in balance are a natural need of human love, though we often judge love's success more through a female lens than a male's—more for an intimacy imperative than for a separateness imperative.

5. Bridge Brains: Exceptions to the Rules

Fifteen years ago, I coined the term "bridge brains" to give a name to the exceptions to the rule. After I had taught gender difference material at Gonzaga University, then began to teach it to couples, workshop attendees, and corporate groups outside the university setting, women would often say, "But you know, I think I fit a lot of the qualities you're presenting as the male brain." This especially happened when I counseled a female engineer or a female CEO of a large company. She would say, "I was a total tomboy as a kid. I couldn't sit still, I didn't like dolls much, which got me rejected, even attacked, by other girls. I was really good at math and science but not so much at reading. I still prefer working alone to talking a lot with people. I'm not very emotional."

Her self-description would powerfully illustrate that she was physically, emotionally, and spiritually a woman—and she wasn't trying to limit or stereotype herself one way or the other—but she had always sensed instinctively that her brain, in some significant ways, didn't work in quite the same way as "other girls' " or "other women's" brains worked. Until she saw brain scans of bridge brains, she hadn't realized who she was.

This same thing happens for some men. A man would say, "You know, this 'bridge brain' thing is a real epiphany: all my life I've known I was a 'bridge brain,' though I didn't have the language for it, and I certainly didn't know there were brain scans that could show it to the world. But I was the boy who liked soft things. I didn't like team sports, I was very sensitive, I have always been more verbal and emotional than most guys. I'm in fashion and love to work with colors, soft tactile fabrics."

This man would point out characteristics in himself that showed him to be a higher oxytocin/lower testosterone male, with a brain formatting that included more "female" characteristics—a greater expression of self through more white-matter processing; more connections between word centers and emotion/feeling and sensorial centers; and more pull toward intimacy with less pull toward independence or separateness.

These women and men bridge the genders. Both Dr. Amen and Dr. Baron-Cohen have used brain scans to show subtle differences between a bridge-brain scan and a more prototypical male or female scan. Dr. Baron-Cohen, for instance, has estimated that around one in seven men and one in five women are in the middle of the brain spectrum (bridge brains). Dr. Amen has shown similar figures, and also shared this third scan, a bridge-brain male (below).

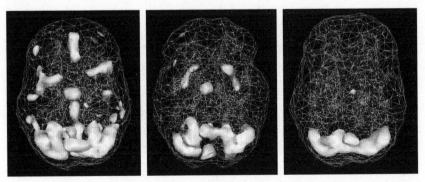

Female at rest   *Bridge*   *Male at rest*

Notice that this man's brain looks a little more "female" than the other man's brain. In this bridge-brain male's scan, there is some activity in memory, emotive, and thinking centers like female brain scans show (which can lead to more rumination about intimacy and more talking about feelings and intimacy). This is an exception to the rule for a male because, in most male brains, as you saw in the scan earlier, there is little or no activity in these intimacy-enhancing centers when the man is zoning out or feeling separate.

By the way, if you wonder why I am not also showing a bridge-brain female's scan, it is because, as Dr. Amen told me, "the female brain has so much more activity than the male in all states of being that differences between prototypical and bridge-brain females are much more difficult to see with certainty, whereas the differences in male brains (mainly because of the nearly complete inactivity in the resting prototypical male's brain) show up much clearer to the naked eye on brain scans."

Analyzing Your Marriage

The overall areas of difference in male and female brains have a lot of consequences and lead to many relational differences. In this book, we are most focused on utilizing the intimate-separateness paradigm. In that context, you look for subtle "difference" clues in your relationship or marriage by seeing if these differences exist in your life. (If you are in a same-sex relationship, see if these appear between more masculinized and feminized partners.)

Instrumentality/Emotionality Difference. Recent studies at the University of Texas, Austin; Southwestern University; and Rutgers University show a male/female disparity in "instrumentality vs. emotionality." The more "male" a person is on the gender brain spectrum, the more "instrumental" he (or she) tends to be. Thus, the *emotionality* (intimacy) life of the relationship may become less important to the male after a few years of marriage than its *instrumentality* (usefulness). "Instrumentality" means that the relationship is, to him, a safe, stable place in which to be in love, have sex, raise children, do hobbies, relax, enjoy life, care for, and nurture others. The amount of verbal or emotional intimacy in the relationship may not be as important to him. Thus, while a woman, wife, or girlfriend may measure marriage success by its degree of intimacy, the man may (quite unconsciously, in most cases) measure that success by its instrumentality. This man may miss the fact that, without more emotionality and intimacy, his partner may feel abandoned—an abandonment that can later become "I am divorcing you because you do not emotionally fulfill me," or "I'm divorcing you because we've fallen out of love with one another." Many men are living out their need for instrumentality without mentoring or counseling assistance; as a result, they do not see the divorce coming and they are shocked by it. Often they say, "But things were going fine—we had a few issues, sure, but the kids are good, we love each other; what more does she want?"

For the woman (or man), the more "female" the brain is on the gender brain spectrum, the more he (or she) may yearn for daily intimacy rituals and daily emotional conversation. Especially in an era of no-fault divorce and economic independence for women, the "instrumentality" of the relationship may be less permanently valuable to her than the emotional fulfillment by which she may measure her success as a lover, wife, and intimate partner. If, over a period of years, the emotional connections become too depleted (or become constant sources of rage and anger), she is likely to leave her spouse for "lack of emotional fulfillment." She will almost invariably be depressed at some point. Her man, unfortunately, may not notice how depleted she feels, how low her self-worth is becoming. Her stress hormone levels have been elevated constantly as she has spent time with and near her spouse seeking "I love yous," date nights, and other sensual, physical, and psychological moments of romance and shared love; she feels she has been rejected by the man she loves, a man who is not seeing her pain.

The bottom line on this instrumentality/emotionality difference for our purposes is to realize that, while a woman has been seeking more intimacy, her husband has been satisfied with more separateness. Neither of these is "wrong." Both ways of love are needed. But no one helped these two people to become aware of this difference and to build intimacy and separateness rituals that could accommodate it. In other words, no one taught this couple the intimate-separateness paradigm—or that not only could they be too far apart psychologically for a healthy marriage but they could also become too close.

The Dopamine Difference. Research at the University of Texas, Austin; Southwestern University; and Rutgers University has also shown male/female differences in the release of the feel-good chemical dopamine. These differences go so deep into our male/female processes that they will not be socialized out of us all one day—they are wired in and they show up to varying degrees on the gender brain spectrum among all individuals.

Whereas female brains tend to release more reward chemical from *emotional connection* as a self-worth builder in a long-term relationship, males tend to release more reward chemical from the *status and worth* they gain by being in the long-term relationship or marriage. Thus, the idea of intimacy vs. instrumentality is so hardwired that it differently affects the pleasure centers in the male and female brains. It is probable that this dopamine signaling dissimilarity actually links back to the X and Y chromosomes and the oxytocin/testosterone differences we noted earlier. Our human history (thus our present DNA) is wired this way:

- Females feel safer and better cared for if they can ensure strong emotional connections with other women and men including (if hetero) one man, as they raise their children.

- Males feel safer and better cared for if they can instrumentally develop family-protective status in competitive hierarchies (in which they can assert their identity and rise up in the hierarchies as they are able) and as they bond with other challengers in the hierarchy in their search for increased status.

From the evolutionary biology standpoint, "emotional safety" and "a sense of emotional reward" feel somewhat different for males and females, even to this day. Females tend to see less aggression and in-dependence as a neurochemically rewarding experience; men may feel satisfied by situations that involve less constant intimacy and more independence.

To test whether this difference between genders holds true across cultures, anthropologists Beatrice and John Whiting studied boys and girls in Japan, Mexico, Kenya, the Philippines, India, and the United States. They found that in all the cultures, both males and females tended to "measure" success in life and relationships somewhat differently. This, then, is something to take very seriously.

When I share these findings with couples, I hope to bring science into the study of love so that we can help both women and men close the gaps between them. With men (or women who are bridge brains), I try to coach them to pull back on some of their natural independence and to seek more closeness:

1. Go on a date night once a week with their partner whenever possible.

2. Provide sensorial love, such as flowers, once a month or at least on important occasions.

3. Have sex and provide equality of sexual intention—make sure she is satisfied sexually, too.

4. Verbally value her at least once a day for all that she does and gives to you, your family, and others with gratitude and a sense of valuing her unconditionally.

5. Say "I love you" at least once a day.

Often, unfortunately, I meet this man (or non-intimate woman) after the relationship has begun a painful downslide. Sometimes the woman or man has said, "About that last one, why should I say 'I love you' when I don't love her/him right now?" I respond, "If there is even a spark of love left, do it. You don't *like* him or her right now, but you do *love* him or her. Would you be here in counseling if you didn't?" I try to challenge this person to understand *the deep nature of his or her partner's need for emotional relationship and verbal-emotional valuing.*

On the other side of this coin, I use understanding of these trans-cultural differences to help women and men develop a greater separateness from the intimacy imperative when it's necessary for love to survive and thrive. This can be especially needed in response to dominant bonding strategy differences between women and men.

Threat Defense/Bonding Opportunity Difference. The female brain is often so active, so white-matter oriented, so able to connect verbal, emotive, sensorial, and memory material, it tends to choose emotive processing as the *dominant bonding strategy.* One of the primary reasons women so often "lose themselves in love" even twenty years after the wedding is the way they set emotional boundaries (or don't set them). A woman (and, of course, a man can do this, too) will be so instinctively focused on bonding and emotional connection that she will not develop a separate, independent self as fluidly as her partner might, or she will relinquish it to her partner and not get it back.

Her mate, on the other hand, might see her complex emotive processing and intimacy not as a bonding opportunity but as a *dangerous territorial invasion*—an invasion of his independent self. This is especially true of men who are more aggressive by nature and more "male" on the brain spectrum (football players, lifelong soldiers, etc.). These males may operate in a "male way" not only because of higher testosterone levels than average but also because of more (or less) *vasopressin,* a male bonding and territoriality chemical. They may see emotionality as invasion of territory and, thus, try to defend themselves against emotional incursion. If they could articulate what they are doing, they might say to their spouse, "You think love is about breaking through your lover's defenses, but I think it is equally about allowing me my defenses."

Remember, this more "male" approach is no worse or better per se than the "female" approach of emotional bonding and relinquishment of her Self for the sake of emotional connection; these are simply two ways of being that come into conflict if we don't understand them. Especially when a very "male male" guy and a more "female" woman marry, this difference can become problematic. As the female-brained partner asks for more feeling-talk, the male-brained partner's fight/ flight instincts may rise; his brain may delay complex emotional reactions (male brains often need more time to connect dots and process emotive material). The male may need to mask emotional vulnerability with aggressive gestures in order to perform and succeed in life (as soldiers must); he may naturally favor physical or sexual emotion over verbal communication; he may in general be more performance driven and less intimacy driven than his spouse; and he may have learned to successfully solve all issues, including emotional ones, through logic and design systems in his workplace, which he brings home to his marriage.

If you are a more "female" woman married to this kind of "very male" man, the intimacy vs. separateness psychology can feel, quite often, tragically different. As you study your relationship, remember that while complex emotional conversation is, for you, a way of bonding your self with his self, for him it may be a threat to his self, not a happy bonding process. He may need safe rituals in which to bond with you emotionally.

A female client, thirty-nine, married to a mechanical engineer, said this after we had worked together for about a year: "We're finally getting this figured out. We do our emotional talks and sharing during one of three bonding rituals—walking on Sunday mornings, riding bikes together one evening a week (depending on work schedules), and, sometimes, after sex. During these times he opens up to me about his feelings and he also hears me better. I can say the things to him I want to say without seeming to scare him away emotionally. I've learned that unless we have these rituals together, he's too focused on work or other things at other times not to feel like I'm attacking or invading him with my feelings and emotions."

When I share this story at a lecture or workshop, someone will invariably say, "But this isn't fair to her. Why should she shut off all her feelings (except during these ritual times), while he gets a free pass to be exactly who he is?" My answer is, "This dopamine/reward system and this fight/flight system are so wired into him that you condemn your relationship by approaching this ideologically. Just as he has made many sacrifices for his wife, children, and marriage, this is a sacrifice she can make not only for him but also the marriage." Many of the other sacrifices he will make appear in the list above; indeed, if his wife alters her approach but he never gives her the flowers, cards, date nights, and other bonding opportunities she needs, the marriage will also be in jeopardy.

Sometimes, however, the immediate "unfairness" of the wife's not pushing her emotions on her husband remains a concern for workshop participants, and we keep talking this out in order to look at it from all angles. By the end of the workshop I find that most people generally come to see the wisdom of a science-based, hardwired look at this matter. One part of the equation that invariably comes out in the discussion is that the wife often has access to five or ten people in her social system with whom she can process her feelings. Her hardwiring is safe. Her husband's hardwiring may be more subtle and need more help from her. So this is a case in which the wife alters her approach to fit her husband's.

Another point invariably made in workshops is this one: "Why didn't we see this coming from day one? Why did it seem early in the relationship that he was very emotionally open?" This, too, has a "hardwired" answer. Women often do not notice this dominant bonding strategy difference when they are courted and fall in love, or even during early years of marriage, because the limbic system difference is overridden by pheromones and other love chemistry in that first year or two, as well as busyness with children and daily life in early years. But by the time the relationship moves past two to four years or four to seven years, it can display this pattern quite clearly, and couples absolutely need to know what they are in for.

When I work with a couple who is obviously in this situation, I teach intimate separateness as a marriage-saving paradigm:

- I task the man with ritualizing his shows of intimacy and holding to the rituals (as listed earlier).

- I work with the woman to understand the emotion vs. threat psychology so that she stops taking his defenses against verbal intimacy personally.

- We talk about how our popular culture portrays true intimacy as being about breaking one another's defenses; in reality, it is also about allowing one another's self-protections.

- I help both the woman and the man focus on finding same-sex friendship groups with whom to practice the gender-specific intimacy patterns they are living out internally. These friends not only can be spontaneous peer mentors, but they can also help both parties to feel the comfort that our ancestors felt when intimacy and separateness pressures weren't felt internally.

THE WONDER OF SEPARATENESS

One of the things we've learned in more than thirty years of providing couple therapy is the importance of helping each person "hear" one another as different voices, even voices that are not always harmonious. In the throes of early love, we want the other person's voice to be in harmony, be the same, sing the same song. But as we love and love and love some more, we need to realize that we married this other person because their song is somewhat different from ours, and therefore complementary.

Vive la différence, in other words. That "other" song needs us as we need it because of our difference—not our sameness. As the many disharmonies emerge between two people over the years, they can become scary or thrilling. If we will be patient with them, respect them, and love them, they will be thrilling—because hearing that disharmony, we hear our best friend, our soul mate, our lover calling out to us with deep need. This need is his or her need, not our need—and caring for this other person's need is one of the most important reasons we are alive. Compassion is our life work, and our mate is a magnet for not only our need to be loved but also our need to give love where needed.

So for us in our therapeutic work, we are teaching: If all two people do is listen for the ways in which our partner's voice is like our own, we will not fulfill our purpose as lovers. We will not make the world safe for another person or ourselves, and we'll feel disappointed.

—Sue Amende-Plep and Gary Plep, marriage and family therapists, married thirty-six years

Love Between Two Brains

When we love, we are two bodies loving one another, two souls mating, and two brains being intimate. Body, mind, and soul, we form a union that we hope will satisfy us emotionally, help us raise children (if we have children), and not be torn apart by adversity. Not until just recently in human history have we scientifically proven how differently our brains operate while we are living, loving, working, and communicating together. Now we know.

In this context, the intimate-separateness paradigm is a middle ground between two brains—it is a rational (and passionate) compromise position in which we can embrace rather than avoid innate differences. To explore what I mean, let's revisit a scenario we looked at earlier and add some new detail to it.

Why Is He So Angry?—Revisited

University of Washington psychologist John Gottman has identified a number of ways of knowing if a couple will last. One of those is whether the man constantly gets angry at his wife. If he does, then Dr. Gottman and his colleagues predict divorce for that couple with amazing accuracy.

The common interpretation of this finding has been that the male's anger is significantly burdening the relationship. Gottman's research has been replicated, and most therapists and mental health counselors, including myself, would agree with Gottman: a pivot point for disaster in a marriage is a constantly angry spouse; male harshness, anger, and criticism, in particular, can become so crushing of a woman's self-esteem that, at some point, the woman seeks alternatives to that belittling of herself, including divorce.

While this is true, something else is also true. We noted it earlier: male anger can also save a marriage, especially if viewed through the lens of the intimate-separateness paradigm. Armed with that paradigm and the gender-based brain research, we can see some potential backstory to that anger.

To do this in your own home, look at your relationship or, if you are not seeing a lot of anger, look at another relationship that is evidencing a lot of anger. Ask these three questions (I use the "male anger" scenario and the male pronoun, but you can substitute female as needed):

- Do we fully understand everything that causes that male anger?
- When in the relationship did that anger show up?
- Why is he so angry?

Some of the anger can come, of course, from the particular man himself—perhaps he's naturally narcissistic and demanding; perhaps he is going through andropause and his shifting hormones are creating irritability; perhaps he is overstressed at work and inappropriately takes it out on his wife; perhaps he has PTSD or depression; perhaps he "has a temper" by innate personality; perhaps he is drinking too much; perhaps he is dissatisfied with his life and thinks of his wife as the cause of his troubles. There are countless reasons he may be angry,

and he must indeed learn to manage his anger; but given the prepon-
derance of couples in the last three decades who fit this pattern, my
antennae go up when I meet a couple reporting an angry man. I want
to know, "What, if anything, in the relationship dynamic might be
causing his anger?"

A powerful answer is quite often recognized among my clients
once I point it out, but is hidden until that awareness takes place.
Quite often these "angry men" became so five or more years into the
relationship. They say something like this:

- She won't let me alone emotionally.
- I can't satisfy her emotionally.
- She has to talk about everything with me.
- I don't have feelings like she has and never will, but she
  badgers me.
- I can't be her girlfriend, but she wants me to be.

Meanwhile, the women they are bonded with say things like:

- He's too distant. I need more heart, more intimacy.
- He never learned how to be close, he doesn't know how, he's
  just like his dad was.
- He'll initiate sex, but otherwise he won't even talk to me.
- He hides his emotions from me; he won't open up enough.
- I need more from him—maybe I just need more than he
  can give.

While the women are voicing the need for more intimacy, the
men are indicating their need for more separateness. That is, behind
the male anger is this hidden conflict. With equal vigor, while women
say, "Why are you so far away, I want you close," the men are saying,
"I love you, but get away, you're too close." As these two apparently
different needs do not get met, the women and men become depressed
and angry, and the female anxiety/male anger pattern emerges ro-
bustly.

Because I was so often seeing this pattern in my first ten years of clinical practice, I developed a number of surveys to help women and men figure out where they fit on the gender spectrum. These surveys allowed them to dig deeply into their common and conflicting needs for intimacy and separateness.

Even if you are not in an angry relationship, please complete this fifth survey in the book. See where you might fit now on the gender spectrum, and then we'll hone in on the intimacy/anger pattern.

Essential Questions Survey 5: Where Do You Fit on the Gender Spectrum?

In your journal or elsewhere, record A, B, or C as your answers for each item.

1. When you are in the car talking with your partner about a party you've both just gone to, and your partner says, "Did you notice Melissa and John seemed to be having marital problems?"

   A. You didn't notice anything between Sarah and John.
   B. You did notice some issues between Sarah and John, but barely.
   C. You noticed a great deal going on between Sarah and John and can't wait to talk about it.

2. When you and your partner sit together in front of the TV to "channel surf," how important is possession of the remote control to you?

   A. You become anxious if you don't control the remote because you believe your partner will want to watch programs that bore you or make you agitated.
   B. You may not enjoy yourself if you give up possession of the remote, but it's okay with you if your partner controls it a small percentage of the time.

C. You don't care what channels she or he surfs during the time you're together watching TV.

3. When you and your partner talk about things that happened many years ago, who remembers more sensorial and emotive details?

   A. You rarely remember these experiences with as much detail.
   B. You often remember these experiences with as much detail.
   C. You have as good a memory or better as she or he does for these sorts of sensual details.

4. Your partner complains that you don't hear him or her or that you don't listen.

   A. A lot of the time.
   B. Some of the time.
   C. Never or almost never.

5. When you are using your computer or doing another task requiring concentration, you have difficulty (and even become impatient or irritable) when your partner interrupts you to talk or to ask questions.

   A. A lot of the time.
   B. Some of the time.
   C. Rarely.

6. Your partner and you have both had a long day, and she or he wants to talk about a problem immediately upon your reunion at day's end.

   A. You generally do not want to talk about it; instead, you just want to go into your cave or do something else.

B. You do listen briefly and try to help him/her solve the problem, but you are not fully present.

C. You enjoy the opportunity to connect with him/her and explore feelings together right then.

7. In a utopian world, where you can spend your free time as you choose, you would prefer to do which of the following?

A. To exercise and/or play something physical and athletic or to play a nonphysical but competitive game (like a video game, chess, poker).

B. To work on a project or hobby that involves building, repairing, or creating something with your hands.

C. To relax and read a book or call a friend and chat about your day.

The Score

You should have seven answers in total. Give each A answer 3 points, each B answer 2 points, and each C answer 1 point. Total up the points. The highest possible score on this test is 21, the lowest is 7. All scores, even the extremes of 21 and 7, are within the range of normal, so there is no "bad" score. Also, the score is only one measure of where you fit on the gender brain spectrum.

If you scored between 14 and 21, your brain probably leans toward the male end of the spectrum. If you scored between 14 and 7, your brain system may exist toward the middle of the spectrum. And if you scored under 7, your brain leans toward the female end of the spectrum.

Now that you've completed this survey for yourself, complete it for your partner (as if you are your partner). Ask your partner to do the survey twice as well, once for him- or herself and once as if he or she were you. See what results you get, and how similar or different you both are with one another. Compare all the results from all four tests and see where your conversation about gender differences goes.

The Gift of Difference on the
Gender Brain Spectrum

When we see that there are male/female differences built into nearly every part of our brains—hippocampus (memory center), amygdala (emotion, anger, aggression, worry center), cerebellum (doing/activity center), brain stem (fight or flight responses and bodily functions), corpus callosum (right/left hemisphere connecting tissue), cingulate gyrus (attention center), frontal lobes (executive decision-making center), caudate nucleus (reward chemistry center), and others, we can hopefully forgive, in advance, a great deal about one another. But for nearly every woman or man I have worked with, the intimate-separateness paradigm, and its basis in brain differences, was nearly always new when we began using it—even among people who were "therapy smart" (had already been to other therapists) and even among workplace teams that did not generally think in terms of intimacy and separateness yet were clearly living out gender-intimacy dilemmas in their work relationships.

Throughout all of this, I found that I had to do some work with most couples, especially most women, to help them value the "male way of love" more than they did. As you continue in your own journey in this regard, don't be too surprised if you find yourself challenged to value the male way of loving, nurturing, caring for others, and being intimate as much as the female way—especially if long-term love is your goal. This valuing does not devalue the female way of love, but it pivots our popular culture (and therefore our relationship advice) toward a deeper love because half of the secret to long-lasting love lies with the male brain, too—an underrepresented brain in our popular literature on intimacy.

The Separateness Solution

Hopefully, now as we end this third chapter, you have three pieces of the puzzle of real love falling into place for you, each of which requires increased separateness.

- You can see the intimate-separateness paradigm, including the need to be aware of and manage the enmeshment/abandonment cycle.
- You can track the dangerous merging, including your merging with ghosts, shadows, and illusions during conflict and intimacy.
- You can study and work with male/female brain difference in love and marriage in such a way that separateness is as valued as intimacy.

While every woman is capable of separateness, and some women are well inclined that way from early childhood, and while some men are far more devoted to daily intimacy than their partners, the differences between men and women in nature, nurture, and culture make the male brain's proclivity for increased separateness a gift to long-lasting intimacy. To see the male brain's relational wisdom, the woman might need to expand her valuation of the way men and boys "do" intimacy, including joining others around her to stand against the sometimes coveted popular idea that males are inferior at intimacy, love, and marriage. If we push beyond the disbelief, we can save many marriages.

To help us enjoy the male brain's proclivity for staying disentangled, here are some scenarios for your conversation and analysis:

1. Think about the man who comes home, gives his wife a peck on the lips, then settles down with exhaustion into his favorite chair to watch TV for a while. He loves his wife, but his brain needs a brief separateness (a rest state) to recharge

and be better able to love her. If his partner does not realize this, she may feel abandoned as he pays no attention to her for an hour, watches TV, or does not include her during this time of neural recharge. She may react with anger at his abandonment of her, and a cycle of conflict begins. (As always with these scenarios there are exceptions and the genders can be reversed.)

2. Think about the man whose eyes glaze over when a conversation or monologue about emotional content goes on for more than a few minutes. He may well be asserting separateness as a self-protection and also as a way of trying to direct his wife away from the entanglements and painful feelings she is having, but she may feel abandoned emotionally by his glazed eyes. She may not realize that, actually, this is his attempt to help her separate herself from her constant, painful feelings, his way of lovingly trying to get her to see her best course.

3. Think about the man who is happiest when he knows his family is safe and provided for, and knowing that, is instrumentally satisfied. This man does not overwhelm his wife or children with a lot of wants or needs; he is not a drunk, he does not have affairs—he just provides for people as they need him, asks that he get a certain amount of sex and love in return, and does what he can to serve others, including his wife. This man is not great at verbal intimacy, but his actions are immensely intimate and empowering for his family.

4. Think about the man who says to his wife that he just wants a garage or other safe place (perhaps a "man cave" or fishing boat) in which to *do* something, *build* something, focus on a productive hobby. This man may not by nature be verbal, but he may challenge others to be intimate in other ways—

ways of *doing*—that may be immensely valuable for a spouse, children, neighborhood, and world. This is perhaps the same man who will say, at the time of divorce, "But I do so much for you and the family—how can you leave me? I clearly love you! Look at how hard I work for you."

This man and these men actually protect and enhance their marriages with more separateness and disentanglement than we have perhaps given them credit for over the last five or so decades. Their intimacy is the kind that allows others to be who they are without imposition of the man's psyche onto others. Their method backfires at times—a wife becomes saddened by a lack of emotional intimacy—but still, if a couple can analyze their marriage from gender-difference and intimate-separateness standpoints early on, they might see that their marriage is more solid than one or both realize, even if not every need of each party is met by the marriage itself.

YOUR WISDOM

Thank you for your survey. Let me share some of our fifty-two years of a good and happy marriage.

I think it is important to admire your spouse, and I admire him and he admires me as we have passion for what we do.

I love to read and have friends over our home. He has his Jazz Band where he plays clarinet. He has a sailboat where he sails down south where there are many channels and fiords. He gets together with his classmate friends once a month at the Navy Club.

Getting away from each other has always been good. When we get back together we always have new things to talk about and to share.

When I was younger, I just wanted him around me all the time. But I figured out that I needed my own life, too. That was what saved our marriage. We did couples things together and still do, but I spend a lot of my time with my women friends and that's been a marriage saver, too.

Don't get me wrong, though. I'm no docile ninny. I insist on my husband being generous, loving, respectful. And whenever we have had health, work, and money problems, we have been able to solve them. I respect his way of solving things, and he respects mine.

You asked for advice, and I guess after fifty-two years my biggest piece of advice is this: don't try to change the other person. He won't change, and not because he doesn't love you, but because he is who he is, just like you are.

Love someone for who they are, and don't waste that love on stuff that's just going to make you unhappy anyway. If you get to thinking you aren't loved enough, retrain him to talk some more and give you what you need, but don't waste your time thinking he's trying to hurt you because he isn't the man you were looking for.

If you're safe, your kids are okay, you have a reason for living, and you have friends and family, you're doing pretty well. Make sure to go on dates and make love and remember this is a long ride, not a sprint, and you'll have many years during this marriage when things will seem dark and grim, but because you love each other, you will work it out.

—Mary Ethel, 76

The Courage to Choose Balanced Love

Tomaso and Cindy were busy with kids, work, marriage, and life's daily stresses; they knew they needed a balanced, female/male, couple-driven, mutual maturation into the next stage of both intimacy *and* separateness. In therapy, Cindy realized that she had tacitly and sadly focused on a lack of emotional fulfillment in the marriage, and was looking toward the freedom from this sadness that divorce would give her. In realizing this, she analyzed her emotional actions and reactions with and toward Tomas, and she saw how enmeshed and dependent she was on him, on his responses, on his life, for her core self. As she was able to see through all of this, she realized that he was not to blame for the end of the marriage, nor was she. There was immense work to do, however, in dealing with abandonment/enmeshment anxieties, conflicts mired in projections, and gender misunderstandings that both parties took much too personally.

Tomaso worked toward more frequent rituals of intimacy with Cindy so that he could improve the couple's sense of emotional fulfillment. In regard to his interrupting Cindy (which devalued her), he decided to practice a trick I have taught many clients. It goes like this:

- When he hears Cindy beginning to speak at a social gathering, he tells himself, "I will only listen, not interrupt. This is *her* time."

- Until she is done telling her story, he only speaks if she asks him a question. He answers it specifically, concretely, and without taking over the conversation.

- When Cindy is finished (and as the conversation organically moves to others in the room), Tomaso makes sure to find an opportunity to support Cindy's story. He says something like, "Like Cindy said," or "Cindy said that really well."

After practicing this for three months, Tomaso gained a better rhythm for interacting in public with Cindy without damaging their relationship by interrupting her. As Cindy explained, "We had been good at being intimate for a few years, then Tomaso asserted the need for separateness and that made me afraid—afraid he was abandoning me. I responded by going into a hyper-intimacy drive with Tomaso, which made him afraid. Neither of us had learned how to be as good at being *both* emotionally close and separate together."

Tomaso, less verbal than Cindy, came to realize that he had instigated the push toward separateness and was now emotionally too withdrawn for the good of the marriage. He saw that Cindy had become so psychologically frightened by her husband's insistence on separateness that she now pursued too much intimacy for their love to last. Cindy cried a good deal in my office, but Tomaso's eyes teared up only once—when he realized how much his emotional distancing had hurt his wife.

Fortunately, the deep love this couple felt for one another has lasted beyond this stage of their marriage. They have remained married and express much greater happiness now. "The most difficult courage to muster is the courage of imperfection," said psychologist Alfred Adler almost a century ago. In relation to the million-year journey of the human brain, and the hundreds of thousands of years of female/male pair-bonding in particular, Adler's comment speaks volumes. For lovers like Tomaso and Cindy today, gender biology is still in play. If we don't factor it into our lives, we will most likely not develop long-lasting love. The biology of our "imperfection" is, in fact, beautiful; if we choose to deal with it well, it adds to the wonder of intimacy. I love D. H. Lawrence's words in this regard:

Love is a mutual relationship, like a flame between wax and air. If either wax or air insists on getting its own way, or getting its own back too much, the flame goes out and the unison disappears. At the same time, if one yields itself up to the other entirely, there is a guttering mess. You have to balance love and individuality, and actually sacrifice a portion of each.

Chapter 4

Living All Twelve Stages of Love Successfully

NAVIGATING THE TWELVE STAGES OF INTIMACY CAN SAVE MARRIAGES

A woman dressed in multicolored pantaloons and a head scarf smiles at the *yabanci's* (foreigner's) joke in a village outside the dusty city of Erzurum, Turkey. She is Kurdish, from a local family, one of four wives, forty-one years old, with the wrinkled face, tired eyes, and bent body of someone much older. She already has two grown children and six grandchildren. Her teeth are so rotten that her toothy smile feels almost painful for me, a young American observer, who wishes he had the money to get her to a dentist immediately. Her hands are gnarled and calloused. In conversations over a period of twenty-four hours, she reveals that she cannot read or write.

Thousands of miles away a woman in a one-piece designer dress carries a Gucci purse toward a waiting car. It is raining in New York; her doorman kindly guards her head with an umbrella. As she smiles at him, he sees perfect white teeth. Her hands show the tender care of a manicurist, and her erect posture, almost like a dancer's, indicates a life of requited ambition and social success. She would perhaps never meet the village woman from Erzurum, and she may not be able to fully imagine how one would survive without being able to read and write.

What do these two seemingly very different women have in common besides gender and age? Many things, actually. Both have children, both are married, both care deeply about family and friends, and both are in the sixth stage of human love. These women come from nearly opposite cultural backgrounds and societies, but they are relatively aligned in their relational journey. The woman in Turkey will probably die before she reaches the seventh stage of relationship, her life expectancy much lower than the woman in New York, who will probably live a full second half of life. But both women are living a map of love that can reveal, if we live long enough, at least twelve stages of intimate separateness.

I interviewed both women many decades ago, as a researcher studying gender in American urban areas and rural Turkish settings. In this early research, I studied maps of attachment and relationship in diverse cultures. Research available at that time (the late 1980s) showed that the human brain evolves through life-stages, thus, I suspected, our ability to attach with a partner, spouse, children, coworkers, new spouse (if divorced previously), friends, and neighbors must evolve in some relatively organized way as well.

It does. As the psychologist Jeff Hedge, who has treated over two thousand patients in his career, recently put it, "Everything happens in stages because that is how human nature is set up. No part of nature is separate from the evolutionary staging process." Renowned addictions specialist John Bradshaw linked natural impulses along these lines to developmental factors in the brain. "Human development occurs epigenetically. This means that one stage builds from the previous one. There is a time of developmental readiness. Nature has her developmental rhythms."

As we know from attachment research, our brains create and use organized systems. While we can argue that chaos is the wild prince in all workings of the world, the king and queen of the human organism are elegantly rhythmic. Scouring psychological science for clues to love-stages, I studied people from the various cultures in which I was doing my research. I asked, "What maps of relationship and love are you using?" The answers were various, and also parallel and complementary.

The map-searching urge is primal to both women and men who focus on long-lasting love. Whether consciously or unconsciously, we all look for maps to love's territory. Women more than men tend to get therapy, read self-help books, and initiate the conscious and verbal search for a map of love—likely, in part, because women tend to pay closer attention to love's daily feelings, trust words more than many men do, and feel love waning more acutely and quickly than men might. But men trust maps, too, once they are engaged in the search. Love is so complex, so fragile, and so intense in its emotional states that maps and a GPS can be love-saving for everyone.

One such map is the subject of this chapter. It is just one look at love, but I hope you'll find it a useful one because it traces the twelve stages of the intimate-separateness paradigm that's lived out over the life span.

Mapping the Stages of Love

As you explore the twelve stages and the hidden patterns they reflect, please keep a few things in mind.

1. The first seven stages of our love relationships mirror the stages of parent-child relationships from approximately birth to early adulthood. Analyzing and tracking these stages in your relationship can be immensely enlightening. We'll flesh out the stages even further in a moment.

2. Wherever you are in the twelve stages, some aspects of past phases exist in later ones, and vice versa. The twelve stages are not a piece of strict mathematics; rather, they are a window into the successful practice of intimate separateness in a relationship beginning from the day you meet your

lover to the day your coupled love ends, either by divorce or death.

3. As lovers, partners, and friends living these stages, we sometimes jump ahead of or fall behind the chronological phase we would seem to be in. For instance, you could be forty-one years old, like the women in New York and Erzurum, developmentally poised for Stage 6, but because of a divorce, which causes a kind of death/rebirth of your love cycle, you might soon find yourself in Stage 1 or 2 with your new lover.

4. Sometimes (quite often, in fact) you and your partner can be in somewhat different stages of attachment even while you live and love together under the same roof. This mismatch is yet another reason why maintaining emotional space (separateness) between you is crucial to your love's longevity. At the same time, one of the most profound influences I hope this book can have on your relationship is to help you and your partner become better aligned in the stages of intimate separateness, so that your love can be strengthened through that alignment.

5. The map you will discover in this chapter is a fluid paradigm meant to sustain and actually grow from *your* input, *your* adaptation. Let it be a focal point for dialogue and feeling-sharing regarding obstacles you've faced or are facing; how you and/or your partner react; arguments you're having; sources of both power struggle and creativity in your partnership. This model is not written in stone—it should be modified by *you*.

6. Seeing stages of attachment and love can help everyone in any culture realize and embrace the *constancy of change*, including our own and your partner's inevitable changes

as the years go by. Mapping the stages of love is a way of accepting who we are and also of bowing to neuroplasticity. The science of love is quite clear: we must evolve as lovers or our love will die. Who we were ten years ago is not necessarily who we are now.

7. Once we arrive in Stage 7, we cross a threshold of intimate separateness that is not perfect love by any means, but it feels both powerfully intimate and separate. This is a very freeing threshold and it brings some assurance of a marriage's chances of lasting for many decades. Thus, getting to Stage 7 is an important goal for a healthy marriage, a goal that is generally not reached without a couple developing a balance between intimacy and separateness.

The Research

The twelve-stage partnership model grows from these four research points:

- My clinical work with more than five hundred clients.
- Application of attachment theory, object-relations, and Jungian analysis.
- Anthropological study of pair-bonding research available from over thirty countries, including my study of American urban and Turkish rural relationship patterns.
- Laboratory studies of human and animal brain and biochemical development in pair-bonding (love).

A special note: in my initial clinical practice I did not have gay, lesbian, or transgender clients, thus my initial observations were with heterosexual couples. I have since worked with same-sex couples and have absorbed clinical research confirming that same-sex pair-bonding does mirror this model. One primary reason, I believe, for the mirroring across racial groups, across cultures, and in all sexual orientations is that human attachment exists a priori of race, culture, or sexual orientation—that is, it is organized in our brains at a cellular level, thus it is universal, even as it manifests differently in various groups.

Make this *Your* Model

As you begin this chapter, please consider opening your journal and, with it in hand, contemplating (without committing yourself or your partner to anything yet) which of the following stages and seasons of attachment best approximates where you and/or your partner together are *right now*. If you are not in a relationship at this point, contemplate which stage your previous relationship reached before it ended.

To pursue this exercise, open your journal to an empty page and write down the seasons and stages listed below on twelve separate pages so you have space for later writing. Put a check mark by the season or stage you think you personally and/or you and your partner collectively are in. Don't take too much time yet on this—just let your gut instinct guide you. We will go more deeply into each of these seasons and stages in a moment. As you read this chapter and study that material, feel free to make notes in your journal near each stage.

The four seasons and the twelve stages are:

Season 1: The Age of Romance (beginning with first glance at the lover and concluding when the couple has decided to end Power Struggle)
    Stage 1: Merging
    Stage 2: Disillusionment (the First Major Crisis)
    Stage 3: Power Struggle (Intense, Mainly Invisible, Enmeshment/Abandonment Patterns)

Season 2: The Age of Partnership
    Stage 4: Awakening
    Stage 5: The Second Major Crisis
    Stage 6: Refined Intimacy

Season 3: The Age of Distinction
    Stage 7: Creative Partnership
    Stage 8: The Third Major Crisis
    Stage 9: Radiant Love

Season 4: The Age of Completion
    Stage 10: Generative Solitude
    Stage 11: The Fourth Major Crisis
    Stage 12: Completion and Death

Even with just these twelve titles in tow, do you have a gut in-stinct about what season or stage you are in? Write in your journal and/or talk with your partner about any initial gut instincts you have.

A More Detailed Map

Holly, thirty-eight, and Travis, thirty-six, came to see me about their marriage of six years. The marriage was Holly's first, Travis's second. Holly was a schoolteacher and Travis a psychologist. They were fight-ing a lot and frequently refusing to speak to each other. Holly said that Travis had begun to work all the time, avoiding her by "using any excuse to work." Travis said Holly had begun to criticize Travis "about everything."

In my office, this conversation ensued:

Travis: I work as hard as I have to work.

Holly: Tell him (Gurian) what that means. Tell the truth.

Travis: The truth as you see it or the truth as it *is*?

Holly: Jesus, Travis. Just talk. Tell him how much you're working.

Travis: I'm working as hard as I need to. I can't get caught up on my patient intakes during the day so I get caught up at night. You grade student papers at night. What's the difference?

Holly: Every night? Till nine o'clock? On my iPad, my iPhone, my computer? Doing God knows what's on there and NOT doing anything that has to do with your spouse? That's you. You don't pay attention to me anymore.

Travis: Everything's an exaggeration with you. Everything's a disaster. Jesus.

Holly (eyes starting to water): You can say your psychobabble shit all you want, but I'm not the problem. You think I'm beneath you. You think you're smarter. When I try to talk to you, you shut down. You make me feel like shit. Shit!

Travis: Holly, come on. That's not true.

Holly: Tell him—your "colleague" (points to me). Tell him the truth. You either shut down or you yell at me.

Travis: What!? I don't yell at you. This is insane. It's you who criticizes me ad infinitum. You are so angry at me you can't even talk to me without us fighting.

Holly: Jesus! I can't stand it! No matter what, you turn everything back on me.

Both Travis and Holly had been in therapy before, so there was some shorthand we could use to help them gain insight, yet the shorthand didn't help them to go deeply into where they needed to go. Conversation between them often returned to this common theme: each blamed the other for their troubles. We worked together for a number of months. At one point in our work, I asked them if either had studied the stages of attachment. Travis had studied attachment theory as a psychologist, and Holly had some familiarity with attachment theory from her own graduate school training in education. We talked about this for a while, and then I asked them if they would let me present a new model to them.

"It will seem obvious, perhaps, but bear with me," I requested, then asked them to look back at their childhoods. "Think back to what it was like to be a child. Of course, no one can remember the early months of life, but you've both described pretty solid attachment to your parents early on, so you would have felt love for your parents like a beautiful parent-child romance of attachment. Try to remember that. Can you feel that in your guts?"

They both agreed they could.

"Okay, now remember the first year or two of being together as a couple. You've described feelings of being one with each other, completely and utterly bonded." They both agreed that that rendition was quite true. Travis wagged his finger at me, and said, "I see where you're going." Holly touched her husband's arm, trying to get him to back off, which was a very interesting gesture—both a show of frustration that he was interrupting and also a show of affection.

I continued by saying, "Okay, now can you remember back to when you were two or three or just think about two- or three-year-olds: the two- or three-year-old is in a different stage of relationship with the parent than the infant, obviously, right?"

"Obviously," Holly agreed. She frowned and smiled. "I see where you're going, too, I think. Remember, Mike, I've read some of your books."

This light jesting from both clients was useful in many ways, and I smiled in response, asking, "Okay, so the question I have for you now is, what stage of relationship are you both in now? Have you thought about it?"

They hadn't.

"Have you talked about stages of love in an attachment framework?"

Travis said, "I'm not big into that kind of analysis. It's pretty pop [pop psychology] for me. And by the way, I have *not* read any of your books." I nodded amiably to his aggressive territory marker, and our time was up for that day, but as the couple left, they went out with homework in hand. The first piece of work was the twelve-stage model (the section you just read and commented on), and another was the seven stages of the parent-child developmental bond (below). Travis and Holly both agreed to read the homework and tell me at our next session which stage they thought they were in. Travis remained suspicious, he said, but "let me give it a look."

A week passed. When I saw the couple again, our session was quite powerful. Both Travis and Holly agreed that they were in Stage 3, the Power Struggle stage.

Travis said, "I see elements of other stages in our relationship, but Stage 3 is probably right."

Holly agreed. "It feels pretty silly to be reduced to this, but I thought about what you said about parent-child bonds. We are kind of stuck in adolescence in our relationship. It's depressing."

The Seven Stages of the Parent-Child Bond

As we've noted, the parent-child bond occurs in definable stages. It is the most formative pair-bond in our lives. Though we are now adults, not children, one of the most powerful things we can do for the sake of love is to pursue the humility of exploring human love from the viewpoint of these attachment stages. It is not beneath any of us—though we do like to defend ourselves, as Travis did, against it.

In the following rendition of the seven stages of the parent-child pair-bond, the stages presented assume (1) a secure parent-child bond and (2) a time span of that bond from birth to approximately twenty-five years old (the age of adulthood). If your parent died early in your life and/or if your bond with your parent was not secure, you will probably find that you consciously or unconsciously tried to move your bonding and attachment needs to another surrogate parent, or matured without some aspects of the parent-child bond noted here. Please adjust this map accordingly.

Stage 1: Birth, Early Attachment. Parent and child are utterly merged as in an intimate romance. Any moments of significant separation can cause anxiety in both parent and child, as they indicate a potential loss of contact and closeness. Exploration of the world occurs in the child with least anxiety if the pair-bond is a secure base.

Stage 2: Early Separation (colloquially called "the terrible twos"). Attachment continues but some separateness is now necessary. Child's developing psyche (independent self) will become overstimulated by too much closeness, needs freedom, seeks to explore. Parent must adjust to child's need for separation; if not, child can become significantly stressed.

Stage 3: Continued Separation/Individual Power Assertion (preschool, early elementary years). All healthy parent-child attachments reach this stage, when both parent and child struggle to assert power. For instance, a child asserts an explorative nature, but the parent grabs the child back from the brink, tries to keep the child safe from risk. Or a child is considered "too shy" by the parent, and the parent tries to push the child to change this approach to life. Parents and children can remain in low- or high-grade power struggles around these differences for a decade or more (and, in some cases, unfortunately, for the life span).

Stage 4: Healthy Separation and Mutual Respect (prepuberty to puberty). The parent and child are instinctively pulled toward more separateness and independence seeking. If healthy separateness occurs, a healthy sense of how to help one another will follow. If healthy separateness is not established at or near puberty and not maintained respectfully during adolescence, significant power struggle will generally occur. At the extreme, the child will rebel utterly.

Stage 5: Middle Adolescence as a Positive and Negative Developmental Crisis. If a bonding tension has not occurred already, middle adolescence serves as both a positive and negative developmental crisis. The adolescent works to wholly establish a separate self, increases independence seeking, and looks outward and away from parents for a large part of self and identity. This separation behavior can cause anxiety in both parent and child.

Stage 6: Refined Core Self-Development, of Both Child and Parent (approximately eighteen years old, "leaving home" to early twenties). By late adolescence, the child is assumed to be "nearly grown up," and thus relatively independent of the parent's everyday attention. If a parent is "too close" to a grown child during this era, the child will generally become angry in some way, whether passive aggressively or overtly. Similarly, if the parent or child is "too far away" (i.e., neglectful), anxiety will be caused in one or both parties. This stage of parent-child attachment is the final stage of individuation before the child becomes a fully independent adult.

Stage 7: Adult-Adult Partnership. By now the child is in his or her twenties (or younger if a crisis or other circumstance has forced earlier maturation, or older if the child is a late bloomer). The parent-child pair-bond is transforming into an adult-adult relationship psychologically, a comfortable friendship, a mutually helpful partnership, a relationship that feels equally safe with both intimacy and separateness. This adult-adult partnership can exist psychologically even if the child is still physically living at home and/or still economically dependent on the parent(s). But if either the parent or adult child clings to the other too constantly, developmental issues will generally result—the child will not fully grow up in early adulthood and neither will the parent feel fully satisfied that she or he has raised "an adult."

• • •

As Travis and Holly talked about this model, Travis and I sparred about his discomfort with "limiting marriage to a simple attachment model" (his words). I felt it was important to butt heads with him for a time in order to push into a deeper analysis of the enmeshment and merging issues he and Holly faced. I have found, especially with some alpha males, a great deal of helpful clinical bonding between client and counselor can transpire through this kind of head-butting.

To challenge and guide him, I asked about Holly's comment regarding his anger. "Can we talk about it now in this context?" He said he was willing to talk about it if we also discussed Holly's anger. At this point, an argument ensued. The couple raised voices; finally, I facilitated some resolution (and distraction) by asking them to notice how those raised voices indicated their power struggle. We talked a great deal about different aspects of that power struggle, and then our time was up. As homework, I now asked them to read the fully annotated twelve-stage map (below) for comparison to the annotated attachment-stage map we looked at previously.

Take a moment, if you would, to read through this model, journal about it, talk about it with your partner or others. Hopefully this can help you move deeper into discovering where you and your partner might be in your relationship right now. We will then return to both maps and compare them.

Season 1: The Age of Romance

You have just fallen in love or are in the first few years of love. You enjoy the blood and brain chemistry of physical, psychological, sexual, and spiritual union with another person.

Stage 1: Romance. It seems to you that your lover has few or no significant flaws; he or she is a source of sweet joy and grace. *Life seems almost impossible without the pair-bond with this other person.* Without your realizing it, these feelings of romance are, unconsciously, like a romance-type dependency of child-parent, but they are also a new, unique, peer pair-bond seemingly without compare.

During this romance, you are projecting illusions constantly onto one another and into yourself, but you don't realize it. And your gender differences—which will have a profound effect on marital longevity later—already hide inside your oneness, though you don't know this yet, either. As biologists Sue Carter and Bruce Cushing have shown, much of the baseline chemistry of love is the same for women and men, but because of the X and Y chromosome differ-ence in bloodstream and brain, romance chemistry also includes sig-nificant differences, such as a woman's "affiliative chemistry" (bonding chemistry) being more self-regulated and self-constructed around the neurotransmitter oxytocin (the chemical at the base of maternal con-nection) and the male's chemistry around vasopressin (the chemical we noted earlier that supports territory protection and paternal con-nection). This is already set in you both during romance, but it won't show up as a powerful conductor of your relational electricity until later (especially in Stage 3).

Stage 2: Disillusionment (the first major crisis). *Flaws emerge* in both of you; some illusions begin to harden, others to disintegrate. Psychological nakedness of the self feels less safe now than a year or two before. Metaphorically, you are Adam and Eve in the garden at the point of eating the apple—you become somewhat ashamed of who you are and/or ashamed of your partner, disillusioned by the loss of perfection. You begin to unconsciously and consciously study your partner for flaws (and so does she or he with you). Because you love this person (and this person loves you), former projections continue and new projections are established, so that bonding can continue, but there is some discomfort in your love now. You may be together three to five years, but the honeymoon is definitely over.

Stage 3: Power Struggle. Four or more years have passed since you first met; flaws have clarified and *now you are in full-out battle mode.* The primary focus of battle is to (1) blame the other and (2) change the other to fit unconscious projections of the "right" or "safe" mate you deserve to have. In Stage 3, we may pay lip service to wanting to change ourselves, but really we want the other person to change. We will attack overtly or manipulate behind the scenes in any way we can to make that happen. Just like a child and parent in the third stage of the parent-child bond, we need much more healthy separateness from the other person and from projections than we realize, but we neglect to develop this psychological separation, in large part because our standard for a "good relationship" is still the intense closeness of Stage 1. This power-struggle stage, in which we are confused by intimacy, can last for a decade or more. Often, it ends in divorce—the couple never really moves into or through the later stages of love.

· · ·

These three stages can happen somewhat simultaneously at times. For instance, some couples start struggling over power from day 1 of the relationship. And after the first few weeks or months of romantic bliss, Stage 2 can begin during Stage 1, with psyches in an overlapping Venn diagram between the two stages: one moment the couple experiences pure bliss and then an hour later, disillusionment. Then Stage 3 can overlap into that.

But at some point, the jesting, joking, fighting-and-make-up sex that indicate some power struggle may become a discernible third stage of constant struggle—this may dominate a relationship when one or both partners enter an enmeshment/abandonment cycle that destabilizes the love. This will be Stage 3 and can remain active for years if they don't get help. The couple may well advance into later stages chronologically as they move through their twenties, then thirties, then forties (if they last as a couple that long), but power struggle (enmeshment/abandonment, dangerous merging) may haunt them for a decade or more.

It is important to note that a certain amount of power struggle is natural to all pair-bonds. It only becomes dangerous if it is not worked through as a stage and transcended developmentally when appropriate. This book is, among other things, a tool kit for moving beyond power struggle. For Travis and Holly, power struggle was now dominating their relationship, and their work would be to move through and beyond it.

A clue to a couple's entrenchment in Stage 3 appears in the anger/anxiety attachment collaboration we looked at in Chapters 1 and 2. One or both people are anxious (overtly feel consciously or unconsciously that the pair-bond is insecure), and one or both people are angry (covertly feel the anxiety, and react to the insecurity with anger). Either party can begin to criticize, judge, manipulate, attack, withdraw. In all cases, one or both partners will relentlessly try to change the other person. Unconsciously, in this struggle, the couple is trying to remove the feelings of destabilization, pain, shame, anger, and disillusionment in their present relationship by doing battle with one another.

Divorce is a possible outcome of Stage 3—indeed, in contemporary pair-bonds, it is likely, and most couples that divorce fit this pattern. While there can be many causes of power struggle—including gender-role battles, lack of closeness, different values about raising children, addiction, infidelity—the startling insight for many people in power struggle, including Travis and Holly, is that a primary cause lies in the lover being *too close*. Dangerous merging is happening in two ways simultaneously:

1. The two psyches are engulfing and enmeshing one another, and neither psyche can feel secure in this feeling—so much so that one or both psyches has become parent-child or parent-adolescent, trying to pull away and disentangle from one another in order to enjoy the necessary separated self of adulthood.

2. Unsuccessful at changing the other or self, the two people generally become even more entrenched in negative patterns rather than less; thus, unsuccessful at maturing the pair-bond, the two people become too psychologically weakened and angry to continue in long-term bonded love.

Except in cases where divorce occurs for reasons of danger, addiction, or infidelity noted before, generally a lack of emotional fulfillment will be deemed the culprit of this broken relationship. Often, the couple will not see or understand the profoundly disabling quality of their enmeshment/abandonment and merging, nor will they understand that they are locked in a brain-regulating, gender-specific attachment/separation cycle that mirrors adolescence. They will not realize until it is too late that they broke up with one another not only because they were too far away from one another emotionally but also because they were so close to one another that they could not disentangle from disillusionment.

YOUR INSIGHTS

We had fallen in love already when she found out she was going overseas for two years for work. I was so in love with her that this two-year absence hurt more than anything, but I couldn't stop my job so I couldn't go. We decided we would have to have a long-distance relationship. Everyone said it would be hard and it was. She left in September, I flew there in February, she flew back here in August, then back there a few weeks later, then I flew back in February. It was very difficult.

But after the two years we both agreed that being separated made us more mature. This blew our minds. We are definitely better lovers now that we're back together. We are better friends than we were. We really need and want each other, we really value each other now in a different way than we did before the separation.

And for me, I'm only twenty-eight, I think I understand love better because we had to communicate so much through social media while we were separate. I had to learn a lot about communicating with her using words.

I'm not glad we were separated for all that time because it was so hard, but in a way I guess I'm glad because I grew up. It's hard to explain.

—Rob, 28

Season 2: The Age of Partnership

Over the course of this season—which lasts for many years—couples develop a new way of loving that releases the hold of enmeshment and abandonment, engulfment, impingement, and dangerous merging. Romance, disillusionment, and power struggle each dissipate (even romance now falls away in favor of child-raising and/or workplace achievement), and the partnership itself absorbs its ebbs and flows into a greater good—partnering for purposes and missions that are larger than battling with one another over power.

All the while, intimacy is kept alive and romance and attachment are protected through a combination of rituals of love, "organized" spontaneity, and other blissful privacies.

Stage 4: Awakening. One partner and soon, hopefully, the second partner awakens to the enmeshment/abandonment cycle, the existence of a parent-adolescent power struggle, the core feeling of being both too far away and too close to one another. *A period of self-awareness and life-change* occurs for the couple as they repair their anger/anxiety (or other) cycle, stabilize their bond, renew romance, apologize for disappointing one another, own their failures and flaws, integrate gender differences into communication, build or recognize separate selves (identities), and inspire the pair-bond to weather the storm.

Stage 5: The Second Major Crisis. Every relationship is tested by *a series of crises and storms at various times in life.* Disillusionment, then power struggle was the most obvious first crisis. Generally, somewhere within the first decade of a long-term attachment there will be a second major crisis (or more)—a significant job loss, the discovery of infertility, a child born with a defect, a troublesome parent moving into the couple's home, war, recession . . . crisis will occur. This major crisis (or series of smaller crises) will occur whether awakening has transpired or not: it can occur during Stage 3 (as it did with the couples featured in the previous chapters) and either inspire awakening or lead to divorce. Should divorce transpire, the divorce itself is the major crisis, and it can inspire new maturation in love as well as a repeat of the first five stages with a new lover.

Stage 6: Refined Intimacy. After a great deal of work, we reach a point of refined love. We realize we know how to love now, we know what the heck we are doing! We now codevelop a partnership, attachment, and marriage that "feels right," "works for us," "gives us each a lot of what we need." If by now a divorce has not occurred, a marriage has probably lasted well more than a decade. Children may be between school age and teens. In this stage, intimacy rituals keep love intimate and thus secure (date nights, game nights, vacations together, kisses, caressing, scheduled sex when spontaneity can't quite work); separateness rituals keep the separate selves safe and thus the love secure (different interests, going out with girlfriends and guy-friends, bowling night, mother-children time that is separate from father-children time).

• • •

As Travis and Holly talked about these stages, they both admitted that they saw this Stage 6 as the stage they wanted to get to. Over many sessions, we looked together at what projections and shadows kept them locked in power struggle, what situations triggered fears of enmeshment and abandonment, and how their struggles linked to each of them working through mother-son/father-son and mother-daughter/father-daughter separation and attachment issues. Throughout these sessions and their own work at home, they used a tool that can have a great deal of experiential success for couples who want to fully enter Stage 4 and move away from the Power Struggle.

A Tool of Awakening: Mirror Images

One of the most difficult things a couple will ever do is move beyond Stage 3 (the next chapter is completely devoted to practical tools for that work). To accomplish this difficult task, couples often need an ongoing practice by which to recognize that they are locked in the power struggle. Awareness of enmeshment has to happen if change is to occur. I helped Holly and Travis to look for this clue. I asked them, "Are you one another's *mirror?*" This needed explanation, of course.

There are positive and negative ways to "mirror" one another in love. "We are so alike," two romantically involved people will say. "We finish each other's sentences," they will add. "Sometimes I complain about something in her, but really, it's myself I'm complaining about." Mirroring is normal and can be quite beautiful. It evolves with every relationship to include helping one another see good qualities. Each of us "mirrors" one another's good qualities verbally, such as, "You are a wonderful mother and leader. You are good at _____, _____, and _____." The husband holds up a mirror to help the wife see positive qualities in herself that she wouldn't otherwise see or articulate.

But the process of psychological mirroring can also go in a more subtle direction. Especially if we are enmeshed with one another, merged, unable to be independent selves, and thus struggling over power constantly, we will generally notice that there are things we "hate" about the other person—things that, if we look even more closely at our relationship, we actually don't like in ourselves. Look again at this piece of Travis's and Holly's dialogue from earlier.

Travis: Holly, come on. That's not true.

Holly: Tell him—your "colleague" (points to me). Tell him the truth. You either shut down or you yell at me.

Travis: What!? I don't yell at you. This is insane. It's *you* who criticizes me ad infinitum. You are so angry at me you can't even talk to me without us fighting.

Holly: Jesus! I can't stand it! No matter what, you turn everything back on me.

Holly and Travis want and need to see themselves as different from one another (and they are, of course), but they are so enmeshed with one another that they actually complain about the same behavior in each of them. Their anxiety is mirrored by their partner's anxiety. Their anger is mirrored, too, as is their criticism. Each of them is anxious, angry, and critical at nearly the same time each time they are in conflict. They are mirror images of one another psychologically—so much so that what one of them "hates" about the partner (Holly hates that Travis is so critical) is actually a quality she would not like in herself, if she could see it and admit it. Similarly, Travis does not like how much time Holly spends doing papers, but in fact he is mirroring this "work addiction" with a work addiction of his own. A clue that a couple has become "mirror images" will show up for you if you do similar things, feel similar things, experience similar things, *and they irritate you.* If you are grating on each other constantly—criticizing each other, disliking each other, "being too hard on each other," "sick of Joe telling those jokes," "sick of Hannah laughing with that weird snort," step back and ask, "In what way am I doing this very same thing?"

Look at yourself and you will often find that *you are doing something similar to the very thing you hate in your partner,* so that unconsciously, when you criticize your partner for that thing, you are also criticizing yourself. Part of your awakening and move toward refined intimacy will depend on recognizing yourself in the mirror your partner is holding up to you (and you to him or her). You may need a good deal of help because it is very subtle. This is about getting so close to each other when we are enmeshed and power struggling that it can be hard to step back and see what (and who) is really there.

I helped Holly and Travis test whether they were "mirroring" one another in this way by asking them to make separate lists (without talking with one another) about things the other did that drove him or her crazy. Once the lists came back, they were analyzed by the couple, and I mediated some of that analysis. Not surprisingly, the two lists were very similar. By doing this list separately they were able to see that when one of them complained about any of these following things, the complaining partner actually did or felt the same things (though perhaps with a different flavor, or with different timing, nuance, or circumstance):

- Each felt hurt or irritated by tone of voice and certain key words each person used to attack the other. Holly more readily admitted that she felt this; Travis defended his vulnerability, but then did finally admit he probably felt the hurt as much as Holly, just differently.

- Each didn't always remember certain things the other had asked him or her to do—both did this, but Holly tended to accuse Travis of it without realizing she did it, too.

- Each became disappointed and expressed disapproval (verbally and/or nonverbally) in the other constantly. Both admitted that they did this without hesitation.

- Each got defensive and responded from a defensive posture rather than fully hearing the other. Both admitted they did this.

- Each misunderstood (sometimes on purpose, sometimes not) what the other was saying, over and over again. Holly claimed not to misunderstand purposefully and accused Travis of doing so; Travis disagreed with this analysis but did admit that he also misunderstood Holly, yet got very angry at Holly for misunderstanding. Neither had realized that they both did this.

- Each needed to be right most of the time. This was overt for Travis, covert for Holly, but both saw how potent this urge was in each of them.

- Each felt constant low-grade anger at the other, expressing it passively or aggressively depending on context. Both admitted to this readily.

- Each felt oppressed, devalued, unappreciated, and victimized. Holly was surprised to see that Travis felt oppressed. She only or mainly associated that word with females in marriage, she admitted.

- Each felt low-grade anxiety while in the other's presence ("I have to walk on eggshells"—Holly), and felt inadequate and blamed the other for that feeling ("No matter what I do, it's wrong"—Travis).

- Each felt abandoned or rejected at least once a day in some obvious or subtle way. Both Holly and Travis felt this, but Holly experienced it more acutely and ruminated about it more.

As we went through this exercise and afterward, Holly and Travis were moved by how similar their internal experiences were: they saw the mirroring. They realized that because they were in power struggle, they had been consciously operating under the common assumption that they were not intimate anymore, and that the cause of their bitter feelings was their anger at one another for "being so far away emotionally." Now they realized that their mutual anger was the mask—they saw that behind it they were so close to one another that they were mimicking each other almost perfectly.

This couple expanded the use of the tool by spending the next week listing (separately) five conflict situations, then they came together to discuss the conflicts (including the two times Travis walked out of the room during an argument and one time Holly did so). In these conflict situations, they were able to see that nearly every one of the mirror images noted above occurred in both of them equally. Now they were able to see that many of their arguments were actually psychological attempts to separate themselves (like adolescents and parents) so that they could fully love and be loved. Holly realized, "We're cloning one another—that's how enmeshed we've become." Travis agreed, "Yes, we've been merged, glued together, and just wanted to get away. We've used friction and conflict to keep some safe distance between us, but most of those conflicts, over so many little things, have been tearing our love apart."

The awakening of this couple, including their therapy and intense personal work, stimulated many months of the following:

- Working to detach from one another.
- Developing rituals that would renew and refine a more balanced intimate separateness.
- Creating a new stage of better working closeness and intimacy between them that would last, they hoped, for decades.

Season 3: The Age of Distinction

At least one child is perhaps grown by now, and perhaps all children will be grown by the time this season of love is under way:

"We know who we are," one or both people might say.

"We are each contributing to the world."

"We are proud of each other."

About the relationship or family, they might say, "We are as in love now as we've ever been before." About life and time, they might say, "Wow, can you believe how fast time went? Just yesterday we were at each other's throats, but now we've had years of creativity together."

There can be an amazing sense of both distinction in the world ("we are good at what we do," "we are accomplished people") and distinction as a couple ("pretty darn decent at this marriage thing after all, thank you").

If a couple has divorced in Seasons 1 or 2, each partner may have remarried by now as well, moving through the previous six stages in an accelerated way in order to protect the children—that is, seeking to mate with a caregiving partner to get help with child-raising and/or looking to find "better love" than occurred with the previous spouse. This new relationship will be, hopefully, the one that distinguishes the person or people as "happy," "content," and "I've finally learned how to love, succeed, be whole."

Stage 7: Creative Partnership. All individuals in this stage of individual life will likely be concerned with forming or sustaining partnerships that allow for and support creativity and life-purpose. For partners who have evolved through the previous stages and developed a healthy, well-refined intimate separateness, stability occurs in Stage 7, allowing each separate self to be creative and purposeful in the world in the ways that the self needs to be—through work, parenting, art, craft, sport, relationships, social causes, philanthropy, and the like.

By now, partners see very little of the kind of long-term enmeshment/abandonment cycles or parent-adolescent projections they saw before. Love is not perfect, but issues tend to resolve in a few days, rather than being "stuck" for months or years. Only a major crisis can subvert this new stage of love.

Stage 8: The Third Major Crisis. Parents die, a child dies or becomes gravely ill, children leave home, a child and his or her spouse decide to divorce, infidelity occurs, one or both partners loses a job, a recession occurs that cleans out savings—a crisis or series of crises can occur. How these new crises or stressors are handled marks the evolution of the partnership. Some couples, married twenty to thirty years, will now divorce. Tacit issues in the marriage, or one individual's changing self, or just the attrition of years, or lack of intimacy, or resurgence of earlier merging and projection issues can meld with an external crisis that causes one or both to need far more separateness than the marriage has provided, which means divorce.

Some couples separate for a year, perhaps regroup, then he or she moves back into the house and the marriage continues. All couples will, at some point, weather sadness, fear, anger, or grief together in this season of life, and that can make them stronger for the future.

THE WISDOM OF SEPARATENESS

Space and some time alone can be a wonderfully satisfying tonic for the soul. . . . Finding that "separateness" shouldn't be difficult. The concept of a "man cave"—or a female equivalent—makes a lot of sense to a lot of people. And then there are those who take the easiest route: candor. They simply acknowledge that, periodically, they enjoy time apart.

—Maryanne Vandervelde, PhD, author of *Parallel Play*

Stage 9: Radiant Love. The couple may be in retirement age now and/or may be grandparents. They are radiant in ways that others—especially younger people—see, feel, and experience as these younger people say, "Look at those two, they've got it figured out." Radiant lovers shine with elder intelligence and radiate stability of pair-bonding, strength of attachment, and a quirky, eccentric, but strong alliance that is enviable.

Even if a couple divorces during this stage, to the grandchildren the couple still radiates wisdom and strength. And for each radiant elder there can be a kind of amazement: "Wow, we made it forty years. How shall we share this gift?" The answer happens over a period of years in which one or both people feel they are sharing what they know, especially with younger lovers.

In *The Wonder of Aging*, I make the argument that every elder couple should mentor one younger couple to ensure the most social stability for our culture. Radiant lovers in Stage 9 generally make great mentors of younger couples. If you happen to be in this stage of life, I hope you will mentor one younger couple in your wisdom. On the flip side, if you are a younger couple locked in power struggle, I hope you will reach out to one or more elders for mentoring.

Season 4: The Age of Completion

If we live long enough to make it to this age, this season can happen over many decades, and much of our partnership may come to revolve around physical and mental changes, illness, dying, and death; but still, there can be an amazing sense of grace in the pair-bond. In fact, in some ways, the new season of life becomes one of our most spontaneous, generative, and intimate. This is largely true because dying is one of the most intimate experiences imaginable between two people. In this season, as we detach more from life and life from us, separateness take on new meaning.

Stage 10: Generative Solitude. For couples who have time together before physical or mental degeneration to travel the world or spend a great deal of time "puttering at stuff we love," many paths of generative (life-giving) solitude emerge. An elder couple can live in one house and share a great deal of life together yet also have different internal and external attentions, concentrations, enjoyments. There is a coming together to bond, eat, enjoy time with others, perhaps sleep together, and also there is a time to enjoy life for its quiet moments separate from one another. There is contentment in separateness that proves, as we look back at our lives, how wise it was to work on getting beyond enmeshment/abandonment and power struggle so that we could really see the beauty and grace that emerge in a lifetime of loving and being loved.

Stage 11: The Fourth Major Crisis. One or both of the partners becomes chronically ill and, finally, gravely ill. The couple's strength and love are tested by crisis after crisis for their ability to remain both intimate and separate, attached and detached, loving and caregiving yet self-focused enough not to get utterly depressed from the caregiver stress. As illness and compassion for the ill become our major life-focus, we can feel a gratitude for our partner's love that we would never have felt if this person had not been in our lives.

Stage 12: Completion. Our partner dies, and then we die. The focus of these last years, months, or days is on completion of spirit, saying the things we need to say for one another, doing the things we need to do to make sure all our family knows they are loved, and finally, freeing ourselves from intimacy with this world into a new kind of separateness that, if we are religiously inclined, will lead to intimacy in another dimension—and if we are not religious, will nonetheless be a new separateness and detachment from the attachments of this lifetime.

Using the Power of Intimate Separateness in Each Stage

Early in my career, I was leading a relationships workshop in which a woman approximately forty years old said to the group, "Love should be hard, it should be hard work, it should be a struggle. If you're not 'in it' with your partner, you're not doing the work, getting into your stuff, healing your wounds." She continued, "For me, the passion between mature lovers comes from the 'stuff' and the struggle; we're meant to get it worked out with each other—that's why we got together—and if it's a struggle for years on end, that's quite okay."

Another participant responded, "But you're not saying you should fight all the time, right?"

"Of course not," was the response. "I'm not saying we shouldn't be kind and all that, but at least from my perspective, it's the emotional and psychological struggle with my partner that shows me I'm alive."

There were many nods of heads to this. At the same time, some other people sat back pensively, not nodding their heads. A powerful discussion ensued regarding how much struggle between lovers is needed for love to be successful. Most of the participants were in the workshop because they had not had the long-term success they wanted in love and relationships.

While I did not work personally with these participants in a clinical way, I sensed that many of the participants—both individuals and couples—were in Stage 3, the power struggle. Sensing this, I took our discussions in that direction. Now, the woman revealed that she had been married three times, once for a year, once for five years, and once for nine. She had also been in a number of other relationships that lasted a short time or up to five years.

After these revelations, a woman in her sixties, who had not yet said anything, now said, "Uh, I don't know if I'm in the right place, but to me, this is wrong. I think the reason your relationships don't last more than a few years is because you like to fight. I'm sorry for being so direct, but I don't think love can last if we do that. The 'struggle' is good sometimes, sure, but in most ways, love can't last until we stop struggling and let be what will be."

Now a new discussion ensued. People who agreed with her position (and who had remained silent earlier) provided stories and insights to support her. During this discussion someone asked me for my position, so I shared my bias: "In my experience, constant struggle (for years on end) probably indicates a tendency to remain locked in enmeshment/abandonment, dangerous merging, and the power struggle stage of relationship." I shared a line from the Sufi poet Jalal al-Din Rumi: "You fill yourself with the sharp pain of love rather than its fulfillment." We talked about the fact that love can be a fun-filled bickering alliance between two strong personalities, but if those personalities are doing more than jesting, teasing, and bickering—if they are at war—they will not reach fulfilling intimacy. They are probably so merged and so constantly afraid of being engulfed that they have become compulsively inclined to give (and receive) the sharp pain of love, rather than love's fulfillment.

Essential Questions Survey 6: Getting at a Cause of Your Power Struggle

Anyone who has ever been in therapy has answered questions about his or her mom and dad. If you have not done so, I hope you will enter therapy right away in order to begin this healthy self-exploration. This work is not about blaming parents; it is about becoming a "love-scientist" who studies his or her own attachment patterns at their source (parents). These attachment patterns give you the ability to love and be loved; and they can hold many secrets as to why and how you engage in power struggle. I am in Season 3 and Stage 7 of love, and yet I constantly return, as needed, to my therapist and my journaling to keep a fresh eye on the issues I brought forward from my family of origin.

In Survey 6, I will assume you have done at least some work on looking at your relationships and modeling regarding your parents' attachment of and with you. This survey is specific to the seven stages of your parent-child pair-bond. After you've answered the questions, I hope you will have some information you can use to more deeply explore any enmeshment/abandonment cycle or dangerous merging with projections that you might be engaged in or might potentially fall into your love relationships—experiences that can lead to prolonged power struggle.

After reviewing the seven stages of the parent-child pair-bond, answer these questions in your journal:

1. Did I have secure attachment with my mom during infancy and early childhood? (If you are adopted, answer the question for both your biological and your adoptive mother.)

2. Did I have secure attachment with my father during infancy and early childhood? (If you are adopted, answer the question for both your biological and your adoptive father.)

3. Did I have mainly normal separation anxieties and experiences with my mother during my first ten years of life (first three stages of mother-child attachment)? What were the "abnormal" or particularly painful times of attachment/ separation during the first ten years with my mother?

4. Did I have mainly normal separation anxieties and experiences with my father during my first ten years of life (first three stages of father-child attachment)? What were

the "abnormal" or particularly painful times of attachment/separation during the first ten years with my father?

5. Did I have some separation issues with either parent, including times I was scared to function in the world without my mother (father) and/or did my mother (father) impinge on my self-development (criticize me constantly and/or did not let me go)?

6. Were there times during puberty and adolescence when my mother impinged on my development, not allowing healthy psychological separation, independence, and growth?

7. Were there times during puberty and adolescence when my father impinged on my development, not allowing healthy psychological separation, independence, and growth?

8. Were there times during puberty and adolescence when my mother and/or father abandoned me or rejected me repeatedly?

Take as much time as you need to answer these questions. Look at old photographs and videos, talk to siblings, talk to parents, if they are living and/or willing to discuss their early relationship with you.

Holly and Travis

Both Holly and Travis made some discoveries about the effects of their mother-child and father-child pair-bonds on their present power struggle. Holly had been abandoned by her mother and Travis had been enmeshed with his father during significant periods of their childhoods. They had been in therapy before and knew this already—in fact, in previous therapy they had both traced back how their abilities to *be intimate and close* were affected by their childhoods. But they had not thought before about how the foundational enmeshments could affect their ability *to be separate* in their love relationship.

Travis's father was, in his words, "definitely enmeshed with me. As a physician, he hounded me, critiqued me, directed me, cajoled me to follow in his footsteps. No matter what I did, it wasn't enough. I was his only child and he lived through me. I couldn't breathe sometimes. It was everything I could do to get away from the heavy criticism and go my own way. I know he is proud of me, but he just didn't realize how unhappy he made me."

Holly's mother was an alcoholic whose early attachment with Holly was solid, she said, but then during her late childhood and her adolescence, Holly felt abandoned by her mother. "She preferred the bottle to us kids. We all knew it and we hated it, but luckily my dad tried to fill in, and we had a lot of extended family who helped." Holly's mother completed a successful rehab after Holly went to college. By then, however, Holly had developed internalized abandonment anxiety in the same way that Travis had developed significant enmeshment anxiety.

By using the tools described in this part, and those that follow in Part II, both Holly and Travis worked to understand the signals of rejection and impingement that each sent out to the other. They worked on anger, rumination, projections, overreaction, and power struggle. This took many months of conflicts and new arguments, and some very deep, frightening silences between them, but it paid off. After many months they assessed themselves to have, in Holly's words, "finally entered a new awakening, thank God." Their marriage became a much stronger, healthy attachment, and their new marital conversation, if it could have been captured in one session, went like this after six months. (I have constructed this from various sessions in order that you can compare it to the conversation on pages 125–126.)

Travis: I work as hard as I have to work, but I can pay more attention to you, and I can be more sensitive to rituals together that keep us bonded. I can also be more patient when you get angry that I'm working too hard. I can understand that some of it is not about me.

Holly: I can work on not getting so angry when you are staring into your computer. That staring of yours triggers my abandonment anxiety. Now I can see it. And I can understand that I grade student papers at night, too. I have my own life; you leaving me alone is not about me and it won't destroy me.

Travis: I need to stop criticizing you the way my father criticized me. I need to stop blaming you for all the same little things I do and feel. I have to get some rational distance. I thought I had it. I thought I knew what was what in our relationship, but I haven't been as wise as I thought.

Holly: I need to stop creating so much drama with you. I catastrophize things that aren't exactly as I want them to be. Once I catastrophize, we get into power struggles.

Travis: I shut down when you talk to me about deep stuff. I do. It's wrong and I apologize. I hear deep, painful stuff from people all day at work, and at home I don't have patience for it, and that is just wrong.

Holly: I know, but I need to work on my critical tone. It's shrill and nagging. I can't even hear myself sometimes.

Travis: And my tone is too harsh, too. My voice is louder than I think.

Holly: I create a lot of chaos and I know that's what's scary for you. And what's scary for me is how quickly you seem to be able to just shut your heart off. It's like you completely go away from me.

Travis: I know. I have to figure out how to be myself without being so distant when I get triggered and scared.

Holly: And I have to be myself without clinging to you so much. It's embarrassing.

• • •

Looking forward to the next stage of attachment and separation can be motivating, empowering, life-guiding. Holly and Travis understood this, awakened to it, and moved into Stage 4. The pain of love still ached for them, it still hurt, it was still a struggle at times, but it also now became a healthy dependency. That "dependency" is something we can all find. It is not a dirty word, though people often think it is. In *Attached*, Dr. Amir Levine and Rachel Heller reveal what science and gut instinct have shown us for generations: *our dependency needs are what keeps humanity going.* While an unhealthy attachment enervates us, a healthy dependency over the long term helps us feel more self-confident, secure, and stable and gives peace of mind. In Stage 3, Holly and Travis had been hyper-stressed about love. Their wake-up call took them to new places, and just in time.

YOUR WISDOM

Note: While this particular story is about a son who feels that his mother impinges on him, it could happen with a daughter and father, daughter and mother, or son and father. I am sharing this particular story here for three reasons, beyond the obvious power of the words themselves:

- Its author, a professor of philosophy, goes into helpful depth on impingement in general, and new projections in particular, through his mother-son pair-bond.

- He is realistically reflecting the length of time it takes to work through this kind of early attachment difficulty, including projections, power struggle, and awakening.

- He illustrates how an individual who is not at this moment in a coupled relationship can still utilize the idea of moving forward through love stages and "separateness" to ground his next relationship successfully.

As you read this, don't be surprised if you feel the urge to read it a second or third time. This writer writes in a philosophical language that packs a big punch once it is carefully deciphered.

• • •

I am a professor of philosophy, born 1964. I'm writing to express my indebtedness to you for your work, in particular the book *Mothers, Sons, and Lovers*. It's been about four years since I discovered your work, and I've been in the process of absorbing it and integrating your insights into my own self-referent thinking. In an extended, and particularly painful, period of reflection, one in which I found myself hating my mother (with red-hot intensity), I realized just how severely she had impinged on my development, not letting me grow up, separate, and become an adult. This processing of this insight has utterly changed my ability to love and be loved.

My understanding now is that when this impingement happens, a mother or father does not let the son separate but instead tries to make him into her projected image of the perfect man—the process of enmeshment and impingement creates a situation in which a boy cannot, as he grows, avail himself of the tremendous benefits of personal suffering because he is in the grip of an internal normative rule that says YOU CAN'T PSYCHOLOGICALLY OWN YOUR OWN POWERS, BECAUSE ALL YOU ARE IS A PSYCHOLOGICAL EXTENSION OF ME.* *This could happen with a father, but in my case it happened with my mother.*

This is the operative ideation in the self, an internalized principle that gets generalized into so many domains of human life: work, academics, and yes, love relationships. It's pernicious and insidious. A parent has impinged on a child and now sent into the boy what I call THE MATERNAL NO = YOU CAN'T BECOME A MAN. Note the ambiguity of "can't"—both in the sense of denied **ability or capacity** and, more importantly, denied **permission** to become a man (the normative "can made into can't").

Thus, when a mother does not separate from her son and does not allow him to separate from her but in fact communicates (in so many nuanced ways) the Maternal No to his becoming a man, she in effect says that "full-fledged manhood and adult ability to be independent and love a mate is not possible for you—you must only remain connected to me, Mother." Thus the boy is, forever, "dancing in his mother's mirror" rather than his own or his future partner's.

It is only by doing the work and gradually moving away from his mother's mirror, by separating fully so that he can love an adult mate, that he can discover a power he must have in order to thrive in love—the power of Personal Authority. This power simply cannot be developed without psychological separateness. Without that separateness, the man will always be in power struggle with projections of mother in a spouse; in this situation, it is difficult for any man or woman to love beyond power struggle and anger.

Ultimately, in its cognitive manifestations, it comes down to being able to assert one's judgments about oneself, others, relationships, and the larger world, in such a way that one's own construal separates one from enmeshment with others, including a lover or spouse. The result is that you feel personal authority in such a way that you don't have to compete with a mate for her personal authority, or steal her personal authority.

Though my calendar age is from 1964, most people think I'm still in my younger thirties. And, for the first time, after four years of work, I feel like the entity inside—ME—is neither a child-man nor a prematurely aged mother's little-hubby. It's wonderful. Over the last four years of fully separating from my mother, I feel that I finally have both the intimacy skills and the separateness skills to love someone and be loved.

—Anonymous, 48

*Bolds and caps are the writer's.

The Pro-Social Journey

Harvard psychiatrist John Ratey has written, "The pro-social urge is the human being's instinct for 'doing for' others, 'turning the other cheek,' pushing beyond personal limits to help family members, even sacrificing him- or herself when necessary for the common good. The pro-social urge makes us human and combines with our reproductive biology and neurochemistry of bonding to commit us to a mate and our offspring."

If you are constantly hurt by love in the stages of a lifetime, your pro-social urge to love your mate will adjust to the constant pain: you will most likely withhold more love than you realize you are withhold-ing and, simultaneously, compulsively and anxiously seek even more love from your partner than the partner can give. Some of the stages of growth during this journey will occur naturally in the life cycle—life happens, our own and our mate's pro-social instincts constantly adjust accordingly—but much of the pain of your relationship will occur be-cause you can't move deeper into new stages in which to express your own pro-social urge.

As you move into the second part of this book, take with you your sense of what stage of relationship you are in. You have worked hard to get wherever you are, and now there is yet still more adventure, wisdom, and depth to discover, including an even more detailed emphasis on practical strategies for developing and sustaining the intimate-separateness balance in each stage. Realization of enmesh-ment/abandonment, dangerous merging, projections and illusions, innate gender differences, and the stages and map of real human love set a foundation for the even more strategic and tactical work of Part II of this book. As you move forward, I hope you will take the time you need to continue exploring the maps provided in Part I—mine them for everything you can before moving too intensely forward, and keep returning to them over the course of your lifetime as you meet new crises and thus need to refresh and recharge your ability to cultivate real, true love.

PART II

Practicing the Art of Intimate Separateness

The farther away love feels from one's touch, the more one naturally speaks of the need for change.

—St. Teresa of Avila

Chapter 5

Ending Power Struggle in Your Relationship

FIVE PRACTICAL STRATEGIES CAN END YOUR POWER STRUGGLES

Toni, thirty-eight, was incessantly critical of Andy, thirty-six, for errors she asserted that he made in the workplace (Toni was the CEO of their small business and Andy, the CPA). She was not a harsh yeller—she did not use a constantly shrill or raised voice; rather, she was what Andy called a "chiseler." Through myriad critical comments per day, Andy said, "She digs her dagger into me, she chisels away at me." Toni's comments often went like this:

"That's not how you should talk to customers, and you know it."

"What are you thinking? You make no sense."

"I can't believe you would do that."

Over a period of years, worn down and wounded by a million little knives, Andy came to feel that nothing he did at work was okay or right; no action really passed muster. "I try to do what she wants, but maybe we just shouldn't work together," he said resignedly. When I asked the couple whether things were the same at home—"Is the dagger constantly plunging into you at home?"—they both agreed that it did happen somewhat, but not as much as at work. In their pair-bond away from work, it seemed—with sex, child-raising, and social life—they were "okay," Andy said.

Given that Toni's criticism wasn't as present at home, I understood that something was going on for Toni and Andy around enmeshment, merging, and power struggle in the workplace that both people were unconscious of. When I asked the couple about previous therapy, Toni and Andy told me that a previous therapist had diagnosed Toni as "somewhat narcissistic" and Andy as a "Mr. Nice Guy," "passive-aggressive." The therapist also noted that Toni primarily was "the one doing the real emotional work in the relationship" (Andy's words).

As we worked together, I helped the couple add to previous therapy with a different angle. I saw them as compartmentalizing Stage 3, Power Struggle, at work and basically colluding in their workplace with dark shadows that kept them constantly anxious, aggressive, and passive-aggressive toward one another. I asked them to celebrate that their home life did not carry as much of this tension as their work life, and as we talked about their struggles, we came to understand the following:

1. Toni felt a deep fear of failure, rejection, and abandonment, which she compartmentalized into her workplace—she was able to do this because she and her husband were so close (in other words, with any other employee, the coworker would have quit, but her husband was not going to leave any time soon, for economic and other reasons).

2. In her compartmentalization of her fears at work, her bond with Andy was "too close." She felt unconsciously compelled to project failure onto Andy, enmeshing him and herself in her own internal struggle with self-worth.

3. Andy felt such a deep fear of success at work that he invited, constantly, a power struggle with Toni. This was happening unconsciously; he enmeshed with Toni but did not know how to separate from her in a healthy way.

4. Andy's natural personality (which he called "passive-aggressive") grated both on him and on his wife; both people hoped for more strength from Andy, strength that would help stabilize the marriage and help the business be more successful.

Variations of these themes are often unconsciously active in marriages in which a "critic" is married to a "conciliator"—one spouse is critical by nature (this spouse is often, though not always, an "alpha" personality, such as Toni), the other spouse is conciliatory (like Andy). While, of course, both people in a relationship may criticize one another and/or be conciliatory depending on circumstance, timing, and so on, the power-struggle stage of marriage can become exacerbated by the two different personality types. We will explore this even more deeply by studying personality types in a moment.

For now, think about whether your marriage possesses a clear "chiseler," a partner with "the dagger always out," a "shamer," or someone like this; and see if the other partner is the one who "takes it," "absorbs the criticism." If you see this pattern in your relationship, look for the ways in which both the attacker and the attackee are actually enmeshed—so entangled in each other's psyches that power struggle (chiseling, criticizing, judging, and doing the things that will be criticized, critiqued, and judged) has become a default mode for the relationship.

During our months of counseling together, Toni came to see that "being the boss" did indeed create failure anxiety for her. She was not an independent, healthy separate self at work (though she thought she was); instead, she was enmeshed with her fears and imagined failures, projected those fears onto Andy, and constantly punished him for his supposed faults in order to quash her own fear of failure. In other words, she was unconsciously (in the limbic brain) saying, "I am always afraid of failure; this makes me feel yucky, ashamed, weak; I will take this out on my lover and partner, Andy, so that (1) I can see failure everywhere and, hopefully, one day, fully confront my fears of it but, meanwhile, (2) also create more and more and more failure because fear of failure is my baseline, it's what I am comfortable with, I will keep creating it until I get help or destroy my love relationship."

This kind of projection and enmeshment can be difficult to see and understand without some help and mentoring. It is the "muck" of enmeshment, of being "too close" both to our own fears/projections and to our spouse's self. One reason for the difficulty in partners seeing this muck is that the criticizing and shaming from the alpha spouse seems, on the surface, to be about judging the other person as inferior, and there isn't much intimacy or closeness in that!

So, the conciliator will disagree that the couple is too intimate: "Are you kidding, when she criticizes me I feel far away from her, not close." Andy did indeed say this: "I want to just get away, not get closer."

But then Toni realized something. She said, "Wait a minute, actually, I think I do feel too close to you when I am criticizing you. In fact, I feel like I'm drowning in all your mistakes and your quirks and slow way you do things. It's like I can't get away, I can't get free, I'm obsessing over your flaws. It drives me nuts." Toni was seeing that she was not a separated self when she became so critical; she was enmeshed, living in her closeness to him, "his flaws," which actually mirrored the flaws she was afraid of in herself.

This is very important work for everyone who looks at power struggles. It is crucial to understand that constant, repetitive battles tend not to occur between lovers who are separate enough from one another to be relatively satisfied with and forgiving of one another; they do occur, however, when we are enmeshed, merged. In this state, we worry over abandonment, we keep pressing the other person to change (we try to remold the other person into the perfect self-image we want to see in the mirror, and do this mainly because of our own fears), and we keep ratcheting up our own failure and other projections, rather than engaging healthy separateness of self that allows for love, affection, and camaraderie to occur.

It is also important to remember that, though the critical spouse is usually the first person everyone looks at for hopeful change, not all the enmeshment anxiety of power struggling is caused by the chiseler. Andy felt constantly afraid that Toni would abandon him, especially at work

("We shouldn't work together," "I should quit," "I don't know why she puts up with my messes," "She's going to fire me one day"). When I asked Toni if she thought Andy should leave the workplace and find another job, she said, "No! I need him. He knows the whole business!"

To help Toni and Andy work through the subtleties of their power struggle, I asked them, as I do all couples who have children, to talk about their kids. The motivation to move beyond power struggle is rarely stronger than when it is linked to the health and well-being of children. For couples who don't have children, observations of child-hoods, as well as observations of other parents and adolescents, allow for understanding the struggles, too. Since Toni and Andy had kids in soccer, I asked if they had been at a game recently and noticed a father or mother yelling at the son or daughter, constantly criticizing the adolescent for failures and errors. Both Andy and Toni had seen one particular father be "pretty abusive" toward his son at soccer practice. Here is dialogue from our conversation about this.

Me: Could that father perhaps be yelling at his son so much because he's remembering his own failures? He's afraid the boy will fail; he's projecting failure onto him?

Toni: Sure. Like, he's not letting the kid just be himself. He's actually remembering his own failures.

Me: Yes. He's projecting his worst, most frightened self-image onto his son. He's not psychologically separate enough from his son to let the boy develop his own self. Unconsciously, the father has made the boy into a mirror object of his own success projections and enmeshed that mirror object with his own issues and fears of failure.

Toni: So that's what "he's too close" means.

Me: Yes. Does that make sense?

Toni: I think I get it. It's pretty abstract.

Me: Yes. Andy, what do you think?

Andy: I agree with Toni. It's kind of abstract.

Me: You're right. But what do you think I'm getting at?

Andy: I think you're saying that Toni and I do that. She feels afraid of failing at work, maybe because of how hard her mom was on her. She feels like she's going to mess it up, but she doesn't know that's what she's feeling and, for some reason, she projects it onto me and hates what she thinks are *my* failures?

Me: Toni, does that make sense?

Toni: Let me think about it. I think so, but I'm trying to understand.

Me: I believe you recall unconsciously how it felt to be constantly criticized by your mom. You project a whole inner world around this onto your work relationship with Andy.

Toni nods. "Yes. But it's not all about me."

Me: No. But one thing at a time. I think you get stressed at work and create power struggle with Andy.

Andy: Why does she do that?

Me: Because you are her husband and lover and she is unconsciously trying to work through all of the shame and pain with you. She projects failure onto you and does battle with it; she does not operate out of a healthy, separated self when she gets stressed at work. She enmeshes all her "crap," as you've called it, in our sessions, on you. You two are indeed "one" as you promised to be on your wedding day, but this oneness is the dangerous kind because a spouse is not the appropriate person to do this stuff with—especially, specifically, because you are her lover; she needs to separate this from you and take it to friends, therapists, journaling, or other tools.

Toni: Wow, really? Could that be true? (Silence as she thinks about it.) Jesus, yeah, I think so. I just don't feel like myself when I'm so mean. I kind of hate myself, but don't realize it at the time. I am using Andy to work my shit out. I am enmeshing him in my stuff, as you say.

Andy: And that's what you (Gurian) mean about the father and son. When Toni does that, she's not letting me be myself. Like the dad with the kid? The dad with the kid kind of hates himself.

Me: Yes, in a way. And Andy, what would be your part in this? We've looked at Toni's half of this power struggle—what are your enmeshments, projections, and merging in this?

Andy was silent and couldn't immediately decipher his part. Before continuing this dialogue, I want to say that it had taken three months for this couple to speak in this language—the language of this book.

Helping them see through the "abstraction" involved the "doing" of surveys and tools, but always also involves engaging the "cognitive" part of the process as much as possible. I have found that if couples can learn this abstract psychological language well, especially as it applies to themselves, they have a tool for their marriage with which, when they leave therapy, they can solve future problems.

Andy: I don't know. Help me. (I waited to see if Toni would say something. She did.)

Toni: I think it's how you always say you should quit; like you'll say, "I suck at this job, obviously, so why don't you just go find someone else?" I wish you would fight me, fight back, be stronger, but you threaten to leave, you don't fight for us, for our relationship.

Andy: Oh. (He nodded, pondering silently. Toni was about to speak, but I spoke instead.)

Me: Do you really wish Andy fought you more overtly? If his personality was as dominating as yours, would you guys be the people that you are?

Toni (pondering): That is an interesting point. We are sort of an "opposites attract" couple, personality-wise.

Andy: You wouldn't like it. You say you would, but you wouldn't. You like being the boss. You say you want me to be as strong as you, but you don't. (Toni ponders this.)

Toni: Maybe. But you can't blame all this on me. It's not all me.

Andy: I know. I know.

Me: Both of you are triggering each other and getting immersed in power struggle.

Andy (to Toni): It's not all about you. Okay, I think I get it. All your criticisms trigger my fear of abandonment, for sure. My mom left my dad, and that fear of abandonment he (Gurian) talks about is real. We knew that when we were seeing the other therapist. I get, like, enmeshed with it or something. (To me): Can we say that?

Me: Yes. Sure.

Toni: Then you talk about leaving, and it triggers my own fear of abandonment and failure, and that just makes me get even more critical of you.

Andy (nodding): Yes. You're right. I do that. (We are silent for a moment to think.)

Andy (to me): Huh. So, are you saying she's also actually being more critical of herself, actually, not just of me? Like, when she is so mean to me, she's actually being mean to herself? So, she's in a struggle not just with me but with herself? Like, if I could understand that, I wouldn't take what she says so personally?

Me: Yes. That seems very likely to me. You need to stop taking so much of what she says personally. You need to see that most of her critiques are about the stress she's feeling. You need to separate yourself from them. Specifically, you'll know you are remaining separate from the critiques in a healthy way when you stop threatening to abandon her.

As these conversations continued, Toni and Andy agreed to keep a journal from their separate viewpoints of what happened every day at work for the next week. They agreed to become love-scientists, observers who used their workplace relationship as a lab. They agreed specifically to see the ways in which they as a couple were actually too merged, too intimate, too enmeshed—and thus, felt compelled to create constant power struggle as a way of trying to break free, a way that was not finding fruition.

Toni especially enjoyed journaling, and her journaling filled forty pages within three weeks. In his less copious journaling, Andy saw that he was enmeshed with Toni as he remembered a situation. Over the last year, he had avoided overhauling the financial reporting in the business enough to satisfy Toni as CEO. She continually criticized him about this lack. He knew intellectually that Toni was right in insisting that the couple's business needed a better financial system; but Andy wielded passive-aggressive power by specifically *not* doing what the business needed. Because of that, the criticism and conflict (power struggle) would continue.

Like most people in power struggle in a marriage, Andy had gotten into a habit over the years of doing or not doing the very things that would cause him more stress and pain with his spouse. Battle, pain, and struggle was the new normal, and each partner made sure of its longevity, tacitly hoping it would heal them of their pains. As they battled constantly, they each felt momentarily powerful (when each "won" something), but then constantly powerless, shifting back and forth. Power struggle became the rhythm of love.

THE WISDOM OF SEPARATENESS

When emotionally injured individuals come together, they sincerely hope that the love of the other will heal them . . . but the reenact-ment of childhood misery is accompanied by childhood feelings of powerlessness. Breaking through this cycle of misery and blame requires making a clear distinction between the past (when we were children with little understanding and few options) and the present (where we have much more power). . . . When personality is constructed around a self-negative belief (e.g., I am no good), changing this belief will shake a person to the core. But with adult understanding of the past and therapeutic support in the present, we can change what we think about ourselves.

—Susan Rosenthal, PhD, Adler Graduate Professional Schools, Toronto, Canada, and Daniel Eckstein, PhD, School of Medicine, Saba University, National Dutch Caribbean

Are You in Power Struggle?

In the first few pages of this book, you took your first Essential Questions Survey. Here is a modification of it that should show you if you are in Stage 3, Power Struggle.

1. Do I and/or my partner try to control one another's "domains"? (Alternatively, in our lives together, are there

significant areas of daily life over which we try to exert
significant control over each other?) Yes ___. No ___.

2. Do we ruminate about and/or get triggered by and/
   or overreact to (take personally) my/or each other's
   weaknesses, personality traits, or vulnerabilities? Yes ___.
   No ___.

3. Do we consciously choose to neglect talking together at least
   once a day? Yes ___. No ___.

4. Do we neglect or purposefully forget to satisfy weekly
   bonding rituals, such as date nights, even when it is
   logistically possible to do so? Yes ___. No ___.

5. Do we neglect to say "I love you" a number of times per
   week to each other, if not at least once a day? Yes ___.
   No ___.

6. Do we neglect to praise one another at least a few times a
   week, if not at least once a day? Yes ___. No ___.

7. Do I believe my partner is rarely or ever right in our marital
   conflicts? Yes ___. No ___.

8. Does my partner allow me to be right in many of our
   marital conflicts? Yes ___. No ___.

9. Do we neglect to apologize to one another within hours or,
   at most, a day, after hurting the other's feelings? Yes ___.
   No ___. If not, which partner (or is it both partners?) does
   not apologize?

10. Do I generally avoid forgiving my partner's flaws? Yes ___.
    No ___.

11. Does my partner generally avoid forgiving my flaws?
    Yes ___. No ___.

12. Do I generally avoid forgiving my own flaws? Yes ___.
    No ___.

13. Do we tend to minimize the importance of gender
    differences in the ways we practice love and intimacy as
    women and men? Yes ___. No ___.

14. Is criticism and judgment my own default position with my
    partner? Yes ___. No ___.

15. Is criticism and judgment my partner's default position with me? Yes ___. No ___.

16. Are we fighting about something every day? Yes ___. No ___.

17. Are we not fighting at all—withdrawn and isolated from one another? Yes ___. No ___.

18. Are we having very little satisfying sex, or is the sex only satisfying after a fight? Yes ___. No ___.

If you answered the majority of these questions in the positive, you are most likely locked into Stage 3 of human love. Your relational "default mode" may be power struggle, especially when you're under stress as an individual or a couple. You will need to focus on one or more personal and/or relational sacrifices in order to move beyond this default mode.

Sacrifices that Help End the Battle

The great sacrifice in a marriage, the great heroism, is to let go of power struggle yourself—separate yourself from it, no matter what your partner does. This is sacrifice and surrender to end a war, even if you are not sure what your "enemy" will do. While working together to move beyond Stage 3 is generally a faster course toward the goal of a healthy future relationship, still, as many of us know, you often can't get your partner on board with change, not at least right away. Each of us has to make the change ourselves first, surrender ourselves to it, and keep plugging away at getting our partner to come along. Luckily, Toni and Andy did this.

The good news is that, much of the time, this works; when we change, our partner feels less stress (a new respect from us, a new rationality, a new simplicity of love, a new self-sacrifice) and rises to the occasion of the happiness, good feeling, intimacy, and love. So the first step, no matter what the outcome will be, is the hardest: changing yourself, even if your partner is not ready.

To take this step, you may need an answer to, "Why let my partner 'off the hook'?" Put another way, "Why surrender power or sacrifice myself and take on this responsibility when I am already caring for ill parents, working fifty hours a week, raising children, and dealing with other stresses of my own? Let my partner make the changes—I'm fine the way I am."

The answer is always personal in this stage of life; at the same time, it is universal. Love can't continue, and your self and soul can't fully grow unless you do this work. This is the developmental work of maturing as a lover. For a decade or more we can say, "That's all about kid stuff, mom/dad stuff, I'm beyond that," or something like this, but if you are in power struggle in a relationship, and if that struggle is not mainly about a highly dangerous situation (violence in the marriage, addiction), the truth is that you are missing something very big; you have not done the work yet that is needed to achieve intimate separateness.

If you lead five or ten years of your life in power struggle, then divorce without having done this work—this sacrifice, surrender—the sense of failure can be acute, often immeasurably sad. If you do commit to doing the work no matter where your partner stands at the outset of your work, you have the greatest chance of living a life of happiness and love after this crisis in love is over. Love, thus, puts us face to face with self-sacrifice: you sacrifice yourself because you know it is the right course; you receive gains at the other end of the sacrifice in yourself at least and, hopefully, for your marriage. But even if your marriage ends, you gain truths about love that you can bring to your next marriage or partnership.

Thus, the sacrifice cannot fail—you will, because of it, live the soulfulness in love that every human being is seeking, even if with another partner.

Sacrifice 1: If You Are Going to Divorce, Create an Amicable Divorce

Mary, thirty-six, and Isaiah, thirty-eight, both worked constantly, she in the medical field and he in software engineering. They had two children, eight and six. They spent their work lives in front of computers and their home lives tending to children, or in front of computers and the television. They had been together for three years before marrying, and had been married nine years. They knew one another well, felt "comfortable with one another," as Mary put it, and "pretty routine," as Isaiah put it. A few of their married years had involved constant criticizing, arguments, power struggle, but they had moved out of that time without therapy—they just stopped fighting, they told me, agreeing to live separate lives. The last three years or so had been years of, as Mary said, "no real sparks. We live and let live. We don't get in each other's way." People thought of them as "the perfect couple." They were anything but.

As counseling continued, more of the hidden distances and dangerous lack of intimacy emerged. The couple had grown apart in nearly every way. This was not the kind of healthy intimate-separateness balance we are discussing in this book: it was 90 percent distance, 10 percent intimacy. Mary confessed in therapy to wanting more children, feeling that another child might help them be more in love. Isaiah said he was too busy now, "and plus," he said, "I think maybe Mary and I would need to be happier before we brought another kid into the world." This comment hit Mary hard; she became teary and then angry, "Whose fault is that?!" she exclaimed. She felt blamed for the marital ennui and distance, even though both Mary and Isaiah had, to a great extent, "checked out" of their partnership.

After six months of marital therapy, Mary and Isaiah decided to split up. The divorce was amicable, and they both felt they had a lot of options. As Isaiah put it, "Mary has been a mentor to me emotionally, but I can't give her everything she wants"; and Mary said, "Isaiah and I had great times and I don't regret our marriage, but I need to find someone who puts me and children first." Mary entered into therapy for a year of work to more fully understand herself going forward so that she would, in her words, "select someone different next time, someone who can be my soul mate."

This couple had moved beyond power struggle by shutting it off completely; they entered a time of being so emotionally distant for so long a counselor like myself almost wished they would re-enter power struggle, just so there would be a spark of hope for them. When I saw Mary about three years after her therapy with me ended, she said she was married to "a wonderful man, who wanted kids. I have another child, a one-year-old." Isaiah's job took him to another state, she reported. "He's seeing someone new." In her quick, faraway look, I saw some sadness about the former relationship, but mainly I saw happiness and a feeling of quietude and dignity.

If you are moving toward divorce, the work of this chapter and of Part II of this book will be about ending power struggle during the divorce so that the divorce can be amicable. As I suggest tools to use to save marriages, for you "saving the marriage" will be about moving the marriage forward by removing enmeshments and projections during the divorce process so that you can have a happy ending and a robust new beginning to your next relationship.

Sacrifice 2: Agree to Disagree

I have seen relationships in which marriages have continued even though the couple was living in *seemingly constant* power struggle. These couples help us understand another sacrifice couples sometimes make—they turn power struggle into a *benign form of bickering*. They continue arguing, criticizing, and so on, but with the mutual covenant in place that they will agree to disagree. Thus, they don't take things personally. Every day is a low-grade battle, and the couple relates to one another mainly through equalizing conflict—theirs is mainly an "intimacy through struggle."

One couple I met socially had been married for forty-eight years and bickered many times a day, correcting one another, criticizing, but the sacrifice they had made was to relate in this way without enmeshment. For them, the "power struggle" was not a battle over the deep power to be separate yet conjoined selves—the two people were actually in the later stages of marriage but appeared, in public, to be in Stage 3 because of the covenanted way their two personalities interpreted love's passions.

YOUR INSIGHTS

I want to start what I want to say with some of my favorite dialogue about relationships—it comes from the movie *The Notebook*.

She: Would you just stay with me?
He: Stay with you? What for? Would you look at us; we are already fighting!
She: Well, that's what we do! We fight! You tell me when I'm being an arrogant son of a bitch, and I tell you when you're being a pain in the ass. Which you are 99 percent of the time. I'm not afraid to hurt your feelings. They have, like, a two-second rebound rate, and then you're off doing the next pain-in-the-ass thing.
He: So what?
She: So, it's not going to be easy, it's going to be really hard. And we are going to have to work at this every day. But, I'm willing to do that because I want you.

From living in the United States, Europe, and China, I have seen three ways of being in love, but both Europe and China seem to have a more realistic view of love than the United States. The *Notebook* quote is more like Europe and China, in my view, than it is like the United States. I don't actually mean all of this completely literally, but I mean it somewhat because it is what I've observed.

I love this *Notebook* quote because even though it's from a Hollywood movie, it's kind of countercultural—it's one of the realest moments in a pretty sappy love story. It also shows that very often the other person pisses you off, in fact, a lot of the time, and for lots of reasons, and who can keep up with them all?—you just have to keep compromising. I think it also shows that for a relationship to be strong, it shouldn't always be gushy, intimate, and emotional.

My boyfriend and I fight a lot, kind of like in the movie, and we aren't afraid of hurting each other's feelings, we say it how it is, but that's just how it goes. I annoy the shit out of him and he annoys the shit out of me. But I still love him and he loves me and at the end of the day we are compatible, and we make up and keep living our lives.

Moral of the story: a lot of people these days seem to think that fighting is a bad thing, and it can be, yes, on a large scale but they seem to think any fighting at all in a relationship is bad because it shows they are bad at relationships or he's not perfect for me because we fight and we don't have this picturesque idea of a relationship. These people get so worried that their love isn't perfect and doesn't always feel good, and they're so afraid of fighting that they end the relationship.

Of course this happens in China, Spain, and everywhere, too, but I haven't seen the picturesque/perfect "we should always be perfectly intimate" stuff anywhere else in the world like the US. I think maybe we would be a little better off in the United States if we could fight and make up without tearing each other's hearts out. I think my boyfriend and I are learning how to do this by not making each other responsible for who we are.

—Danielle, 24

Sacrifice 3: Deal with Non-Relational Pressure Points Separately

Most clients who come into my office have read books and articles about relationships that seem to say to them, "My relationship is supposed to heal me." They will not realize, unless they awaken and get help, that there are specific issues and "pressure points" both partners have that are not very much the business of the love relationship at all. We can be daily helpmates to our partners, but we can't fix, heal, or remove the stresses, pressure points, or areas of self-imposed error our partner is involved in.

Hopefully, from reading the first four chapters of this book, you will have begun an internal journey of identifying merging cycles and working to separate from them. As you do so, a great deal of power struggle will end. As this work continues, "non-relational" factors (pressure points) need to be understood and worked with immediately—in fact, mutual separation from some of these pressure points will automatically end a great deal of the power struggle that you previously believed came from relational tensions. Toni and Andy increased their ability to work through their power struggle issues by looking at the Essential Questions and listening for clues to non-relational sources of struggle.

Essential Questions Survey 7: Analyzing Your Separate, Non-Relational Sources of Power Struggle

These are areas you will be able to disentangle from relatively quickly—separating from them, getting them in perspective, and making changes to accommodate them will exponentially aid you in solving power struggle issues all around:

1. Do I (or my partner) suffer from alcohol abuse; substance abuse; sex, electronic, or other addiction? If you answer yes, the addiction is most likely a primary cause of the power struggle between you. Ending this abuse or addiction is the thing you need help with—this needs to be separated from the marriage/relationship-as-cause and be treated as its own discrete cause.

2. Do I (or my partner) suffer from a physical health issue (e.g., chronic pain, disease, physical disorder) that affects mood? If so, your marriage may be struggling over power and relational needs that cannot be met or solved through emotional changes; instead, the marriage must adjust to a new reality of one partner's changed health situation. If

you hear yourself making arguments that "blame" your marriage (or the other person) for mood changes that are actually related to the new health situation, it is important for both parties to get assistance in separating the marital relationship from the health problem.

3. Do I (or my partner) suffer from a food allergy or food issue such as low blood sugar, or a lack of sleep, or a lack of exercise that affects personal mood? For instance, is my partner especially critical and angry before she or he eats dinner, or am I? If so, you should adjust to this new environmental reality. You will most likely need to avoid emotional conversations before dinner or after a bad night's sleep.

4. Have I (or my partner) been put on new medications or changed our medications or vitamins/supplements? For instance, have your own or your partner's medications changed from proprietary to generic? Trace back when the "relationship issues" started in order to see what blood and brain chemistry has been affecting personality and mood and for how long. If a pill or medication has entered a person's system, it may trump some other relationship or emotional struggles as a primary causative element in your present power struggles.

5. Have our battles begun commensurate with hormone imbalances and cycles, including pregnancy and post-pregnancy, and/or menopause and andropause? Two cases: in one, in which the man no longer initiated sex and even daily affection, the woman worried that she was at fault somehow and that twenty-two years of love were going to be lost. She began to fear that he'd abandon her. Actually, the man's testosterone levels had fallen significantly because of early andropause, which depleted his estrogen as well.

Biology played a key role, but she thought emotional and relational struggles were the cause. In another case, the couple was arguing daily, and the husband had moved out; divorce was imminent. The wife's doctor recommended a hysterectomy because of fibroid cysts and other issues. The hysterectomy was performed and, as the woman herself said two months later, "Our relationship is no longer insane." Women should check out books by Christiane Northrup and others on midlife, as well as *Women's Moods* and *The Female Brain.* Men should read books by Jed Diamond, such as *Male Menopause,* and Louann Brizendine's *The Male Brain* and Daniel Amen's *Sex on the Brain.*

6. Am I (or my partner) under significant workplace stress, stress around children, caregiver stress around aging parents, any external stressor that is bleeding into our love-relationship and creating a struggle between us? Couples often attack one another and engage in power struggle with one another as an unconscious response to external stressors. If you are doing this, it is crucial that both partners engage in whatever work is necessary to "not take things personally" and to operate, for a time, with some close intimacy, but also a good dose of respectful, helpful separateness. The external stressor may go on for a long time, and the party least affected by that stressor will generally need to make the sacrifice of "weathering the storm." (Obviously, if the person under the stress becomes abusive, self-protection necessitates a less patient course.)

7. Am I (or my partner) suffering post-traumatic stress triggers? If you or your partner was physically or sexually abused as a child or physically or mentally harmed in military service, much of your or your partner's present mood change and resultant relationship problems can be related to PTSD. New research shows that adults who

were abused as children are significantly more likely than other adults to experience chronic anxiety. Working with a therapist to discover the triggers and the extent of the PTSD will be crucial to relationship survival. If one partner suffers PTSD, the other partner will need to sacrifice some closeness for perhaps many years while the sufferer makes the sacrifice of getting help.

8. Do I (or my partner) suffer from depression, personality disorders, or other chronic or newly presenting mental health issues? More than one in five Americans has a mental disorder or illness. You could be one of these or married to one of these. If so, much of your relational stress is related to the disorder or illness, and consciousness of this can help you separate your love relationship from the disorder. For instance, a client complained that he could not trust his spouse, and so their therapy was about that "trust issue" until we realized in therapy that the accuser was significantly depressed. "Trust" between the parties (a relational diagnosis by the couple) was actually not the primary issue. The depression, which was difficult to read in this man, needed separate treatment via medication, new exercise regimes, vitamin supplements, and therapy—the marriage needed to take a step back from blaming itself (via the two parties) for the marital distress.

9. Am I (or my partner) suffering from family issues that require personal and, perhaps for a few months, *separate* therapy? Couple therapy needs to involve both people, but many individuals need individual therapy, even if they are in a couple relationship. Issues that go back to projections and shadows of Mom and Dad in the family of origin—an absent father (or mother), an enmeshed and dominating mother (or father), an alcoholic father or mother, etc. . . . These issues can't ultimately be solved through power struggle

in a love relationship. For a relationship to last, the person who suffered childhood parenting issues must heal from these issues not only with the partner's help but also with a therapist or other professional and/or group of peer mentors (friends, men's group, women's group) that does not involve the partner.

10. Have I bought into an ideology—religious or social— that pits me competitively, as a man or woman, against my partner because of his or her gender or other creed or belief system? A most common source of power struggle in the area of gender occurs at religious and social ideology extremes—one partner is an ardent feminist, perhaps, who approaches love as a gender power struggle from the outset, while the other partner is not; or one partner may take a religious teaching regarding gender roles and obedience almost literally, while the other does not. Either because of the social ideology or religious ideology, power struggle can occur. The parties need to make the sacrifice (and feel the courage) of separating themselves from the ideology to see if, to a great extent, it is causing unnecessary power struggle.

These ten pressure points do not encompass all issues, but they are like curtains that need to be opened for light to illuminate the marriage. The profound act of self-sacrifice for you—opening the windows so the relationship can find the light—will not only involve getting help for your pressure points and separate issues but also separating or disentangling yourself psychologically from your partner's issues, *even if your partner will not get help.* You can ask your partner for help in supporting your separate journey (she or he will, perhaps, join you in therapy and the work of this book), and/or you can encourage your partner to get help for his or her issues, but you will not have success if you avoid the issues by trying to increase intimacy and, thus, enmeshment with your partner.

Toni and Andy

As I worked with Toni and Andy, they decided to make some sacrifices commensurate with opening curtains and letting light into their external (non-relational) causes of power struggle.

- We discovered that Toni tended to get angriest when she was hungriest and on days when she got too little exercise. So she learned to eat healthy snacks and to do thirty minutes of cardiovascular exercise at the beginning of her workday. This food-and-exercise element had nothing to do with Andy or the partnership; this was *her* issue. She needed to deal with it. In fact, the issue was so separately hers (and understandably so) that if Andy asked her to exercise, she got angry and accused him of calling her fat and of being ready to abandon her because she was not attractive to him. This was an enmeshment-power struggle. Andy had to learn to back away and trust that she would realize how important exercise and healthy eating were to herself and her marriage. Toni got help in therapy to work through body-image issues so that she could change her course.

- Andy's testosterone had fallen to less than half of its levels five years before. This was affecting *his* mood and motivation, and it was an element of self totally separate from Toni. Andy asked his physician for assistance with a testosterone patch. This helped his mood and his sex drive, which brought more joy into the marriage. He worked in therapy on his low self-confidence and "my inferiority complex I've had all my life." He came to understand that he couldn't enmesh with Toni anymore, "as if Toni will be the one to make me believe in myself. I have to believe in myself. I have to take this pressure off Toni."

Sacrifice 4: Loving Who You Got

During both their separate and their couple time in self-discovery, Toni and Andy completed a comparison of personality and temperament types (to do this yourself, please consult the Appendix at the end of this book). Through this work, they came to know one another and themselves in ways they had not before, which helped them gain healthy perspective on the following elements:

1. Their inborn, natural, core personalities, which will not change in the relationship (we are born with these personalities genetically—they are here to stay).
2. The natural and learned complementarities of core personality (new ways two separate personalities can coexist without power struggle).
3. The parts of their personalities that would probably always cause some friction (knowing this helped them be more patient with one another).

Love beyond Stage 3—moving beyond power struggle—requires us to remove most illusions from our relationship and learn more about the core personality living with us in our house. If we don't do this, we will continue projecting selves and personalities onto the other and ourselves, and we will vacillate hourly or daily between hyper-watchfulness of the other's personality and withdrawal from that personality altogether.

Given the importance of personality to power struggle, please take time separately and/or together to do two or more of the personality surveys noted in the Appendix. To do this, you will need to take this book and your journal on a trip with you to the bookstore and/or through the Internet.

Genome Mapping (Official and Non-Official)

Constant anger and constant rumination are, as we've noted throughout this book, powerful enemies of marital tranquillity. A tool to help you look at both anger and rumination has emerged in this last decade and will solidify even more fully in the next decades: genome/DNA mapping. Genome mapping is becoming less expensive every day, and more and more people are utilizing it to gauge susceptibility to physical and health issues; it is not yet a perfect mechanism for pinpointing the brain's functions, but it will most likely advance to this goal at some point.

Until genome mapping fully reflects the brain as much as it now does the body, and bloodstream, you can do some of the psychological mapping yourself, realizing from genome research that many of your own, natural marriage-stressing qualities (and your partner's) are inborn. These realizations can help you end power struggle because they can assist you in self-regulating aggression, anger, rumination, and anxiety.

Here is an example you can track right now through your own observations of yourself and your partner: the alleles on your 5-HTT gene, which regulate serotonin in your brain. Studies by Emory University primatologists J. D. Higley, Steve Suomi, and their team were some of the first to qualitatively identify the 5-HTT alleles. They and other geneticists over the last two decades have found that:

1. Short alleles on the 5-HTT gene tend to make naturally aggressive people even more aggressive.
2. Short alleles on the 5-HTT gene tend to make people who are inclined toward anxiety even more inclined to dwell on things, both naturally and/or under stress.

So, if you are the "aggressive" person or the "anxious" person, you are most likely "wired" that way. Researchers have further found differences between people with two short alleles, one long and one short allele, and two long alleles. The exact number of people with these three distinct allele sets is unknown—it can't be measured until absolutely everyone on earth has a genome map done—but researchers estimate around 17 percent of people have two short alleles. These people can tend to be more anxious or aggressive than those with two long alleles. A 2013 study found that approximately 70 percent of people would qualify as "less sensitive" on a spectrum of "naturally resilient, relatively nonreactive to aggressive emotions," but that the remaining 30 percent would qualify as "sensitive or very sensitive." Of this 30 percent, a little over half are likely to have two short alleles and slightly less than half have one short and one long allele on the 5-HTT chromosome.

In your marriage, you may fit one of these categories, as may your partner. Perhaps you have two short alleles or one short and one long, and fit on the "more sensitive" end of the spectrum (like Andy), but you are married to someone who has two long alleles, so he or she is relatively unconscious of the damage that can be done with aggressive and insensitive words or tones of voice (perhaps like Toni). Exacerbating this situation, your sensitivity may lead you to dwell for hours or days about the unconscious "attack" by your mate (excessive rumination), which can lead to significant enmeshment with him or her as you try to get your spouse to change who she or he is in order to protect yourself against your own sensitivity, anxiety, rumination, and sadness.

This scenario can happen to both genders—both women and men can be more "sensitive" and have the short alleles. It is believed that one potential reason more men practice the aggressive end of this spectrum, even when having short alleles, is their high levels of testosterone; but many men have lower testosterone and two short alleles, and can be married to a woman with higher natural aggression, an alpha personality, with longer alleles. All of this can create a scenario in which the husband is more sensitive and the wife is more aggressive, as with Toni and Andy.

The point here is not to limit you and your partner via genome research but to add this information to the personality profiling in the Appendix so that you can develop an increasingly fuller and more mature picture of exactly who you are (as exact as that can be!) and who your partner is. The more exact you can be, the more mature everyone's expectations can be. Knowing that you and your partner will not change, you can work out a way to meet in the middle. When she or he gets angry, your partner can apologize relatively quickly; you will feel your feelings, but also remember who you are. You will, thus, call a friend with whom you can process your partner's angry words and your feelings, but you will not passive-aggressively blame or try to change your partner. Nor will your partner think there is something weak about you and try to change you. At calm moments—over the dinner table, for instance, or while sitting on the beach—your different genetics may come up in conversation and you might even smile at how "different we are."

As you explore "who you each are," you can look back at your family lines to see who else in your families were "just like you" or "just like me." This is a powerful way of separating yourself and your potentially negative reactions from your mate's psychological and emotional life—it is a way of taking judgment, criticism, enmeshment, and power struggle out of your relationship. Your interactions might sound like these words from my clients:

- Okay, I get it, this is who I am. I am a ruminator. I probably have two short alleles. I have a very active cingulate gyrus (concentration/attention center in the brain), so I get anxious, run thoughts through my head, can't let them go. So, knowing this, I need to realize that many things about Ismet that I dwell on and create power struggle over are not real; they are part of the way my brain works in the world; they are not my partner; I have to separate them from her. My mom was like me. I wish she had done that.

- This is who I am. I get angry and aggressive pretty quickly. I probably have two short alleles or one long and one short. Probably when my amygdala (aggression/stress center in the brain) gets swelled up from stress, my blood floods with stress hormones and I lash out. I need to separate my partner from this. This is me, not my partner's responsibility. I have to count to ten before I react. I also have to walk away for a few minutes to gather myself so I don't react and hurt him. My dad was like me. I wish he had done that.

As you take time to look at yourselves this way, fill out the personality profiles in the Appendix not just for yourself but also for your partner; ask him or her to do the same. Then go further: take the personality and other available tests (as it is possible to do so) as if you are one or both of your parents. Ask yourself in a kind of mock test: "What were the core personalities of my/our parents?" Because you and your mate will have pieces of each of their genetics regarding personality style, the more you know, the better. With your own and your partner's personality typologies in mind, trace your and his or her genetic personality predilections. Ask, "How does my personality complement his or hers, and vice versa?" If you discover—as most of us do—that there are also ways in which you are noncomplementary, spend much-needed time exploring this. Two alpha personalities, for instance, in the same house, can be problematic in love if boundaries are not set and separate domains are not established.

As much as possible, give yourselves a month or more to delve into your personalities, temperaments, communication styles, and natural ways of being. As you go through this process, remember that you are learning who you are; this is your identity, your "separate self." Once you know this self, you will have a deeper understanding of the core personality you each bring to the table—it is a large part of what you are fighting over.

Sacrifice 5: Utilizing New Rules for Love

Another sacrifice we must make involves accepting new rules for love. We have to throw out some of our old, unconscious rules and make new ones. I ask my clients to "Please write your new rules down." Here are the new rules Gail and I developed in our fifteenth year of marriage. I hope these will stimulate your own dialogue and creativity.

1. I will remember to let women and men love one another differently. More men love more instrumentally and more women more emotionally, and both forms of love are equally important forms of love.

2. I will remember that none of us gets everything we want from love. Love is an embrace of two different souls, not a shopping mall. Emotional fulfillment ebbs and flows over the decades—it is not always present, so I shouldn't expect it to be.

3. I will remember that love is both unconditional and transactional, not one or the other. When we are not feeling unconditionally loved, let's look for ways in which we are, nonetheless, getting something important out of the economic and other transactions in our marriage.

4. I will work to make a marriage of dependency in which we each also enjoy some safe independence. Interdependence can't come from power struggle, so I will work to move beyond that stage of love whenever it appears.

5. I will remember that we can provide for, protect, and nurture one another, but we cannot live the other's journey or be inside one another's heads. I will watch for, and when needed, study our enmeshment/abandonment cycles every day.

6. I will remember to compliment my partner every day or otherwise as much as possible when we are together or apart. If I know you are going through a particularly fragile

time, I will adjust my expectations and compliment what I can, even if I am dissatisfied with certain aspects of what you are doing. This is a form of devotion.

7. I will remember to give you credit in public for who you are and what you do. Love can't be sustained if we are not constantly valuing the other person, in both words and deeds, among friends and family. In this way, love is a communal effort, and marriage can be supported by the community.

8. I will remember that love is about many things that go beyond emotions. I will grow to the point in life where I can measure love by all its elements, not just by my feelings.

As you apply your own rules for your love, you will most likely find that the standard of a good marriage will gradually shift in your partnership. The standard will no longer be your own or your partner's feelings per se but, rather, the actual success with which you are practicing a *balance of intimacy and separateness* in your bond. The insights, tools, and strategies you institute to protect that balance will become new habits, and the cumulative success of those habits will best protect your long-lasting bond. Your feelings will ebb and flow, but your relationship will remain strong.

Two New Tools for Ending Power Struggle

Perhaps without being conscious of it, you have committed to making sacrifices for the sake of love, making new rules, and taking steps forward. Thus far in this book, the steps and sacrifices are set up to help you emotionally disentangle and thus move beyond power struggle in your relationship. To do this, you have to confront the sources of your deepest fears. So, in looking closely at intimate separateness, you will need to assess the ways in which you *create and feel fear* in your relationship. Tracing your feelings back to the internal experience of fear is a simple, ongoing way of finding peace in love. Here are two practical tools you can use to help with this right now.

The Trace-Back Tool

The trace-back tool can be used in many areas of conflict to root out fear. It is a tool that helps you rewrite your relationship toward Stage 4 and beyond. If you are already in a later stage of marriage and power struggles show up situationally (as you'll see below), this tool can keep you from reverting permanently back into Stage 3. To give an example of how it works, let me reveal a dynamic between myself and Gail. The relationship about which I am perhaps the best love-scientist is my own, so I can see certain details in it, in myself, and in my and Gail's core personalities that creep up on me and potentially cause reversion in my psyche to power struggle, even to this day.

Over the decades, one of the ways in which I was enmeshed with Gail appeared when we had friends over for dinner. I picked a fight with Gail, before the friends came over and while Gail was preparing food. The fight involved—at least on the surface—the fact that Gail likes to spend more money on food than I do. I am by nature more parsimonious (cheap?) than she is. This especially creates issues when we prepare dinner for friends because preparing dinner for friends is Gail's domain (we have agreed on this for two decades). My enmeshed and projection-laden dialogue went like this:

Mike: Why do we need three hors d'oeuvres? We're having eight people over? This is too much! This just wastes money.

Gail: Back off, Mike. This is my domain.

Mike: But Gail, this is insane! We'll waste all this food and money!

We go back and forth like this a bit, then Gail cooks and I set the table, and we take a break until I continue with some critical, irritated points that spoil her enjoyment of the preparation and her self-valuation as a friend and hostess. Sometimes I have continued my argument and power struggle even after our friends arrive. I'd say, "Check it out, folks, we've got a buffet for you; Gail went a little nuts with the food." Gail either ignores me or tells me to shut up. Some friends laugh and some feel uncomfortable.

I have had to apologize to Gail for this many times over the years, and I have never felt at peace with my compulsion to create this fight. The whole thing is rude and disrespectful, or as my daughters have said, "nasty." They were right. Finally, I stopped doing this by using the trace-back tool. In employing this tool, I realized I was attacking Gail out of fear and I decided to trace the fear back to my past. Sitting by a river one day, I sorted through the recurring situation and was able to trace back my behavior to how my mother hit me when I was a boy whenever I wasted food; that trauma created anxiety in me that I still felt, and that anxiety got triggered when food was being prepared, thus I "hit" Gail verbally when I felt the anxiety.

I realized that accusing Gail of being "crazy, insane" showed that I must be suffering from enmeshment with ghosts/projections from the past. Because of my own family history (my parents both struggled with mental illness during my boyhood), I am prone to be hyper-vigilant about what is "crazy," or "insane." The upside of this is that I have devoted my life to helping people with their mental health; the downside is that I was hurting my wife. Because of Gail's family history (her mother's depression), "insane" and "crazy" are words that trigger a deep array of feelings in her—feelings I should know better than to trigger. But my dagger was out because of enmeshment with my shadows and projections of my own family past.

You can use this trace-back tool in any recurring situation that causes marital tension. You know yourself and your partner. You are the most qualified love-scientists to trace back toward a potential source of your enmeshment, daggering, and encroachment on your lover's domain. If you need help in seeing the steps back, let a counselor help you. Start with an easy opener: a domain you have agreed with your partner is his or hers. Study that domain and look for why you are causing problems there, then use the trace-back tool to probe your rationale for causing those problems.

As you use the trace-back tool, be ready to feel humbled. Here is my journal's entry language of trace-back from May of 2009. I still find it humbling to this day.

Trace-Back Clue 1: My comments about "crazy" and "insane" are very telling. Hearing them shows me I have to keep going deeper and farther back. Chaos, insane family, depression, abuse . . . all of these are creeping through in "insane" and "crazy."

Trace-Back Clue 2: Gail becomes nervous when we have people over because she is introverted; so, even though she adores our friends, her brain goes into stress mode from the stimulation of all these people coming to her home. One of the best ways she has found to calm the stress and enjoy her domain and our friends is to buy and serve more food than is needed, but this triggers me to get entangled, lose my separate self, and enmesh with Gail's domain. Why?

Well, first, in my family of origin, we had very little money and I was hurt in relation to it—two sources of trauma there, the desperation for food/money and my mother's physical abuse of me in that context. Thus, to me, food is not to be wasted, and I go into an internal stress situation (unconscious/limbic) when too much food is served. While stressed in this way, I lash out at Gail. I am a dominant personality anyway, and this all coalesces to the detriment of my relationship with Gail.

Second, I feel inadequate in comparison to Gail when it comes to family and friendships. While I have a number of good friends and a pretty happy family, my self-image is that Gail is empathic, well loved, the person our friends come to see, while I am not. This has been my lingering self-image since there was a great deal of abuse in my own family of origin. Putting together these elements, I can trace back my criticism of Gail to enmeshment, trauma, and self-image issues. I enmesh with Gail as if Gail can heal me, and this is always an illusion of love. I need to make changes immediately.

This trace-back can become (and it has, for Gail and myself) a conscious tool for disentanglement between you and your partner. While I had always apologized to Gail over the years for creating the tension, nonetheless an apology was not enough; I had to stop the practice. Gail and I were married twenty years before I finally removed this marital tension from our relationship—it took me until I was nearly fifty years old to fully understand the power struggle in the "friends are coming over" dynamic. That means Gail and I were well into the seventh stage of relationship by then, but I brought residuals of power struggle to the relationship.

Now, I have stopped the bad behavior by making sure to be conscious of the trace-back when we are having friends over. I remind myself that Gail is not my mother who knocked it into our heads that not a single carrot should ever be thrown away. I also tell myself that Gail is the independent owner of the domain of cooking, so it is not any of my business anyway what she cooks, or doesn't cook, provides or doesn't provide, by way of food and drink. (This issue of "domain" and "separateness-regarding-domain" will be much more fully explored in the next chapter.) Overall, I try to stay out of the way; and I have recently practiced humility around this by making fun of myself with our friends, confessing to how enmeshed and silly I've been.

This situation is an example of a "little sin" in a relationship that can destroy a marriage if it accumulates with other little sins to become a constant power struggle. You most likely commit these little sins in your relationship—no one is immune to them. Being in love for decades is a process, not a static "sinlessness." The cure for the little sins will almost always require a trace-back to figure out their root causes, going back to your core personality traits and primary relationships, usually with your parents and during your childhood. Those set you up for the situation that triggers you to enmesh the self with your partner, then break free via criticizing, passive-aggressive behavior, direct conflict, nagging, victim/rescue dynamics, or another method.

The Tracking-Disillusionments Tool

Underneath a lot of power struggle is disillusionment: we have become disillusioned with who our partner is and who we are, so we battle over power. Very few people engage in ongoing Stage 3 Power Struggle who feel adequate and happy about either themselves or their partner.

An Exercise: List Your and Your Partner's Inadequacies

In your journal, make a list of the ways in which this other person has disappointed you.

You can begin with the sentence stem, "_____ disappoints me when she or he does _____."

You can also write, "I get so mad when _____ does (or says) _____."

As you work with your own memory to see areas of disappointment, write, "When we were in _____ (or doing _____), she or he did _____ and/or said _____."

List everything you can remember over a period of days. Once you have a list of disappointments to work with, start categorizing them. You may notice that the disappointments and disillusionments fit into at least one of these four categories. Attach these numbers to the items on your list:

1. Your partner has disappointed you by accusing you of being deeply flawed for *who you are*. Your very person and self were not respected, as she or he said something similar to what I did to Gail: "You are crazy." The words used or actions performed will overtly or covertly be saying, *You are somewhat worthless, flawed, not well, weak, a failure . . . thus, you are not worth loving; you are worth abandoning.*

2. Your partner will have devalued or rejected you for certain things *you did (or did not do)* that you believe have an upside, a goodness to them, a deep worth that your partner is missing. Perhaps she said, "You're lazy. You don't help out." Or he said, "You do things for everyone else, not me." In hearing this, you think, "She is focusing on my flaws only—what about all my good stuff?" Or, "He does not know me, after all these years. I do these hundreds of things for him, but he doesn't praise them."

3. Your core personalities have clashed, and you feel either that you have too much power (she or he disappointed you by not standing up to you or "doing his or her part") and/ or his or her personality dominates yours. Either too strong or too weak, your partner disappoints you by not adjusting and adapting better to *what you need.* Thus, you often feel that you are not being cared for, protected, nurtured, or treated in a way that feeds your needs. Both Andy and Toni felt this.

4. Your partner disappoints you by being *just like you* without your realizing it. You loathe yourself, feel yourself to be inadequate and disappointing (low self-esteem), and unconsciously want your partner to be different from you— better than you—but she or he just acts as you act, and those actions feel (unconsciously) too familiar; they trigger your own disillusionments and fears of failure in yourself, as they did with Andy and Toni.

Once you have this list and have attached a 1, 2, 3, or 4 to each bullet in the list, make a new list. List the ways in which you are *disappointed with yourself.* This list may be difficult to write, so take time and get help from counselors or close friends. If you need some extra internal help making this list, enter the perspective of your partner—

that is, *be* your partner. Look through your partner's eyes at yourself from his or her eyes; study yourself for what you say and do in your relationship that you know is disappointing, hurtful, unnecessary, weak, immoral, and that is destructive of yourself and your relationship.

After you have this full list, apply the 1, 2, 3, or 4 to the list items. A brief example of this list might look like this:

- I'm disappointed in myself when I get angry at the kids and Tarza. When I get angry, I lash out and make them feel like they are terrible people. **1**

- It's my own fear that I'm a bad lover that makes me keep asking A.J. if the sex was any good. I wish A.J. gave me more direction or just generally talked to me more about what he wants. I feel like I screw it up. **2**

- I give in to Naina on some things, and I fight back on other things, but I'm not confident that I make the right choices in either case. Like, yesterday, she said, _____ and I fought back but then I realized she was right. A week ago, she said _____ and I didn't fight back and I should have. **3**

- No matter what I do, it's not enough, and no matter what Sam does, it's not enough. We both hate each other. He just wants a few minutes a day of contact and intimacy, and I withhold it, punishing him for his weaknesses. He does the same with me. **4**

Mirror Images, Redux

Complete this exercise as many times as you can (hopefully your partner will, too) until you notice that you and your partner are both feeling inadequate and disillusioned for many of the same things. You are each giving voice not only to your own fears of inadequacy and disillusionments but also to your partner's feelings of inadequacy and disillusionment. You are mirror images in this department, to at least some great extent.

For couples in power struggle, feeling that commonality as deeply as possible can lead to positive conversation and change, especially if they do this work with a therapist. In fact, to move beyond power struggle, you have to feel the commonality of disillusionment consciously and for a long time (weeks, months, maybe a year or more) as you struggle to disengage and disentangle.

From Power Struggle to Intimate Separateness

As you trace back each of your conflict situations and gain perspective on inadequacies, desperations, traumas, and deep fears, you must also choose to alter your daily practice with your partner. Even if your partner does only a few of the following right now with you, if you do them yourself, you will be doing your part to grow, evolve, and move beyond dependence on power struggle as your default mode of pair-bonding.

Here are ten daily practices to institute right now and forever forward—as much as you can.

1. From now on, before criticizing my partner, I will see if I in fact do the same thing (even if with a slightly different subject or area). If so, I will try not to harp on this thing anymore. (Perhaps you press your partner to eat differently, lose weight, take better care of him or herself, even though you are not eating well either, and not taking care of yourself well enough).

2. For one week, I will try only criticizing and judging "dangerous" actions—that is, my partner needs to be doing something clearly dangerous to me, my kids, or him- or herself for me to get angry about it. After that week, I will

see how this feels and if any positive changes have occurred
in my marriage.

3. I will avoid criticizing my partner in public at all costs. If
I do lash out at him or her in public, I will avoid shaming
(these are attacks on the self, such as "you are crazy," "you
are worthless"). I will also apologize in private, later (if
the public gathering is finished) and then, if my partner
wishes, apologize to any friends or people who were
witnesses, via phone calls, email, or an apology at the next
gathering.

4. Unless my partner was 100 percent in the wrong, I will
apologize immediately or within 24 hours for my part
in verbal and relational mistakes I made, no matter what
part my partner played in causing them. (Hopefully, your
partner will do the same for you.)

5. I will stop blaming my partner for fears I bring to the
partnership from previous marriages or relationships. Thus,
I will work to keep my partner separate from projections of
my previous pair-bonds with family and other partners.

6. I will stand up for myself when I am verbally attacked. I will
tell my partner to stop attacking me; after we cool off, I will
look for an opportunity within twenty-four hours to discuss
how hurt I felt. If the attacks are physical and dangerous,
I will seek social services, police intervention, or legal
separation.

7. When approaching my partner for conversation, I will start
with my own concrete feelings and with concrete situations
or exact words—*not general complaints, but clear descriptions.*
"I felt terrible last night when you told our friends that I'm
always making mistakes. I felt like I'm stupid. Here's exactly

what you said that triggered that feeling: _____
_____."

8. I will look for ways in which my partner's and my personalities—which I understand to be relatively set for life—can become more compatible. If I tend to be more spontaneous and she or he tends to be more naturally micromanaging, I will accept that and study how to maximize it, work around it, accept its assets, and vocalize, appropriately, its liabilities rather than struggle to change something unchangeable.

9. I will make a list of my pressure and stress points, as well as my partner's, and study and update that list over the years of our relationship. Many of my angers, fears, pain, shames, trauma residues, and relational errors come from external stresses that trigger my (and my partner's) non-relational pressure points. I will quickly forgive those.

10. I will seek mentoring and assistance immediately for any addiction, personality disorder, stressful situation, physical or mental cause of significant pain, or other non-relational (separate) action or process I have or am involved in that creates the need for power struggle in my relationship.

YOUR WISDOM

Healthy communication is critical. It is important to communicate authentically with the goal in mind to benefit the relationship.

Come from a perspective of trust that your partner is not intending to hurt you with their actions or words.

Be willing to be wrong. Be willing to listen and see things from his or her point of view.

The other important aspect for me is to be committed to lots of things in addition to my husband. All my romantic eggs are in his basket, but not all my emotional ones. I have emotional relationships with friends, other family, kids, parents, and God.

In difficult times, I remember I made a promise to God to love my husband and be with him. Or if a person isn't religious, still, the promise is important: you can think of it as making a promise to the relationship, and that promise means not putting so much into the relationship that it sinks into a sinkhole.

I also recommend date nights, especially for couples with children, which can literally be marriage savers. They certainly were for us. Even just a lunch or meeting or a coffee is a great way to reconnect.

Treat the person the way you want to be treated. If you want more romance, be more romantic. Don't rely on the other person. You can go through weird years where he is not romantic anymore and you have to make the romance. That's okay. Take the long view. Make it happen.

Always remember, life is precious, and everyone is doing their best under lots of stress. Spend more time seeing the good and enjoying life than finding fault.

When arguing, beware: it is too easy to slip into insults. Avoid insults and sarcasm.

It is important to tame that anger and that need to "win" and focus on the relationship and what it needs.

My husband taught me how to communicate openly and calmly and to understand each other's perspectives. I used to want to win each battle and be right. I learned there is compromise, there is understanding, and out of that is a deeper love and trust.

We avoid low blows and mean comments. We avoid speaking poorly about each other's family.

We, well mostly I, avoid bringing up the past. I used to spend way too much time rehashing past wrongdoings. That was not fair to my husband or our relationship. Once you've moved to a new stage of life together don't spend lots of time rehashing everyone's inten-

> tions and craziness in the past stage. Move on. Life moves on and
> so should we.
>
> —Marny, 64, first marriage, sixteen years;
> second marriage, twenty-three years

Love as Personal Devotion

One of my greatest professional pleasures has been officiating at weddings. The first couple I married was twenty-five and twenty-six years old, the next was twenty-four and twenty-five, and the latest was seventy-seven and seventy-eight.

Ethel, seventy-seven, and Floyd, seventy-eight, were two of the nicest people around—gentle, caring, delightful. Both had been married before—Ethel for forty-five years and Floyd for forty-three years—and both had helped their spouses through disease and, ultimately, through the process of death. They had not seen each other for decades while married to their spouses, but one day, a few years after each of their spouses had died, they met again and reminisced about high school (they had gone to the prom together sixty years before!). Gradually, now, they reunited as two elders, and after a few years of reconnecting, they decided to marry.

Ethel, a personal friend, had attended other weddings I had officiated. She and Floyd honored me by asking me to marry them, too. Each in separate ways during the marriage preparation process said, "I loved my husband (wife) more than life itself, and now I will love Floyd (Ethel) more than life itself—but this time, we don't have to go through those immense struggles like before. We know how to accept each other." Ethel said, "We are not trying to get back to some old garden where we expect perfection from a spouse—we just want to be happy together."

Ethel and Floyd are both Jewish, and the garden and perfection reference resonated well with the Garden of Eden. Both Ethel and

Floyd had already, figuratively, eaten the apple long ago in their first marriages—and gone through the struggles over power that marriage is and can be. At seventy-seven and seventy-eight years old, they no longer hoped to be Adam and Eve—they knew who they were, and they were much farther down the road of life than that.

In the context of pair-bonding and love, Adam and Eve realized, in eating the apple, that love was not perfect; they sacrificed perfection to do the generative work of loving one another in the real world. And from the generative work of Adam and Eve came, at least in metaphor, all the future generations. For Ethel and Floyd, those were their children, grandchildren, and great-grandchildren, as well as their vision of a peaceful, elder marriage.

So, too, it can be for all of us—we start out in a romantic garden, become disillusioned when we really see the other person's naked psyche (and our own, as well), and battle by becoming too close and too far away in response. But the journey can continue beyond this, if we walk carefully together, and one day we can become rooted in real love, not in ideals of perfection.

The psychologist John Welwood has put it this way: "While the 'high' of falling in love provides a taste of heavenly expansion, the earthly demands of two different individuals working out a day-to-day life together are what ground love and help it take root. . . . When love comes down to earth—bringing to light those dark corners we would prefer to ignore, and thus encompassing all the different parts of who we are—it gains depth and power."

Ethel, Floyd, and I worked together on developing language for their wedding ceremony that fit their sense of this new relationship. Here are my ministerial words of devotion from their wedding ceremony:

> Dearest Ethel and Floyd, your family and friends join you today
> in this tender hour you'll remember from a dream,
> when you stood together in this garden, near this fountain,
> and the whole history of human love stopped here as well,
> to stand with you in joy.

Two good people who first met more than sixty years ago—
        with more than one hundred and fifty years between you—
                you know already the courage of a journey.
You know the unique dance of marrying your best friend:
        as one of you moves to master the art of loving,
                the other must master the art of being loved.
Today, you celebrate this dance with ancient wisdom and new possibility.
        By placing rings on the other's finger,
                and in the ritual of wine and wineglass,
you'll show your willingness to trust another person with your deepest fears;
        and even more: to trust yourself with another heart's secrets.
The vows of life you share here, now, are your way of saying everywhere:
        "We want the words 'I love you' to be, again, holy."

                                    •

And these words will be holy, for you will make them so.
        From this day forward
may you commit your most loving patience to your best friend.
        Forgive in advance all anxieties, stresses, disagreements, messes.
Promise to repair, even with knots, the threads of love you will inevitably tear.
        Promise to help one another through all seasons of adventure,
                even autumn and late winter.
Promise to walk hand in hand, wherever you travel in the world,
        so that you will both be protected, woman and man.
Promise to remain so devoted to your best friend that, whether sick or well,
        you will live for just one more chance to rescue from the wind
                even your lover's most discolored leaves.

                                    •

And as the years pass, find opportunities to sit peacefully together,
        near a fountain, or at a lake, or around your family dinner table . . .
admire your children, grandchildren, great-grandchildren;
        look, just then, into one another's eyes and smile,
                for you will know the truth of human love:
                not mainly from ourselves, but from our family's radiance
                        we are fully seen.

As I've interacted with Ethel and Floyd over the years, I've seen two people who say "I love you" to each other generously. I think of them when I talk with clients who say, "If I'm mad at my spouse or disappointed in him, should I still say 'I love you'?" Another client put the question this way: "Look, I don't like her a lot of the time, so I don't say 'I love you.' I want to be authentic, not false, so I don't say it." Another client had this to say: "I don't know why she needs me to say 'I love you' all the time. I'm not a words guy, I'm a doer. I *show* my love."

To these clients I say what I think Ethel and Floyd would say: "Your days are numbered—be humble and devoted every moment you can, no matter your 'feelings' at that moment." "I love you" is a holy phrase of devotion, it is a prayer. It is worth uttering, even when we are not sure the prayers will bring peace—still, we speak our holy words. If our marriage is over, it's over, and we won't say "I love you," but if there is still hope for us, we can respect our initial choice of this person by being devoted enough to say "I love you" and sacrificing even our own ego with excuses about "authenticity" or temporary feelings of not liking someone.

Real life comes at us as a huge wind. We need the power of love to push it aside.

Chapter 6

Practicing Intimate Separateness for Life

TO BE HAPPY IN MARRIAGE, WE EACH NEED OUR OWN DOMAINS

S evda and Tarik, a Turkish couple in their late thirties, were friends of Gail's and mine during the two years we taught and conducted research in Turkey. At parties or social gatherings, Sevda, a university professor, insisted that Tarik, a physician, was an "interruptor." She also insisted that she was expressly *not* an interruptor. And she confessed that Tarik's tendency to interrupt created significant marital difficulties. She was right—it did, and Tarik was oblivious to the damage.

As we've seen in this book, and as you've probably seen in your friendships, this obliviousness often happens with men. Male heart rates do not rise as high as women's during a marital conflict or stressful situation, and males don't notice as much (in general, with exceptions). Scientists Janice Kiecolt-Glaser and Ron Glaser have found that not only women's heart rates but their stress hormones epinephrine and norepinephrine rise during stressful situations in marriage, and again, men's much less so. Men's hearts, literally, may remain "oblivious" to possible damage in their actions, and so too do their bloodstreams and brains.

Tarik and Sevda were both alpha personalities, both leaders in their separate workplaces, and both enjoyed talking. They were examples of what my mother used to call "people who love to hear the sound of their own voices." Luckily, they were both fascinating people, so their friends enjoyed their conversations, insights, and banter; but in their marriage, their commonality was obviously creating friction. Tarik wanted to talk when Sevda did, so he obliviously interrupted her. This was often uncomfortable for the rest of us because we could see Sevda's frustration. We could almost see her heart rate and stress hormones rise. Simultaneously, there was even more complexity: Sevda was also an interruptor, but because she did not do it in public, she was unaware of the behavior and its effect on Tarik.

I overheard this conversation:

Tarik: I was reading an article about asymmetry in both mammary glands and testicles that posited why one mammary gland and testi—

Sevda: One's bigger than the other, so of course they'd be asymmetrical.

Tarik: Yes, I know, but the size doesn't create the genetic—

Sevda: Hand me that picture—

Tarik: What the biologists were positing was that the asymmetry delivers a message—

Sevda: Do we really have time for this now? We've got to get the pictures hung.

I had arrived early to Sevda and Tarik's apartment and had used the restroom. Coming out of the restroom, I could hear a conversation that a therapist would never otherwise hear because it wouldn't take place in a therapy office or laboratory; it was one of those hidden conversations in a relationship that reveals the *mirror images* we live as couples. This is what we discussed in the previous chapter, in which the very thing that drives one partner nuts about the other is probably something she or he is actually doing as well. The very thing that drove Sevda crazy about Tarik in public also drove Tarik crazy about Sevda in private. For any number of reasons—some of them cultural, involving gender roles in Turkey perhaps, Sevda did not interrupt Tarik in public; but in private she devalued him the same way he devalued her.

When I've brought this example up in workshops and with colleagues, some interesting dialogues occur. One of them regards analysis from a feminist colleague: "Because Tarik interrupts and devalues Sevda in public, Sevda returns the favor to Tarik, but because of gender roles in Turkey, she does it only in private. She is able to equalize power in the relationship only in private." This puts the behavior in a power context, and that is certainly one aspect of the behavior.

At the same time, marriage works not only because we struggle to equalize power but also because we practice intimate separateness in our emotional and psychological life on a daily basis. To do that, Tarik and Sevda needed to take a deeper look into their *mirroring behavior*. They needed to understand that in the romance and early attachment phases of love, we human beings to some extent "marry ourselves" (i.e., in many ways, we marry our mirror image) and later we must learn to *separate ourselves from ourselves*. That is another mind-bender, but it is crucial. If we can learn to do this, we will be more forgiving of (and take less personally) the grating habits of our partner.

We will realize that those grating habits are also our own!

An Exercise: List Your Bad Marital Habits

Take a moment to list your "bad marital habits." You will have no doubt noticed what many of them are by now. Your partner will no doubt have complained about them. Own them for a moment in your journal. For instance, do you:

1. Interrupt your partner in public or private? Perhaps you interrupt your partner in *both* settings. If so, give some examples of both. If just one setting, give some examples of dialogue of interruption in one setting. Some interruption is normal between best friends, but do you do it too much? Own this if you do.

2. Avoid doing things you know make your partner happy? Perhaps you know that your partner would be very happy if

you cleaned the house, but you avoid doing it. Perhaps you don't just avoid doing it *some* of the time (some of the time would be a compromise), but instead, you avoid doing it *all* the time. Or you do it only when your partner forces you—perhaps through bribery, begging, or anger.

3. Avoid doing things sexually that either you really want to do and/or that you know your partner needs and wants to do? Give examples of sexual experiments you or your partner want to try—write down why you avoid them. Be specific. If you remember conversations you and your partner have had about these things, write down at least one of those conversations.

4. Criticize your partner in public and/or a great deal in private? Some amount of critique, judgment, moralizing, and correcting of a partner's behavior is normal in any long partnership. You care about your partner and figure you know what's best for him or her. But do you criticize, judge, become reactive, or correct your partner on more than just a few things? If so, list those things.

5. Let your partner criticize, judge, moralize about, and correct you more than is safe for the development, growth, or stability of your own separated identity and self? It's normal for all of us to defer to our partner's critiques sometimes—if we didn't, we'd lack an essential humility in our relationship. But if you are getting critiqued every day, and if you constantly assume your partner is right and you are much more flawed than him or her and deserve constant criticism, your self-confidence is probably being significantly debilitated. List the critiques you "take" from your partner.

Whatever number of "bad habits" you come up with, study them, think about them, and sit with your answers for a while. Then, list five bad marital habits your partner possesses. If your partner is reading this book with you, she or he will hopefully by now have listed five personal bad marital habits as well. If she or he is not following this book with you, do this exercise as if you were him or her.

Assuming for a moment that you've both done this, compare notes, talk, then use your lists and anecdotes as grist for relational improvement. As needed, talk with a counselor alone or together about what will now be two or more lists between you.

If, as you talk about these things with your partner, one or both of you become either blaming or defensive, try setting a timer so that neither of you goes on and on (which can make the partner defensive or bored or blaming). I suggest three minutes for each description or example of each bad habit. If either of you takes more than the allotted time, start the particular point over. If one of you tells the story by blaming, start it over. If one of you becomes defensive, start it over.

As you talk about these bad habits in a timed or other safe way, and as you gradually (or immediately) do it without blaming one another or becoming significantly defensive, *you will be practicing intimate separateness.* Before you realize it, a few weeks of conversation will go by, and you will feel that something different is happening in your conversations together. This can be a liberating, empowering, and maturing feeling.

As needed, do this exercise with a therapist mediating.

One thing that will help immensely is if you can see the mirror image: see how your partner's bad habit is, in some way, also your own. Talk about which habits mirror one another. Joke about them, as you feel comfortable. For instance, if your partner refuses to ever clean the house, you can generally think of something equivalent that you are refusing to do. Talk about this, see the mirroring, take ownership of the mirror image. For example:

"I am not into doing housework as carefully as you are, but you rebel against my sexual experiments in the same way, you know."

"You interrupt me in public, that's true, but at the same time, I interrupt you in private."

If you run into any trouble seeing the mirrored habits, it can be important to get help from a counselor.

Personality Patience, Intimate Separateness, and Attachment Security

Intimate separateness must be practiced in the same way that one practices any art or craft. A pianist practices the piano. A computer programmer practices coding. A hairstylist practices hairstyles. Practicing one's art or craft is so common that a person might joke, "I've become addicted to rock climbing." Or, "I hate the cello sometimes but I've just got to practice—it's a part of me, it's in me, it's who I am." Or, "I don't feel like I really know myself unless I'm dancing." Practicing takes time, but it pays off.

Intimate separateness needs to be practiced, too, if you are to build a marriage that will last. Dakota Hoyt, the executive director of the Gurian Institute, said to me recently, "Jack (her husband) and I practice intimate separateness as much as possible. We didn't realize what we were doing until you named it for us, but it's exactly what we've learned to practice. We had to learn it over the years because, frankly, we drive each other a bit crazy. Some of our habits are similar, but some are different, like we go to bed at different times.

"One thing that really works for us is to take some time off from one another. Every week I do my own things and let him do his own things. It took us a while to learn this rhythm, but now it feels great. And it makes important discussions much easier. We're not always trying to be 'together' and 'connected' and 'deep' every moment of every day. We save things up, and when we focus, we really focus; we shut everything else out to be intimate. And when we're separate, doing our own thing, we aren't thinking too much about becoming intimate again, but I really think the intimacy is always there in the separateness. It's like we are unconsciously building up desire for one another's thoughts, feelings, even bodies because we practice the separateness."

Dakota was married to her first husband for eighteen years, then divorced for six years. She has been married to Jack, her second husband, for twenty-seven years. At sixty-nine, she is in a different stage from her daughter or granddaughter, and she knows it. But she said, "I tell my kids and grandkids about the importance of separateness and the habits Jack and I have developed because I want them as young people to have an easier time of relationship than I did. I want them to see that it is not just intimacy but also separateness that proves your marriage is secure."

Dakota continued, "The intimacy is wonderful, don't get me wrong, but it's not the only thing that proves you really trust one another. The trust is also proven from being separate enough from one another that when you come back together and look over the dinner table and see the other person for who she or he is, you can finally say, 'Wow, that's who I love. Not bad. We give each other space, we care about each other, we have passion, and we're also our own people.' To me, sitting across the dinner table and feeling that comfort and joy really proves to me that our marriage is here to stay."

An Exercise: Feel How It Feels to Be Separate

Think about the last five times you were separated from your partner for more than a workday (i.e., for at least a few days). List each time in your journal. Ask and answer these questions:

How did I feel? Did I feel like my attachment with my partner was secure, or did I worry during any of the five times that my partner was too far away?

Did I feel anxiety or worry or jealousy, even if just for a few minutes or an hour or two?

Did I feel lonely, not just alone?

Did my aloneness transfer into negative emotions about my partner? Distrust? Anger?

As you answer these questions and contemplate these feelings, think about how it feels generally for you to be separated from someone you care about. Among your girlfriends or guy friends, do you constantly worry that you've said the wrong thing, let them down, need to talk to them again to see if everything is okay between you?

When a friend of yours spends time with another friend and not with you (for whatever reason), do you worry or recriminate yourself, as if you caused something wrong in your friendship, or as if you are not worthy enough of being a true friend? Overall, do you ruminate a great deal or get angry (jealous) very quickly?

Process those feelings by writing in your journal, talking with your partner, and/or with a therapist. Sometimes your fears of rejection, abandonment, loneliness, and worry will be justified. For instance, if you have been betrayed by your lover (we will study marital infidelity in the next chapter), distrust, worry, fear, even self-blame are normal, as is rumination. If you have been abused or otherwise significantly hurt in a previous relationship, your fears and worries now may be a logical post-trauma reaction. If you can't hold on to friends or are constantly rejected by friends, this personality issue needs careful attention. If you have a diagnosed personality disorder, constant anxiety of this ruminating kind can be normal for you; if it is destructive, you will likely need therapeutic or medical assistance.

At the same time, if many episodes of prolonged separateness from your lover or friends bring up worry, anxiety, and some low-grade (or high-grade) form of abandonment fear (which correlates with rumination and/or anger), then it is probably essential you get help with this pattern right away. Your internal situation will probably stop you from developing and nurturing attachment security, gaining personality patience—both patience with yourself and your partner. It will probably stop you from trusting your relationship, your partner, and yourself enough to protect your love by practicing intimate separateness. Absent healing, treatment, or new skills in this area, you will probably either feel constantly devalued until you finally have to leave your relationship and/or you will try to control your partner constantly, making her or him leave you. The very abandonment and loneliness you most fear will come to pass, and for a while—even a few years— you may blame your partner(s) for fulfilling your prophecies of marital failure. But one day, you will start the desperate cycle again, and at some point, separateness will cause the same deep fear and loneliness in you. If you feel the fear and loneliness when you are separate from your lover and/or others, get help right now. Your ability to love and be loved may be at stake.

An Exercise: Look for Clues of Personality Impatience

Patience is a hallmark of intimate separateness. It is part of the daily devotion of love. No matter your personal issues (or lack of them), we all need to increase our patience with our partner's separate self. To improve your patience, try asking these five questions and studying your relationship through their eyes:

- Do you immediately feel like opening your mouth to talk when you hear your partner talking to you or another person near you?

- Do you feel the urge to change your partner's behaviors and perhaps, even, his or her core personality?

- When you watch your partner with your family or friends, do you feel judgmental?

- When your partner gets angry with you, do you generally (all or most of the time) decide she or he is wrong?

- When you get angry at your partner, do you sense you are often overreacting (often in anger) and/or ruminating too much and, thus, becoming unnecessarily anxious?

If most of your answers were yes, you may be enmeshed. If this is the case, and as you do the work provided in the previous chapters, add this tool of focus to help you develop what I call *personality patience* on a daily basis. Take time in your journal to answer these questions with lists:

What exact traits in my partner trigger me to become anxious or worried in private?

    a.
    b.
    c.
    d.

What exact traits in my partner trigger me to become anxious or worried in public (with others)?

    a.
    b.
    c.
    d.

What exact traits in my partner do I tend to overreact to in private (overreact would be measured by feelings in you that your partner did these things to hurt you in some way—making you anxious or angry—when she or he most likely did not)?

    a.
    b.
    c.
    d.

What exact traits in my partner make me irritable, angry, very frustrated?

    a.
    b.
    c.
    d.

These lists can go beyond "d" and should reveal to you a number of repeated items. The questions should help you focus on a few traits you get angry and anxious about and/or overreact to. Once you have that list of repeated items, you will have in front of you the exact traits and behaviors that you can focus on to become more patient with, forgiving of, letting them roll over you, and not reacting to. You can murmur mindfully and silently:

> When _____ starts talking, I will listen, not speak, at least until the end of his/her story.

> When _____ says _____, I will try saying something supportive like, "Okay, sure," rather than something judgmental.

> When _____ does _____, I will not react; and I will watch how not-reacting feels.

There is a great deal of trial and error in this daily practice, so don't worry about being imperfect. Over the weeks and months, as you keep working at having patience with your partner's personality, you will develop new habits and rhythms. This can be true even if you have a diagnosed personality disorder, or your partner does.

As you work on this patience, hopefully your partner is also doing these same things. If he or she is not, you can still increase your own patience by filling out the above questions as if you were your partner looking at yourself. That mirroring will bring insights and inspiration as you see, through your partner's eyes, that many of your overreactions to her or him need new, kinder practice.

While you are focused on this work, talk with your partner about behavioral changes you absolutely need him or her to make for successful love to be sustained. Every couple has to decide these lists for themselves, but many of these guidelines might fit your list. Gail and I as a couple try to practice these as much as possible:

- Make sure to remember my "big days" like birthdays, anniversary; show you love me by planning something really nice for us; give me flowers once in a while.

- Kiss me at least once a day, even just a quick peck on the lips would be great. I need that, even if you don't.

- Give me more space when I first come home from work. Don't talk to me right away about anything big. I just need space and time to get my bearings.

- When I ask, "Do you love me?" or say, "I love you," say "I love you" back to me and reassure me that you love me. I need to hear the words.

- Don't worry if I don't initiate sex as much anymore. I'm exhausted. But I love you, so if you initiate it, I will try to follow you into it.

Anything personal and private can go on this list, and you can do your best to satisfy it with devotion. Even when you are unsure what to do, choose the simple, beautiful things you can do (things only you know about because only you know your partner this well). Cooking a meal, taking out the garbage, loading the dishwasher, changing a diaper, trying a new sexual position, holding your partner's hand when she is sad, telling him his actions are needed, gazing together at your children's sleeping faces—everything can feel different, love-laden, meaningful in the small measures that add up to long-lasting love.

And always remember that intimate separateness, the most passionate and yet stable form of love, involves transactions. While you are asking your partner for more patience with your personality and self, and as you express your needs, make sure you let your partner know that you have in mind his or her list of needs and personality quirks, and you are becoming more patient and forgiving about as many items on the list as you can.

Practicing Domain Security
and Divisions of Labor

Some of the best proof you will ever have that you have moved beyond power struggle and are successfully practicing intimate separateness will come in your mutual comfort with *divided domains*. This will be a division of labor regarding the most primal drives in a relationship: food, shelter, clothing, child care, sexual life, emotional life, social life. The division of labor will feel both intimate and separate. By this I mean the division will not feel like a source of loneliness or of power struggle but, rather, as a way of giving one another the gift of love. As you work on these domains and divisions of labor (and if the practices continue), you should immediately see less marital tension in:

- housework issues
- parenting
- work/life balance
- conflict
- sexual intimacy
- money issues
- communication issues

Our ancestors, as we've established, practiced intimate separateness (and, sometimes, far more separateness than intimacy) by default in their long marriages. Up until recently, the gender roles between couples in a marriage were defined, thus labor was divided and many sources of tension were diminished considerably. This led to human survival, yet also to power imbalances between the genders, and we entered a feminist process of breaking down the old gender roles in order to empower women's independence and identity. This was a powerful evolutionary step in our civilization, and one that continues.

However, this deconstruction of gender roles has also disrupted a primal protector of marriage—agreed-upon divisions of labor. The old gender roles, without our realizing it, protected long-lasting marriages. The cost was high for many people, but the protection did occur nonetheless, as it occurs today in countries such as Saudi Arabia, where divorce rates are quite low. Although we in the West don't want to return to oppressive gender roles, it is crucial we understand the importance of division of labor portions of a healthy marriage. While we need not buy into any stereotyped gender roles—women stay home, men go to work—couples today need to remember that human nature is at work within us. You and your lover are profoundly different people with profoundly different talent sets, interests, ideas, abilities, competencies, and areas of courageous innovation. To not divide your married lives along the lines of those differing assets is to disrespect one another inherently. It is our nature as human beings to survive and thrive by respecting one another's assets and dividing our labors, working together in the ways that are compatible, not competitive.

YOUR INSIGHTS

I used to think most things that went wrong were my fault, especially when I was in my early twenties; then, after we got married, I thought most problems we had were her fault; then we got into therapy and I learned that everything was fifty-fifty; at least it should be; we should just start out thinking that everything was equal so that no one person takes on all the responsibility for change and improvement.

Now I realize that all these things are true at different times. Sometimes, it really is mostly my fault. Other times, it really is mostly her fault. Other times, it's about fifty-fifty.

One thing I know that was mainly my fault had to do with getting jealous of how satisfied and content she was with life. She had me, her work, her volunteering, our kids . . . she was stressed, sure, but content. But that happiness of hers made me jealous, angry, envious. I got mad at her, told her she was spending too much time with other people, not me. She said, "You work sixty hours a week and I never know when you'll be working so I've formed my own happy life—you can't get mad at me for not being home exactly when you get home. You have to become content with your life like I'm content with my life."

I didn't believe her until I got into therapy again and you (my counselor) said the exact same thing to me without knowing she had said it. When I argued with you, like "No way, this is fifty-fifty, so she has to change 50 percent," you said, "In this case, it seems like it is *you* who has to change—*you* have to find meaningful activities besides work that will make *you* content. You can't keep attacking her meaningful identity and self because she has one and you don't."

So I learned something. I never realized what feeling abandoned was about, or how I was like a kid clinging to her. Now, every time I think, "Hey, why should I change, why shouldn't she?" I think about identity. I try to think: What's *my* identity? If I have an identity, if I know who I am, if I have activities and people, including my wife, who make me happy and content, I don't need to keep telling her it is her job to make sure I'm okay. That's just bullshit.

—Manuel, 51

Essential Questions Survey 8: What Are Your Domains?

This survey asks you to become a love-scientist of your labor and domains. Look for ways in which your two personalities are similar in exercising these domains, but also different. Look for ways in which you have divided these domains in a healthy way, and ways in which you may not yet have divided up this labor and ought to do so as soon as possible.

- Who gets more satisfaction from focusing on planning, creating, and preparing most meals in our marriage?
- Who gets more satisfaction from caring for the inside of the house?
- Who gets more satisfaction from caring for the outside of the house and the yard?
- Which one of us pays more attention to what clothes each family member wears?
- Who is better at managing the money in our marriage? Or, if we're both good at it, how do we divide up that money management?
- How do we divide up child care?
  - Who offers more hands-on care?
  - Who provides more discipline?
  - Who provides more mentoring in risk-taking?
  - Who teaches more skills in direct empathy?
  - Who teaches more skills in how to use competition as a success tool?
- Who initiates more sexual encounters between us and comes up with more sexual experiments?
- Who guides emotional conversation more constantly between us?
- Who is more concerned with safety and health in our relationship?

These are primal questions that will take time to process and discuss. In many cases, the "who" will shift as the stages of your relationship shift. One of you will want to control certain domains when both of you are working, for instance; then, when and if children come, and if one of you goes to part-time work or becomes a stay-at-home parent, the domains might shift accordingly. At any point in a relationship, answers to the above questions can be "both of us equally all the time," yet as you dig deeper and have longer conversations about these domains—and especially if your marriage or partnership has lasted for four to seven years or more—you will most likely find that you both inherently need separate domains so that you can cut back on power struggle, respect each other for your strengths, and know that these separate domains enhance intimacy.

The Domain of Food

Who does most of the shopping for food in your family?

Does one of you do all of it?

Is one of you better at it?

Are you and your partner comfortable with how you've divided your labor in this primal domain? If not, get help to smooth this out right away. Like the other primal drives and domains, this is a receptacle for many other issues and power struggles in a marriage.

Similarly, who does most of the cooking in your family? Perhaps you both cook the same amount. This can happen, certainly; in most cases, however, one partner wants (even needs, at a primal level) to do more of the cooking, organization of the kitchen, etc. Have you divided this labor joyfully, or are you in power struggle about it?

Power struggle can show up even after one person has taken over this domain but the other keeps trying to give advice (as I did in the trace-back tool in Chapter 5). It can also show up when one tries to force the other to do more in a domain where he or she lacks interest or competency. For instance, a couple may be happiest getting takeout food, but as a part of a power struggle, one might criticize the other for not cooking more.

Food is primal—it carries a lot of our enmeshment/abandonment and merging patterns, replete with overreacting, ruminating, controlling, manipulating, becoming anxious, feeling rejected, feeling hurt, getting angry. If you see these things happening around food in your pair-bond, take that seriously: it may indicate deeper issues.

YOUR WISDOM

One of the most important things in our marriage of fifty-two years has been an attitude of gratitude between us for our jobs, our work, our ways of doing things, many of which are different, but can fit together cohesively and in a complementary not competitive way if we really look at them closely.

Early on when my marriage wasn't going so hot (we got married while still in college, we were quite young, and there was a lot of immaturity), I talked to a counselor about how things were going. She told me that one of the things that made her marriage good was that her husband always thanked her for the things she did, especially at mealtime. No matter how simple the meal, her husband always thanked her and told her how much he enjoyed the meal. I made that a regular practice in my marriage, and I believe that has helped.

Another piece of advice that I was given at the very beginning and that I made a habit of was to always kiss my wife before I left for work in the morning and tell her that I loved her and what I appreciated about her. There were many times that I didn't feel loving or appreciative (we might have had an argument or unpleasant disagreement the evening before), but usually I would force myself to tell her I loved her in a nice way before I left and sometimes I would thank her for something that needed my gratitude—I did this because I kept thinking "what if something were to happen to one of us today and we never saw each other again, what would be the last memory?" There were occasions when I was just too upset to give her a fond farewell or thanks for the day but that never lasted more than one day.

—Dan, 68

The Domain of Shelter/Habitat

Who is naturally more interested in the internal aspects of the home?

Which of you cares more about colors, drapes, furniture?

Which of you cares more about dust, neatness, clutter?

If you get into hassles with one another regarding housework, study those hassles closely. They are primal arguments concerning the "nest," which is your shelter that conveys safety and identity to you as individuals, as a couple, and as a family. Few things are more primal to our happiness than safety and identity.

Often, if one person in the pair-bond is more interested in the house as security (working out of the home to pay for it), she or he might not be as interested in the sensorial details of how the house looks. Conversely, the partner who is concerned with safety may also be the one who pays closer attention to where dust collects, how neat the place is, how the home "presents" to her or him and to others. If the person working hard to provide for the house is also being critiqued ("You don't do enough housework," "You don't load the dishwasher correctly," "You don't know how to dust"), the domain of shelter/habitat is probably causing stress in the relationship.

The partner who cares about housework the most will need to let go of power struggles about housework and accept that the other is not as interested in how nice the house looks. This is even the case when both partners are equal providers (breadwinners), but one sees the condition of the nest differently. As long as the more sensitive partner is empowered to do what he or she wants to do in regards to the housework—including more hands-on work and the control of hiring of housework helpers, if available and affordable, there should be no more power struggle.

The primal needs of shelter/habitat can also inhibit and derail the practice of intimate separateness when it comes to house remodeling. Many divorces follow house renovations because the construction or decorating questions that come up expose basic differences in beliefs and attitudes. Should you and your partner be considering such a process, determine in advance who will be making which decisions.

Otherwise, you risk tension and power struggle, which may result in less sex, more verbal arguments, anger, and criticism of one another.

This is primal stuff, remember. A remodeling of your shelter, your "nest," is not a cosmetic thing—it is a reflection of your nature, personality, identity, and primal drive to provide, protect, and nurture the life around you. Consider this example: a couple came to see me—"near divorce," in the wife's words, "because of this friggin' remodeling." The woman was the primary breadwinner; her husband, the stay-at-home dad; the husband had hands-on control of the remodeling work being done, therefore. His wife understood that she had to let go of lots of decisions, but her husband was spending more money than planned, without concern. His lack of accountability stressed his wife, who was a mother of two, CEO, wife, and provider of the money. I had to coach the husband to realize how much he devalued and disrespected his wife by overspending. "You are basically dissing your wife," I told him. "Yes, you control the minutiae of the work, but you must listen to your wife better and bring her into the decision making more respectfully, or you will pay dear consequences."

The Domain of Child Development

If you have children, look at which of you provides what kinds of love and services to your children. These include kinds of affection, discipline, material goods, rules, risk-taking, empathy development, competency development, resiliency development, moral and character development, skills training, art and craft development, reading and literacy development, math and science development, and general and specific nurturance.

As you look at these, think about how you already divide up child care and how you can do even better, in new ways that respect your separate gifts (and cut down on tensions).

- How do you divide fun time with the children, and who controls which domains in this time?

- Is one of you the domain controller of after-school activities? If so, perhaps the other ought to control certain aspects of the weekend or vacation time?

If you are divorced, domain control can be easier, but also more difficult. Watch out if one of you is giving up far more control than is healthy for the children's nurturance; this usually involves the father, who is forced into a position of becoming a friend to the children rather than a domain-controlling parent.

And remember, there is nothing wrong with the word "control." In a strong marriage, security comes not from sameness but from our evolving both separately and together a sense of control over respective domains. Happiness in a marriage comes because we blend our separate assets, including controlling those separate assets, for the good of the whole: the couple, the family, and the home.

The Domain of Sexuality and Intimacy

Sexuality and other forms of ritualized and spontaneous emotional intimacy are crucial to intimate separateness. In long-lasting couples, this domain also reflects divisions of labor, and that can be quite healthy.

A client came to see me because his wife had stopped initiating anything sexual with him. If he initiated sex, she would go along and enjoy it, but only if he initiated it once a week. She was in her twentieth year of marriage, she was in menopause, and sexuality was more complicated for her than for him. Simultaneously, she did not realize that as she reduced sex over the last year, he started losing one of the primary ways he was emotionally intimate with her. This loss created too much distance—triggering abandonment fear.

In essence, the woman had taken control of her declining need for sex but was losing her husband. This couple, then, went through a transformative therapeutic process of developing new ways of being emotionally and physically intimate—the development of intimacy rituals and intimacy protectors around gift giving, talking every day, hugging or kissing once a day, eating more meals together, saying "I love you" once a day.

They also developed new ways (for them) of giving the husband sexual intimacy—more oral sex, more masturbation while she tickled his testicles, the use of lubricants during intercourse to combat her vaginal dryness. The husband, as he accommodated the new stage of life he and his wife were in, smartly paid compliments to his wife. Once, when she joked in my office, "Listen, I want to keep my man satisfied, but I can't do it the way I used to, so I hope he's grateful," he touched her hand and said, "Honey, I'm very grateful for the changes. Believe me." His eyes became teary with emotion and she hugged him tightly. A new division of labor occurred in this couple's sexual life, and it helped them regain attachment security.

In this case, as in every case of domain division and respect for one another's domains, there is a gift giving we do with one another. It is transactional and often needs verbal acknowledgment.

Practicing Equality, Not Sameness

One of the many myths that have plagued marriage and intimacy for the last few decades is that of sameness—that we will be happiest if we are the same. In fact, the practice of intimate separateness happens when we are just different enough to be interesting to one another. Our gifts are meant to act in *complementarity* rather than *sameness*. This is true throughout the natural world, because pair-bonding in all species is about dependency. We depend on one another to fill in where we are weak. We do not have to be strong in every area. We are not the same as one another in every (or even most) areas. We can disagree on a lot of things, banter, argue, fight about lots of things.

We can divide roles in traditional gender ways for a period of time or become gender benders in the way we divide roles. We can each be selfish in one area but selfless in another, and we notice that our partner is, too, in his or her way. If we tried always to be the same, we would live with a relentless drive to remold the other to be "the same," and anyone who has been successfully married for a long time knows that the long-term killer of a marriage is an attempt to change the other person.

An Exercise: Study Your Complementarity

Take a moment to see if you and your partner fit any of these a/b pairs. If so, you may be quite complementary in ways that are healthy for your relationship's longevity.

ONE OF YOU:
   a. May more often automatically and quickly submerge the needs of the self in order to help others, while
   b. the other may help others, but set clearer boundaries on the relinquishment of the self.

ONE OF YOU:
   a. May become anxious without constant verbal contact, including receiving compliments or praise, while
   b. the other becomes overwhelmed by constant verbalizations, finding them to be somewhat intrusive.

ONE OF YOU:
   a. Lacks self-confidence in most (though not all) key areas of performance, achievement, and success, while
   b. the other has genuine self-confidence and/or bloated self-confidence in similar areas of success.

ONE OF YOU:
   a. Bases a sense of life's meaning on success in everyday attachments and relationships, while
   b. the other bases a sense of life's meaning in performance, success, and competition.

ONE OF YOU:

a. Finds joy in most things, sees the positive in most things, has a spontaneous attitude toward life's vagaries, while

b. the other sees catastrophes imminent, tends toward negativity, is regimented, and may enjoy complaining.

ONE OF YOU:

a. Tends to take things personally, feeling more easily hurt emotionally, while

b. the other tends to forget or move on more quickly from slights and small issues.

ONE OF YOU:

a. Tends to ruminate for a long time on emotional and relational experiences, while

b. the other tends to avoid dwelling for a long time on emotional or relational experiences.

ONE OF YOU:

a. Sees worst-case scenarios first (glass is half empty), while

b. the other tends to figure that "all will be well, things will be fine" (glass half full).

ONE OF YOU:

a. Overthinks and micromanages in many domains, having difficulty trusting the other or other people to fully figure out things for themselves, while

b. the other is more likely to "go with the flow," trusting others to manage their own intricacies of life, and only micromanages in one or two domains.

ONE OF YOU:

a. Is calm in a crisis, but otherwise becomes overstimulated by stress more easily, while

b. the other freezes in a crisis but otherwise does not overreact too often to everyday stressors and demands of multitasking.

ONE OF YOU:

a. Gets easily agitated by myriad details, becoming easily angry, while

b. the other multitasks fluidly, with less anger.

ONE OF YOU:

a. Worries constantly about offending people, while

b. the other worries less about offending other people.

ONE OF YOU:

a. Is better at negotiating with business colleagues or strangers, such as car dealers, than the other, while

b. the other is better at working successfully with people (family members, children) who need empathy to feel comfortable negotiating.

ONE OF YOU:

a. Is generally more rigid in behavior patterns, while

b. the other is generally more adaptable and flexible.

As you take time (a month or more) to look at these (and other relevant) characteristics, and find any complementarities in the list items, you will discover areas where you are indeed very much the same. But you may also notice areas where you and your partner are a/b pairs who have been trying to push for sameness. You can assess this complementarity and decide, both individually and as a couple, whether "letting the other person be him- or herself" is okay.

If you see that you have been trying to push your partner to be more like you in lots of areas, talk about whether this practice is a way of one person impinging on the other, and thereby creating power struggle. See if the will-to-sameness that was essential to early attachment is now an expression of frightened desperation in one of you. The phrase "opposites attract" has a great deal of truth to it. More accurately, it should be "complementarities attract."

Marriage is a *realistic* union: it thrives on what's natural, and complementarity is natural. Ultimately, when it comes to morals or values, both partners need to be on the same page (both agreeing that cheating, lying, stealing, or violence are bad), but in the emotional and psychological drivers of long-term love, we do not need to be identical. In fact, letting go of that need for sameness may save your marriage or, if your marriage is already strong, move it toward a deeper intimacy.

Protecting Complementarity

Each time we choose to do something loving, we build healthy bonding, which in turn builds more love. Each time we try to force sameness on our partner ("Do it this way, my way, I'm right"), we impinge on our partner's free, independent development. Then, as our partner resists or passive-aggressively capitulates, we feel less self-confident in our own rightness. The spiral goes on until we break it. To protect complementarity in your relationship, try these new practices:

1. For one week, stop yourself every time you are about to correct your partner (as suggested above), and internally correct *yourself*. This humility will retrain you to see gifts, be grateful, and restrict your urge to make your partner the same as you. As you put this into practice, remember that much of what you are critiquing in your partner is what you don't like about yourself.

2. Live with passion *in your own way* and let your partner do so *in his or her own way*. Compliment your partner's passions and hobbies, acknowledge their validity. Even if your passions are not all the same, the joy you bring your mate through the compliment will incite a common passion between you.

3. Talk together until you agree on transactional gifts. "If I do this for you, will you please do this for me?" "If I say _____, will you say _____?" "I'm willing to do more of this (this might be something sexual!) if you will do more of _____."

4. Negotiate time and space to follow both people's passions by promising and accepting support for that time and space. Take the time you deserve. Take the space you need. Help your partner do so, as well.

5. If you are not romantically or sexually passionate in your relationship right now, let your spouse know that your passion has been diverted by the stress of another project and then reassure him or her it will return. Give a timeline for the return of attention to everyday needs for sex, intimacy, and mutual passion.

6. Ask your partner, "What support do you need this week so that you can pursue and fulfill your passions?" This can never be asked enough. And remember, if you alone are asking, you might be paying back for previous gifts your partner has given you concerning your own passions. Once you are practicing intimate separateness on a daily basis, the long-term memory of gifts given to partners leads to a return on those gifts. That said, if you ask this question and your partner never does, the marriage is unfair, and that unfairness may well need to be dealt with in counseling or with other interventions.

7. Privately and publicly, pay one another compliments regarding your separate passions and selves. Even if you don't like your partner, when in public, compliment him or her when appropriate. Your partner's feelings of being valued and loved will pay big dividends.

8. Speak your needs clearly and acknowledge your partner's needs constantly. Love is not a struggle over whose needs come first. Love is an ebb and flow that entails meeting and not meeting one another's needs. Some weeks, months, even years, one partner may seem to be sacrificing more than the other. As long as, over the many years or decades of marriage, these phases even out, your love will probably be fine.

9. Make sure your partner knows you want to give and receive unconditional love. This will not mean you *respect* everything your partner does, nor that your partner respects everything you do. *Respect* and *love* are not the same thing, though they can come hand in hand. Even when we don't respect something our partner has done, we can still love our partner.

At its core, complementarity creates a safe emotional container—a sense of trust and safety—that sameness generally does not do. The will to sameness is a will to power struggle; the will to complementarity is a will to stability. When we try to be the same as our partner or, more likely, make our partner the same as we are, we make both love and respect conditional on a sameness that, ultimately, is impossible. Gradually or quickly, both respect and love devolve to power struggle, then the demise of a relationship.

YOUR WISDOM

My wife and I have been married forty-two years. I've learned these things about love:

• Turn off the TV, the computer, the iPod, the whatever, put down the book, the newspaper, etc. . . . and pay full attention to your spouse. I remember that I used to sit and watch a lot of TV while my wife wanted to talk to me. My mind would be concentrating on what was happening on TV rather than what she was saying. At one point while I was particularly glued to an episode of yet another inane cop drama, she said, "You are a TV addict," and with that she walked out of the room. I asked myself then and there if I was going to be married to the TV or her. I turned off the TV and didn't turn it back on again for years, and then it was only to watch the news or a special sports event. From then on the TV never went on in our house other than on weekday evenings when we would watch a movie together or the aforementioned news and occasional sporting event.

- Remember first of all that true love is not how you feel, it is how you act. Always act as though you were in love, no matter how you feel.

- Don't be so concerned about who you marry as who you are. Make sure that YOU are the right person, an honorable person who treats all with respect, even your spouse.

- Keep remembering your spouse's positive traits; concentrate on those and remember that no matter who you were married to, they would have negative traits and you have to take the good with the bad. There is no such thing as a one-sided coin. Every spouse, like every coin, has two sides and you have to take both, the more attractive side with the less attractive side.

- Remember that you, like that coin, have a less attractive side also and your spouse is putting up with that.

- We humans have a tendency to love conditionally. That is a sure recipe for failure in marriage. Make sure your commitment is a covenant based upon how you will treat your spouse, not on how you feel. You have made more than a commitment to another person. You have made a commitment to be a certain kind of person, one who is patient, kind, forgiving, and loving, no matter what the circumstances.

- Treat your spouse as more important than yourself, as if he or she were your boss, or a person of great importance whom you are glad to serve.

- Study their love language, and treat them accordingly (see Gary Chapman's *Five Love Languages*). Become a student of your mate.

- Respect and accept that he or she is different, that they will not see the world the same way you do no matter how hard you try to make them see it that way.

- Use I messages, not YOU messages. Avoid criticism other than the most loving, constructive kind. Also, understand that your spouse will almost never see your criticism as loving and constructive.

- Take romantic getaways. They don't have to be expensive, but take time away together.

- Guys, continue to date your wife all your life, and treat her with the same courtesy you would treat that cute gal at work or down the street if you took her out! Never even think about taking that cute gal at work or down the street out!!!

- Guys, be a protector, help your wife feel secure. While you are looking for physical intimacy, she has a deep need to feel safe, protected, secure, in both your love and life, and she looks to you to help provide her with that sense of security. If she feels you are risking her welfare, she will turn off and become sexually unresponsive. That is a sign to her that you don't really love her.

- When she is being difficult (not if, but when) keep loving her. She has a need to know that you love her at all times and will never leave her even when she is being difficult.

- In the words of a song from *Camelot*, "How to Handle a Woman," the answer is "Love her, love her, love her."

- Realize that you will fail in many of your attempts to be a loving spouse, even with the best of intentions. Forgive yourself and keep on trying. You will have successes!

• • •

In our marriage there have been many times that both my wife and I have felt like we wanted out, but we have never given up and the love has always returned. I am as in love as when we first married. After all these years I still find her to be a wonderful person to whom I am fortunate to be married.

—Dan, 68

Protecting Your Marriage

Love is a lifelong journey of daily choices. It has no clear destination except . . . love. Our flaws can be stimulated in this journey by too much closeness or too much separateness. During this long journey, what is a lover's job? In response to one client's request that I "boil it down," I created this list.

A Lover's Job

A partner, lover, and spouse is a helpmate, not a doctor, therapist, priest, or judge.

When I'm sad, it is not my lover's job to make me happy, but to help me find answers to my despair.

When I'm constantly angry, it is not my lover's job to manage my anger, but to help me find someone who can help me do so.

When I'm anxious, it is not my lover's job to cure my anxiety, but to help me learn to trust the world.

When I ruminate too much over my lover's flaws, it is not my lover's job to change for me, but to help me find ways to quiet my mind.

When I'm hurt, it is not my lover's job to heal me, but to bandage my wounds as much as she or he can, and then help me heal myself.

When I'm involved in any unhealthy activity, it is not my lover's job to make me stop, but to help me find people who can.

My lover has come into my life to be the cocreator of my home, the co-parent of my children, the lover of my body and soul, but my lover is not that other part of myself I can ask to do everything I myself don't want to do.

My lover is not inside my head, and if I need something, I need to voice the need, and I need to remember, even as I voice the need, my lover can fulfill only some of it.

In all this, my lover is not the source of my resilience nor my fragility but, rather, the friend who stands with me, both close and separate as needed, so that we can give to the world the gifts of our love.

· · ·

Ultimately, we marry someone who will help us heal ourselves of our flaws, but that person is not responsible for our healing, and we can never be "fixed." Rather, we marry someone with whom we can be safely and comfortably dependent and independent—always knowing we must also create safety and independence for ourselves on a daily basis. Practicing intimate separateness protects long-term love because that love is always in process.

We are always working at love, never finishing it, and each beautiful moment with our partner is like a music recital; the performer has practiced for months and then proudly shows his or her abilities, gets some applause (the dopamine rush of feeling rewarded by a beautiful moment of "mission accomplished"), then it is time to practice again for the next moment. The guarantee of all the daily practice is not the erasure of suffering or struggle but the enjoyment of life together, one moment at a time.

Given all the vagaries of human love, there is only one way to fully protect yourself from feeling or getting hurt: never love. But if you do love, you will be hurt, over and over again. Lovers have swords, we draw blood, we cause each other pain, we neglect to practice gratitude, we become selfish, and we blame the other for our woes.

But if we live in intimate separateness, we can weather all of that. In fact, we can thrive in it. We can come to laugh about ourselves and our partners. We can create together a kind of glow, like musical performers in duet, who get so good at what they are doing they appear, to others, to be radiant with joy and love.

Chapter 7

The Powerful Lessons
of Affairs and Infidelity

EVERY CRISIS, INCLUDING INFIDELITY,
CAN TEACH US ABOUT LOVE

When I was about six years into my counseling practice, I received a call from Sanford, a man who was well known in the public sphere. He had read my 1992 book *Mothers, Sons, and Lovers.* "It's as if you were writing about me," he confessed, explaining that he had had a complex relationship with his mother, and that complexity affected all his relationships with women. Now he was in a dark time with his second wife; she had just caught him in an affair. Sanford wondered if he could come from New York to Spokane to work with me. He also wondered if I would be willing to then fly back with him to meet with him and his wife to "help us patch things up."

"I'm ready to take whatever responsibility I need to with her," he promised.

I warned him that working with him would be fine, but then I would be aligned with him, which would weaken my chances of helping him with his wife. Despite this caveat, he did fly to my location in his Lear jet, we worked together in a two-day intensive, then he went back to his wife to see what he could save of his marriage. A week later, as arranged, his Lear jet came to pick me up and flew me to his location, a car drove me to a palatial house, he greeted me at the door, introduced me to his wife, and we talked for no more than five minutes when it was clear to me that his wife had already "packed her bags"—in every way except the physical.

"I'm not interested in you or any of this psychobabble bullshit," she yelled at me and him as this short conversation ended. "I'm taking him for everything he's got, and I'll get the kids, too. Go back the hell wherever you came from!"

A car service drove me and Sanford back to the airport. Sanford and I shook hands and said good-bye. A young counselor, I walked back onto the Lear jet, feeling inadequate. I felt for this man, too, who hoped wealth and an outsider could save him, and this woman in whose eyes I saw some love yet for this man, but also so much fury as to destroy any chance of reconciliation. From working with the man and hearing (albeit from his point of view) about his wife, I saw classic enmeshment/abandonment issues writ so large as to inevitably end a family, with three children torn between warring parents. This case was like many others in which the counselor providing therapy walks away feeling powerless.

But even in this case, lessons emerged. Over the decades I have worked with a number of couples in which one or both of the clients has been sexually, emotionally, and/or romantically unfaithful. Few of these involve Lear jets and a wide-eyed young counselor traveling across the country, but all of them have taught me lessons about intimate separateness that I could not learn in school, or even from couples who had not faced infidelity. While infidelity survivors often become convinced of their own ugliness and destitution, then face internal and external shame in profound proportions, they are also some of the bravest people we will ever meet. And even the actors (those committing the affairs) are not evil—affairs are nearly always matters of emotional/sexual hyper-intimacy or hyper-separation rather than evil intention.

Given that approximately 35 percent of men and 25 percent of women will have some form of an extramarital affair in their lifetime, there is a great deal of wisdom to be derived from such a large population (in the tens of millions in the United States alone). According to psychiatrist Scott Haltzman, author of *The Secrets of Surviving Infidelity*, infidelity in total most likely affects approximately 40 percent of the population.

A Personal Story

As a marriage and family counselor, I have found myself sympathetic to people with sexual issues, including promiscuity and infidelity, for the normal professional reasons—it is part of my work. At the same time, I believe I also feel deep sympathy for people in this situation because I have personally lived the complexity of sexual infidelity. I lived it as a boy who was sexually molested at the age of ten by his psychiatrist, a man who was married to someone my family knew socially. As a ten-year-old, in 1968, I knew almost nothing about sex yet—had not masturbated, did not really understand the birds and the bees—and I was thrown from total ignorance and innocence very quickly into constant sexual stimulation. This was immensely confusing and traumatic; it took me many years of therapy to work through the trauma of both physical and sexual abuse during my boyhood. At the same time, it taught me, through difficult life experience, some things that have helped me in my work because they hide very deep in the human condition:

- The very thing you know in your guts is absolutely wrong can feel better than anything you have felt before—thrilling, freeing, amazing, even growthful.

- Someone other than the people closest to you can hold the power (even if illusory) to take you to joy and bliss much more quickly (so it feels at the time) and far more deeply than can the people you love.

- The very parts of your body (and brain) that everyone else says are wrong, flawed, sinful, and dangerous can take you to places that seem to feed your soul like no one place or thing has seemed to do before.

- Our central features as human beings—sexuality is one of these—are neither purely moral nor immoral in their content, but straddle every part of life: psychology, morality, intimacy, individual personality development, and social life.

- Everyone responds to sexual trauma differently; there is no single right way people "should" respond to being hurt sexually (including being betrayed). Trauma of this kind is as complex as are the diversity of people's responses to death. In my case, I ended up being non-promiscuous and I ended up monogamous; I have had few, rather than many, sexual partners (seven between twenty years old, when I lost my virginity, and twenty-six, when I met Gail; seven was considered "few" for a young man raised in the counter-culture world who came of age in the 1970s and early 1980s), and I selected (unconsciously at that young age) a monogamous partner, Gail. Though a victim of sexual violence, I went in the direction of non-promiscuity; but many people who have been sexually abused move in the direction of promiscuity. This diversity has been important for me to know and study as I help people with sexual issues, including people who have been sexually molested or harmed in the past.

- The way that worked best for me to heal sexual trauma and difficulty was to practice intimate separateness in sexuality: to enjoy its intimacy but also to be open to its experimental nature—that is, to separate myself from seeing sex as only about emotional intimacy and emotional closeness. To explain this, I think about prostitution. Prostitution is about getting sexual needs met—which involves physical intimacy—while maintaining (for the most part) emotional separateness. While some individuals who see prostitutes form emotionally intimate relationships with them, most do not. Sex can be separate from love. Understanding this has helped me treat couples who face infidelity.

Overall, my personal story and experience with sexuality have helped me see that sexuality, sexual addiction, affairs, infidelity, and sexual promiscuity can give many gifts even in the trauma they bring to our married lives. One of those gifts is the lens of intimate separateness, and another is the healing power of separateness. Without practicing separateness, we can feel so completely devastated by infidelity and other similar sex-based emotional trauma as to lose ourselves. Without separateness, we can feel we are dying in our intimacy, and if we feel that, we will get hyper-angry, ruminate, become anxious and afraid. The intimate alliance with the apparent death of the self will be a focus for us that devastates love for years or decades to come. It does not need to do that.

The Gifts of Infidelity

When people come into my office to talk about affairs, they are battling the lost trust, the shame, the hidden needs and desires of infidelity that radiate onto everything else in their lives. Part of their bravery at this time is that they are often more positively vulnerable to healing, personal change, and personal growth than are many individuals and couples who seek therapy for reasons that appear more opaque, and thus healing may move at a slower pace.

As we explore this area of human marriage, let me say that, in my experience, every affair is like a fingerprint—unique. One couple came to see me ready to confess both of their affairs right then. "Let's get it over with," she said. "Yes, we're ready to move on," he said. Another couple, in which only the wife had had an affair, was not so sanguine; our first session was filled with vitriol and threats. In another, in which the husband had had affairs but not the wife, he sat in silent shame while she listed his faults.

Also, let me disclose that since just over 80 percent of the infidelity cases I have seen involved marriages with children, saving the marriage (under the caveats I noted in Chapter 1) is the disclosed first intention of the couples. Thus, I tend to work with the "actor," "survivor," and "children" as a triumvirate, in hopes of helping the couple stay together.

YOUR INSIGHTS

The design of the brain means that we very often have little or no control over when we are swept by emotion, nor over what emotion it will be. But we can have some say in how long an emotion will last.

—Daniel Goleman, author of *Emotional Intelligence*

Defining Terms: What Do *You* Mean by "Infidelity" or "Affairs"?

Before going any further, we should define terms. In the scientific literature, the correct name for a man who has stayed sexually loyal to his spouse is a "monogynist," for a woman it's "monandrist." Similarly, a man who has been unfaithful is a "polygynist," and a woman is a "polyandrist." Within these labels, there is a great deal of discussion about what exactly constitutes having sex or being intimate with someone else and what the boundaries of an emotional affair are.

So that you can discover where you are in all this—your place in this is the most important thing now—please answer the questions in this survey. I suggest you and your partner do this in separate rooms, so that you do not see each other's answers or emotional expressions ahead of time. Try not to discuss this ahead of time, either. After you've both completed the survey, have a discussion (or series of discussions) about your answers. If you need help with this, have some sessions with a counselor. This material can bring up a lot of personal feelings and thoughts that link to your own nature, nurture, and social-cultural frameworks.

Essential Questions Survey 9, Part I: Defining Terms

Read these actions and check off one or more answers. "Unfaithful" means you consider it damaging to your relationship but not a relationship destroyer. "Dangerous" means your relationship could end because of the action. "No problem" means you perhaps have an "open marriage" and/or may not consider sex with another person a problem.

	UNFAITHFUL	DANGEROUS	NO PROBLEM
Sexual intercourse with another person	_____	_____	_____
Oral sex with another person	_____	_____	_____
Anal sex with another person	_____	_____	_____
Kissing ("in a moment of weakness")	_____	_____	_____
Sexual acts with a same-sex partner (not spouse)	_____	_____	_____
Emotionally intimate relationship with another (but no sex)	_____	_____	_____
Constantly looking at the attractive bodies of other people	_____	_____	_____

	UNFAITHFUL	DANGEROUS	NO PROBLEM
Constantly flirting with other people at work or at parties	_____	_____	_____
Forming an emotional bond with another person who is potentially a sexual partner, even if sex never happens	_____	_____	_____

Which of these do you think is worse?

1. My partner has sex with another person(s) while also in a sexual relationship with me.
2. My partner stops having sex with me (or only has sex with me once in a very great while) and has sex with another person(s).

1. _____ or **2.** _____

Do you agree with this statement?

Seeing a prostitute is considered an affair.   YES _____   NO _____

Do you believe?

SEXUAL AFFAIRS CAN ACTUALLY BE HEALTHY FOR A MARRIAGE WHEN:	YES	NO
1. Both partners agree to explore other partners together	_____	_____
2. Both partners agree to let the spouse explore other partners	_____	_____
3. Both partners agree to "try new stuff" or "explore other options"	_____	_____

SEXUAL AFFAIRS CAN ACTUALLY BE HEALTHY FOR A MARRIAGE WHEN:	YES	NO
4. One partner has a health problem (i.e., obesity, mental illness, STD, AIDS, other illness) and the non-ill partner needs sex	_____	_____

Essential Questions Survey 9, Part II: Why You or Your Partner Might Be Unfaithful to a Spouse

Go through this list of causes of infidelity both privately and with your partner. See which, if any, of these causes of infidelity connect with your life right now. Put a check mark by it. After going through this list, if you see any red flags at all, reach out immediately to a therapist for help. Also, as you go through this list, and as you discuss it with your partner, you will be walking through an exercise in intimate separateness. This will become clearer further on in the chapter.

1. The unfaithful spouse may lack "the monogamy gene." There is a genetic component to infidelity (see below). If you or your partner (or both) had multiple, parallel, and/or serial emotional and/or sexual partners previous to marriage and then more than one during your marriage(s), you and/ or your partner may need to check this item for discussion together with one another and with a professional.

2. It is culturally acceptable (and even encouraged) in certain ethnic groups and many cultures to have more than one mate, especially one mate for marriage/child-raising and another for sexual intimacy. Are you or your spouse a part of such a culture or upbringing or genetic line? If so, this is a cultural and genetic element to look at specifically with your trusted counselor or coach.

3. One or both of you are in love with two people at one time. It is neurobiologically possible to love two people at once. The whole brain (brain stem, limbic system, and neocortex) can all experience what we call holistically "being in love" with more than one person. This possibility is another natural element to infidelity that needs to be discussed and analyzed carefully as partners attempt to understand what the lover receives (and gives) to both wife and mistress or husband and second lover.

4. The affair is comorbid (runs parallel to) andropause and/or menopause. A great deal of infidelity occurs during the decade or so when a man is going through andropause and/or a woman is going through menopause. Because male hormones are testosterone based (testosterone is a sex-drive hormone), it is logical that somewhat more men have affairs during this time than women, but an increasing number of women also have affairs during menopause.

5. The affair is compensating for and/or an escape from a significant stressor in the marriage—the stressor could be an overwhelming workload, an addiction, a two- or three-year absence from spouse because of work in another country, a long-term sexual absence of the spouse due to pregnancy, a long-term emotional absence of the spouse due to child-raising, the death of a child or other significant stressor of this kind, mental illness of a spouse, or marital distress that has been building for years. In the case of transitory physical, sexual, or emotional absence of a partner (from pregnancy, for instance), the "affair" is more generally related to the human need for sexual and physical companionship than to emotional abandonment.

6. The affair exists because one or both parties need it in order to build or rebuild self-esteem, self-worth, or self-confidence

after a trauma. If one partner has been constantly denigrated by the other partner (or by parents or others at work or elsewhere), an affair, especially of the sexual kind, can feel like survival of self or identity. This may also be the case during andropause and menopause, when a person's identity can become significantly distressed. In either case, identity and self can become shocked by internal changes, and sexual or romantic affairs may be the result. Similarly, if a partner is constantly being psychologically impinged upon by the other partner, an affair can feel like a life-saving escape or separation activity.

7. To get ahead in the workplace or in a social group—that is, an "instrumental" affair. The instrumentality can be completely self-serving (that is, "I want this promotion and will do anything to get it") and/or practiced on behalf of one's family assets ("a promotion means more money to provide the family, so I will take the risk"). The person having the affair generally uses risk-benefit analysis to decide whether to have the affair. It is generally important for the nonactor to study the "I am doing this to help the family" element of the affair when she or he learns of the infidelity. This can even be true when the affair does not involve the workplace but does involve acquiring assets from someone in a social group (perhaps a husband needs funding for a project and someone in the social group will give that funding if the wife has an affair with him).

8. Spontaneous and convenient sexual and/or stress release (a "happy ending" at a massage, or a one-night stand at a sales conference away from home). This kind of infidelity is often of physical value only, without an in-depth psychological element. It is often, though not always, connected to the use of alcohol or substances that diminish inhibition. While a "sudden lapse" or "one-night stand" of this kind will

and can be relationship destroying because of its breach of trust, it is important to look at whether there is a pattern to this behavior. If, in a many-decades-long marriage, this has happened once, it is generally not as reflective of a deeply destructive marital pattern as it would be if it recurs constantly and/or recurs specifically in a pattern involving alcoholic behavior.

9. Sexual or other disease of spouse that has made sexual intercourse (and/or emotional life) difficult to nil between spouses. This reason for stepping out of a marriage sexually and emotionally is more common than we may realize. The sexual or other issue can be that the spouse has HIV, a sexually transmitted disease, or a long-term disease that has diminished one partner's sex drive or ability to function, such as cancer or obesity. This latter is becoming more common as some spouses gain so much weight that they become sexually dysfunctional and/or visually/sexually repugnant to their spouse.

10. The affair is, either unconsciously or consciously for the actor, a device by which to heal, end, or otherwise challenge the marriage. The actor needs to pull away from an enmeshed spouse or to practice being close to another person because his or her spouse is distant; this actor may hope that his or her marriage will benefit later from the affair. The affair, thus, is seen as instrumental to the difficult marriage. Also, the affair can be, either unconsciously or consciously for the actor, a device by which to end the marriage. Similarly, the affair can be a payback challenge to the marriage: "My spouse did it to me, so I'll do it to him and let's see how he likes it!" In all these cases, the affair will be "instrumental."

11. The affair(s) relates to addiction—the sex itself, thus, is secondary in causation to the porn, sex, love, alcohol,

drugs, or other addiction. Infidelity genetics are often comorbid (again, run parallel to) the genetics for addictions; affairs are often interconnected with the behavior of addictions. This is both a genetic function and a strictly psychological function of the stress that the addictions put on the human brain's ability to love one other person singularly and responsibly.

12. To explore sexual fantasies that a spouse will not try or finds repugnant—that is, to protect the spouse from one's own embarrassing fantasies or from fantasies the spouse has specifically said are repugnant and will not fulfill. Given that millions of Americans enjoy BDSM (Bondage, Discipline, Sadism, Masochism) activities, and given the new research showing that many of our most visceral needs have a genetic component, it is not unlikely that a genetically marked dominant or submissive person may be married to a person who is not marked at all for this kind of "alternative" sexuality. Affairs often result when two people are naturally so different in their sexual needs that they have thus far been unable to understand themselves or the other enough to figure out solutions to the differences.

The Separateness Solution from Different Viewpoints

In looking at all potential causes of various degrees of infidelity, you are already adding a "separateness mode" to your thoughts, feelings, and discussions about infidelity. If you are involved in an affair as actor or survivor or both, that separateness will be crucial to healing your marriage and/or your own personal growth from and through this crisis.

Gauging Infidelity-Culpability as the Actor

If you are the actor in the infidelity, your constructive mission at this point involves taking responsibility; helping rebuild trust; getting help to understand yourself and your culpability in the affair; understanding causes in nature, nurture, and culture; understanding causes in enmeshment/abandonment; putting your spouse and family first again; and changing your behavior. Your best chance of doing all these things psychologically is to focus not only on regaining intimacy with your spouse but also on developing more healthy psychological separateness than ever before.

Some of that separateness will come in understanding your enmeshment and other internal (and your spouse's) cycles of intimacy, as we've explored earlier in this book. You may want to go through the exercises in this book to help you analyze your and your partner's patterns of abandonment and enmeshment. Separateness may save the marriage. At the same time, if you remain too distant (don't take enough verbal and emotional responsibility, don't engage in counseling together, avoid dealing with your own psychological issues), you may well lose this marriage quickly, too.

Your spouse's culpability for the affair will no doubt be on your mind, but bringing it up just after an affair is discovered may not be useful. You will most likely want to reach out quickly to a therapist or others to help you think about what was said in Chapter 6—personality, core self, and other parts of your spouse and yourself—to gauge how best to manage discussions of issues your spouse brings to the infidelity. Your therapist can help you with each one.

With my clients who have had affairs (actors), I use the twelve points in Part II of the faithfulness survey as discussion points for gaining the internal separateness to work through the "why" of "Why did I do it?" and then plan out a future course for the development of the self and the happier marriage.

Healing the Survivor's Wound of Infidelity

There is almost always an unspoken question in the survivor's mind: Surviving this will ultimately mean forgiving my spouse, but how do I forgive him or her?

Forgiveness requires a great deal of psychological separateness. When we are initially in shock, we feel angry, ashamed, and grieve the hurt of the affair. We are not able to focus on separateness (beyond just wanting to distance our partner through animus), and thus tend to withdraw from our spouse—this is natural and an important part of our grief. At a certain point, however, especially if we are hoping to (1) rebuild the marriage or (2) divorce but rebuild the self, we need to gain a position of psychological separateness in multiple areas of focus, including forgiveness.

Here now are seven primary areas of separateness that help build survivors' selves toward forgiveness. Even if you have not been involved in an affair, I believe their content and focus can be helpful. If you have been involved in an affair, working on them in yourself, with your spouse, and with a therapist is more likely to bear fruit if you have already done the previous work in this book. If you've opened this book just now and come straight to this chapter because you or your partner have had an affair, but you haven't looked at the rest of this book, I encourage you to go back to the beginning and return later to this portion of this chapter.

THE WISDOM OF SEPARATENESS

In humans (like prairie voles) male love circuits get an extra kick when stress levels are high. After an intense physical challenge, for instance, males will bond quickly and sexually with the first willing female they lay eyes on. This may be why military men under the stress of war often bring home brides. Women, by con-

> trast, will rebuff advances or expressions of affection and desire when under stress.
>
> —**Louann Brizendine, MD, author of** *The Female Brain* **and** *The Male Brain*

Forgiveness 1: Dealing with the Biology of Monogamy

Scientists Louann Brizendine, David Buss, Helen Fisher, and others have pointed out that biology plays a powerful role in all matters of sexuality and intimacy, including monogamy. From a genetic viewpoint, you or your partner may or may not be naturally monogamous. As human genome mapping becomes more advanced in the next decade, your genetics will clarify early in love relationships. (I think we are only a decade away from this happening, with most people getting genome maps in early adulthood by 2025.)

How will the future of your relationship look, given that there may be a genetic component to monogamy? This is a crucial area to focus on while you are concentrating on the emotional and psychological hurt of the affair. You may have married a person who does not have the chromosome markers for monogamy, or you yourself may not have them. (To go deeper into the science of this, check out my book *The Wonder of Aging* [if you are over forty-five], *The Female Brain* by Louann Brizendine, or *Anatomy of Love* by Helen Fisher.)

While knowing this piece of genetics does not itself forgive the misbehavior, the deeper into studying genetics and monogamy you can go, the more health you can bring to your healing. You will gradually see less fault in yourself for co-causing the affair or other spousal misbehavior, and thus forgive yourself more quickly. Over time, if you choose to move through the steps of re-trusting your spouse, you should also be able to forgive him or her more quickly.

This area of focus alone does not solve all marital distress regarding infidelity, but it does give couples a new baseline for stepping back (separating psychologically) and understanding what is going on. At the same time, biology is not the only arbiter of destiny. Your own and your partner's deepened knowledge of the biology of monogamy should be a tool in the toolbox, not an excuse to avoid keeping promises to partners.

Forgiveness 2: Reframing the Lying Behavior

If your spouse lied to you (which he or she inevitably did at some point), the lies have nearly destroyed your sense of trust in that person. The lies, too, are part of the shame you may feel, as well as the rage. These lies must be dealt with if you are to move forward. It is important for you to gain a healthy separation from them.

One way to do that is to analyze them in retrospect to discover multiple motives for them. You may notice that many of the lies your unfaithful spouse told were not just self-aggrandizing or "selfish"; many were motivated by his or her need to protect you and your family—that is, marital and family devotion. No matter your partner's behavior with another (or others), you and your partner were bonded and attached throughout the affair. That bonding and attachment brought with it the natural protectiveness of your spouse, for you and your children with him or her. As you study the particular lies your partner told, look for ways in which she or he, by lying to you, worked very hard to make sure you and your children were not hurt. While the lies ended up causing a lot of hurt (you found out about the affair and your relationship is now at risk), this end result does not negate the fact that your spouse loved you, as evidenced by his or her protectiveness of your feelings and the stability of your marriage for months or years of lying previous to the moment you discovered the lies.

As you work to regain trust, see your partner beyond the crime of the lies to the other motives for lying. Get help understanding his or her protectiveness. A client whose wife cheated on him told me, "This has helped a lot—still seeing that she was trying to be a good wife and protect us by lying. I am more angry about it than I can put into words—the lying has hurt me more than even the sex, I think—but still, stepping back from it and seeing that element of protectiveness has helped a lot."

When I mentioned my own sexual abuse as a boy, and talked about how it has taught me the importance of separating all the various elements in sexual misconduct—seeing that there are many gray areas—I did so in hopes of inspiring people to see gray areas in infidelity. A primary mistake made by survivors is this one: a survivor focuses so constantly on the breach of intimacy that she or he (1) cannot separate the spouse's whole self from that breach, and (2) cannot separate him or herself from that breach. The result is that both the actor and the survivor's selves and ability to love and be loved become enmeshed with the breach. The actor becomes evil (no gray areas there) and, in turn, the survivor becomes, unfortunately, unlovable. As this happens, the survivor focuses only on "I must be innately stupid or worthless if I attached to a completely bad person." This manifests in thoughts or spoken words such as, "I must be a piece of shit to be treated this way by her." Or, "He is a piece of shit and that piece of shit never loved me." Either the self or the other becomes unloving and unlovable in our post-discovery thinking process, and at a certain point, for very many people, the unlovable person becomes the self.

If you face either or both sides of this pain, work within yourself and with others to separate yourself from these emotional overreactions and their black-and-white and non-gray ideas. Look at the ways in which your partner's affair did not have to do with you (e.g., he or she may not possess the monogamy gene) and/or did involve deep love and caring for you and your children.

I had to do this in healing my sexual abuse trauma. I had to see that in something this complicated, my abuser was sick and, yes, I believe, evil, *but* the sexual contact involved a number of gray areas; for instance, my world opened up, I learned about myself sexually (I learned that masturbation is okay), I felt new feelings, sexual feelings, that though they traumatized me also freed me to become a sexual person. Once I was able to get healthy separateness from the trauma, and find a balanced sexual and psychological self, I was able to mature relatively quickly in some ways because I no longer held on to black-and-white illusions and projections about sex, intimacy, my developing psyche, and the "perfection" of others.

Every survivor can gain from developing this sense of separateness from black-and-white projections. Significant therapy may be needed to do so, however.

Forgiveness 3: Discovering How I Am Also an Actor, Not Just a Survivor

It is a common thought in therapy and the psychology field that in a marriage, "things are caused fifty-fifty by both people." This is generally thought to be true of infidelity, but like all generalizations, it is more a code that opens a door of study and realization than a truism. Especially in the realm of affairs and infidelity, the "blame" can parse out to eighty-twenty or sixty-forty, or any other possible ratios of moral and emotional culpability. If the actor lacks the monogamy genetics or has significantly operative addiction genetics, that spouse's biology is going to outweigh most if not all attempts to stop affairs from happening. No matter what you do to become more intimate or separate with your spouse, these other factors will work to destroy that intimacy, so you are not in a fifty-fifty situation.

That said, the fifty-fifty code is still useful for walking through the door of infidelity to further understand the separateness solution. In most marital situations, survivors are playing some part in the reason the affairs happened. Generally, you can track your part of this equation to both intimacy and separateness: If you're the survivor, in what ways have you been *too distant* from your spouse, and/or in what ways have you *enmeshed (merged too much)* with your spouse?

Beyond the biology of monogamy and non-monogamy, infidelity often happens in response to these stressors in marriages. If you spent all or most of your time away from your spouse, paying no attention to your spouse, or distancing from your spouse, your part in the affair may constitute that portion of the problem. Also, if you are facing significant mental or physical disease (including obesity), your changed body and brain were most likely a part of the affair's commission; your partner is still more than 50 percent responsible, but you may have enough responsibility to be able to work on things from your side. If for years you have engaged in intimate power struggle with your spouse—badgering, criticizing, clinging, possessing, attacking, impinging—you are this portion of the problem.

No matter what happens in your marriage, you need to get help for this portion. This help will be a gift for your self-development that will arise from the affairs and infidelity whether this marriage lasts or not. You will finally get help with developing a more successful intimacy/ separateness balance in your future love relationships. Ultimately, no matter what happens in this marriage, you will be happier in the future, and the infidelity will have brought you the gift of separateness.

As you explore this enmeshment/power struggle in the affair, one way you'll know you may experience long-term growth is that you will most likely gain separation from a "victim" stance. You will feel like a survivor, yes, but you will gradually sense yourself to be more of a victor than a victim.

Forgiveness 4: Deciding Whether There Are Gradations of Affairs and Infidelity

All affairs are about many things, of course, and we must explore all causes in order to heal the pain of affairs. At the same time, I have found it important to talk about the sex as sex. If we don't do this, we skirt a large part of why the sexual affair occurred. With some clients, given that I have written about being sexually molested, I even mention my own story, telling them that I understand that sex is sex. Even when it comes in a traumatic way, it still carries with it the brain chemistry of euphoria, and that sexual euphoria is something people do need.

In some cases (certainly not all) of sexual infidelity in marriage, the offending party has stepped out in the marriage because sex has left the marriage. Were sex still a primary mode of sharing love in the marriage, the unfaithful partner might not have stepped out to go find it. The important question in this area of forgiveness and separateness for you is: Where does my spouse's affair fit on this spectrum?

Sam and Sally, two clients of mine, fit the situation of sex leaving a marriage. As I began working with this couple, Sam said he thought he did not have the monogamy gene, but had stayed faithful to Sally physically while bonding with porn, masturbation, and a number of fantasies he asked Sally to act out (which she enjoyed). "But I was on the edge of infidelity for years," he confessed. "Sally was a great lover, and I was able to fight my demons thanks to her being so into sex, but when she got pregnant, I became stupid. Stupid! I had an affair. It was a sex-only affair. Then, a year after Isabel was born, Sally still didn't want to have sex, and I began seeing a prostitute, then I started having a sexual affair with a coworker. None of these was more than sex, but I know how stupid I was. The pregnancy was the best thing and the worst thing in my life."

By this latter statement he meant he gained a child—who defined him now and gave him immense joy—but also learned not only that he was non-monogamous genetically but also that he did not have the psychological resources to remain separate from his fear of abandonment when Sally went inward during pregnancy and paid no sexual attention to him. By the time Isabel was two years old and Sally was again pregnant, she discovered her husband's affair. By now the couple had only had sexual intercourse twice in three years. As I worked with this couple, I found that the basics for healing were there:

1. Sam was willing to take responsibility for his actions and apologize and rebuild trust and make things right.

2. Sally was open to the understanding that healing could take years—that is, healing had to happen in increments.

3. Sally was open to the possibility of forgiveness as a part of her own spiritual path.

4. Sam and Sally still loved one another. There was, as Sally admitted, "still a spark in me."

5. Sally was open to looking at sex as sex. When Sam said, "It was never about love, I've only loved Sally. It was only about sex," Sally got angry at him, as would be quite normal, but was also able, later, to return to the conversation about her and Sam's sex life, and understand sex's role in love better.

In this particular case, this "sex is only sex" piece helped greatly. Ten years after I worked with this couple, I saw them again at a symphony performance. Sally pulled me aside and said, "We're still married, you know, Sam and me, and I have a different attitude toward sex now. His affairs were the worst thing that happened to me at that time, but also the best. I don't see sex the same way anymore."

I needed to disengage from this dialogue in public as soon as possible to protect confidentiality, and I never saw Sally again nor learned what she meant exactly, but the couple's marriage had clearly survived. I assumed that Sally, who had been brought up in a very strict religious family, had developed a sense of liberation about sexuality—experiencing growth as a painful gift of her husband's infidelity. This is not the preferred course for personal change, of course, but in this marriage something had happened regarding the survivor's sexuality during the forgiveness process that appeared to help Sally and Sam a great deal.

"Above all, sexual love is the most intense and dramatic of the common ways in which a human being comes into union and conscious relationship with something outside himself," writes Alan Watts. "It is, furthermore, the most vivid of the human being's customary expressions of his organic spontaneity, the most positive and creative occasion of his being transported by something beyond his conscious will." Sex is that powerful, that important, to love.

We can all get very busy and forget to have sex with our partner; we can have children who need us and we don't have sex with our partner; for many very good reasons, we can forget that for all of us sex is a form of union with a sense of full divinity of self and other; and that for some people (Sam, for instance) once this mode of contact, communication, adoration, affection, spiritual intimacy, and union is removed from the relationship, the person loses one of his or her primary ways of achieving the spontaneity and the spiritual and physical union of self, soul, nature, love, and lover.

The reproductive physiologist Joanna Ellington, author of *Slippery When Wet* (an in-depth resource on the role of sex in love) recently highlighted this idea in an interview. She said, "I know I'm generalizing, and this won't be true for everyone, but in thirty years of studying women and men I have learned that for some people—some women and somewhat more men—if sex is taken out of the marriage, the marriage won't survive." This is a stark statement and surely controversial, but it is worth pondering as we take a holistic view of marriage.

For Sally and Sam, returning sex to the marriage helped a great deal. It helped ensure a more intimate attachment, and it helped Sally become braver in some ways than she had ever been. She faced religious and other issues around sexuality beneath the surface that had unconsciously been embedded in the self. Sam betrayed Sally, and it hurt terribly, but also, Sally gained separateness from religious and other internal issues, and Sam and Sally absorbed the sexual affairs into the twelve stages of love as a gift.

Forgiveness 5: Deciding Your Seat of Worth as a Woman

If you are a woman survivor of a husband's or partner's affairs, your identity not only as a person but also as a *woman* will likely need study and growth. You will have to forgive your partner for bringing your sense of your own womanhood, femininity, sexual attractiveness, and female identity to a point of self-denigration. As one female therapist, who became my client, told me, her husband "doesn't realize it, but he has been saying to me for the whole year of his affairs, 'You are subpar as a woman.' He hasn't just hurt me as a person—he has destroyed my sense of what an attractive, lovable woman is."

As she and I worked together on these issues and talked about this over a number of sessions, she quoted a book by the psychologist

Robert Johnson that she particularly loved. She read these words aloud to me that Johnson wrote in the context of why we are in love relationships and marriages: "So that we can learn that human relationship is inseparable from friendship and commitment. We can learn that the essence of love is not to use the other to make us happy but to serve and affirm the one we love. And we can discover, to our surprise, that what we have needed more than anything was not so much to be loved, as to love."

This therapist and survivor looked up from the page and said, "I think I'm learning through this painful process (post-affair healing) that the essence for me of being a woman is not just feeling like I'm attractive and wanted; it's also this feeling of wanting to serve my partner, affirm him, and thus have him affirm me as his friend and his lover. That's what I could never get him to realize. His affairs dug away at this, and we can't be married anymore (the couple had already divorced) but this is what I have to forgive—that his actions spit in the face of who I knew myself to be as a woman; he basically said, 'It's not enough even that you take care of me. A woman should do even more than that for me.'

"But you see, Michael, I can't do more than take care of people. He doesn't see it, and that's why our marriage is over. I gave everything I had and everything I was as a woman, and it wasn't enough for him. He just doesn't get it. He won't get it. He has someone else now. My healing has to stop involving trying to get him (either in person or in my inner dialogue) to 'finally' understand me and thus make me feel loved. I know already what I was born to do, and that's to care for my children and others; for a while now I guess I'll have to practice this without a husband, and that's okay. I have found myself because of that damn affair."

If you are in a crisis around an affair right now, the idea that we fall in love with someone "not so much to be loved as to love" may seem anathema, even downright absurd. And perhaps "to love" is not your core definition of yourself as a woman. Indeed, you will probably have many core definitions of yourself as a woman. This therapist was just one woman with one set of core definitions. Her wisdom is universal,

I think, in its honesty about connecting healing and forgiveness to gender. We are all people, *and* we are women and men. Setting gender aside may actually inhibit forgiveness and personal growth.

As you work to forgive, journal about how the affair affects you *as a woman*. Talk with friends about it. Explore "womanhood" or "being a woman" as you perhaps never have before. Talk about what you as a woman want. In the 2013 Tyler Perry movie *Temptation*, which is about thirtysomething relationships, Judith says to her husband, Bryce, "I don't want a good guy, I want a phenomenal guy." Is this woman you?

Do you as a woman want more from a man than a spouse can give? Are your expectations reasonable?

Do you want something other than healthy love?

Talk about enmeshment, abandonment, and power struggles from the viewpoint of "woman." As you do so, and especially if you get help and support, you may find that a gift of the affair is new growth for you not only as a person, lover, or mate but also as a woman. From that growth will come a dissipation of some of the pain and advancement in the forgiveness of yourself that may help you move forward.

Forgiveness 6: Deciding Your Seat of Worth as a Man

I worked with a man, forty-five, married eighteen years with three children, ages eleven, eight, and four, whose wife was repugnant to him sexually ("she's gained seventy pounds") and repugnant to him emotionally ("she nags me all the time," "she tries to control everything I do," "she's not who I married anymore"). This man came to me because he had fallen in love with a coworker and started an affair with her that had thus far lasted four months. He felt guilty and came to see me so that I might help him "sort out what to do."

As soon as my normal intake and survey questions were completed, I asked him to tell the story of meeting and falling in love with his wife, then to do the same for his girlfriend. He told each story, and our session ended with some homework for him to do regarding what he liked about his wife, what he liked about his girlfriend, and what he liked about himself when he was with each of them.

The next session involved discussing all of his homework material, then my asking him if he was aware of all the research on the possible effects of a divorce—especially if his affair came out—on his children. He was somewhat aware of the possible stress, but now promised to contemplate the future of his children—that is, that for a decade or more they would live a life full of hurt, feeling torn between the bad father and the hurt mother. This thought moved him; he wanted to avoid it because of his love for his children, so he gained some motivation to work on things.

Over a period of sessions we explored the "who, what, where, when, why, and how" of the two women he loved, and I also kept returning him to his children's lives. Over the period of a month, I slipped these two questions into every session: "What kind of man do you want to be? What kind of father do you want to be?" His homework became, in part, to keep thinking about those questions. At times this was difficult for him. In one session, he became angry. "I don't want to talk about my kids," he hissed. "I came here to talk about what to do with _____."

"What to do," I countered, "is nothing if it's not about your kids. *As a man,* what do you believe would be best for your kids?"

He stomped out of the room and did not talk to me again until a year later. I saw him, his wife, and his children at a local shopping mall. His wife—whom he had refused to invite into counseling—knew nonetheless who I was from my books. I remained conversationally distant, of course, keeping things light, since I could not reveal that her husband had been my client. I also sensed that he had not mentioned my counseling role to his wife. But it was clear that he had decided to stay in his marriage.

I also saw that this husband and wife seemed happy; she held her husband's arm and he grinned more than once, trying to communicate something to me, something genuinely joyful. At least from outward appearances, this woman was not the woman he had physically described; she looked to be only slightly overweight, clearly having lost more than fifty pounds based on his earlier description. This man had decided that the kind of man and father he wanted to be was the man and father who stays with his wife and children.

I walked away with a lot of unknowns (was he still having an affair with the nurse or someone else?), my mind also whirring with *Did I push too far? If I had been less honest about my views on the role of divorce on children's mental health, would he have stayed in therapy? Could I have gotten her into therapy with him?* But I also walked away feeling that I had done the only thing I could do in this situation: while being mainly nonjudgmental and empathic, I had challenged the man to look at manhood itself. "Manhood" for him meant sexuality, love, work, and children. "Separateness" in therapy meant my helping him detach from the sex and intimacy of his relationship with his secondary love object and gain perspective on who he wanted to be as a father and husband.

YOUR WISDOM

Some of the keys to a long-lasting relationship for me as a person and therapist are:

First, I'd say that "couple relationships" are difficult. I think of them as "the graduate school of life." Before we are in a committed relationship and are dating, things can look easy and wonderful. But as soon as we commit, we are no longer on "good behavior." Old hurts and fears emerge, and we have to learn to deal and heal. Relationships aren't about "living happily ever after," like we learn in movies and fairy tales. They are about learning how to love deeply and well. And that takes time and effort for most of us.

After my wife and I had been married for three or four years, we went to hear the legendary therapist Carl Rogers talk about therapy and relationships. He and his wife had been married for fifty-four years at the time. He told us that he and his wife had gone through some difficult times, it wasn't all wonderful, even for this famous man who had helped millions. Roger's wife smiled and said to him, "Yes, I remember there were those difficult seven or eight years when nothing seemed to be working." What? Seven or eight years? I couldn't believe that someone could hang in there that long and not leave. But having been married now to Carlin for thirty-five years, I can understand that sometimes there are long stretches where things just aren't working.

Second, when things are tough in the relationship, try not to blame yourself or the other person. "No blame, no shame," is a mantra I use. I can say, that's the hardest work I've ever done. It would seem so clear to me that "if only she would just (fill in the blank), things would be all right." It seemed so obvious that she was the cause of the problem. At other times I felt like I had screwed things up and I was the cause of our unhappiness. I learned there is no "cause." My anger and hurt feeds her anger and hurt, and things just go downhill from there. The more difficult action, but the one that works best, is to work on myself. I would repeat over and over "the problem is not my wife. The problem is my life." When I focused on my own life and what I could do to love and support myself better, things would always improve in the relationship.

Third, in this time of impermanence and constant change and turnover, it's easy to let our relationships be another thing we "trade in." We move to a new job, a new house, a new neighborhood, a new car. Why not trade the old partner in on a new one? Particularly when there seem to be so many other opportunities, and relationships can seem so difficult and painful, sometimes for years. Why continue to suffer when we can "start over" with someone else who doesn't carry so much of the old baggage? I followed that pattern and so did my wife. We've each been married twice before. And we each had times in our thirty-five-year marriage when we thought "Maybe I'm just not cut out to be married" or "He/she just isn't who I thought they were. Maybe I should cut my losses and move on." Too many people give up too soon and too many "marriage and family" counselors actually collude in the

process by focusing attention on our individual desire to "be happy"
and not enough on our mutual desire to have a joyful relationship.
It takes work, but it is so worth it.

—Jed Diamond, PhD, author of *Male Menopause*

Forgiveness 7: Returning to Morality

If you are the third party in the affair—the person who has an affair with a married person—you can play a part in the healing and
forgiveness in the marriage by focusing on the children. You may be
able to justify the affair sexually and romantically, but the existence of
children will, hopefully, bring a moral compass to your considerations.
Protection of children is the seat of all human morality and thus ought
to supplant personal needs for intimacy and euphoria. This belief has
been another gift of the sexual molestation I experienced; I saw that
the sex created intimacy and euphoria for my abuser, but I grew and
matured to understand that when children are involved in any way,
intimacy and euphoria must be subordinate.

Our laws concerning sexual abuse are written to reflect this prem-
ise, of course. I tell my story and mention those laws to adults involved
in affairs with people who have children so as to help them gain separateness of a moral kind. "By having this affair," I suggest, "you are
harming children." Then, I ask, "Would you agree that it is immoral to
harm children?" If they agree, separateness from the sex and the affair
is necessary for the children's protection. Often, my counseling ends
before much of this gets acted upon, but in some cases I have seen the
object of the affair break it off to protect the children and/or become
friends with the children's other parent (usually in a situation in which
divorce does occur and the actor and object marry). At a visceral level,
this can work if the object (now the stepmother or stepfather) constantly works to prove to the survivor (the ex-wife or ex-husband) that
she or he is a good co-parent. The survivor is more likely to forgive

the affair if the new parent bends over backward to do right by the children and lets the survivor retain most maternal or paternal control.

This is messy work, and no therapist has the answer to promoting forgiveness on all fronts. What I add to the conversation is the concept of separateness. Whatever ways we can gain psychological detachment and separateness in response to these affairs, we will generally not regret. We will go through times of self-doubt, pain, anguish, hatred, self-hatred, depression, anxiety, and numbness and indifference; we may lack a moral standard for what we should do now, how we should act, and how we should love others, but if children are involved, the moral standard is obvious.

The Gift of Separateness

When affairs have created one of the major crises in a relationship, we must, at some point, "move on." One woman whose husband had had an affair talked in counseling about watching the TV series *The Good Wife* over and over again to help her move on. She spoke of Hillary Clinton and how heroic she felt Mrs. Clinton to be. This client found inspiration to live in a new present, not in the past, in order to rebuild trust. When her husband had another affair five years later, she felt devastated for a number of months, but she was also stronger. She said, "This time I left him, but I don't regret that we had five more years after that first time. He's got a flaw in his psyche, but my kids are almost grown, and I just need to get away from men now. I just need to find myself, stop blaming myself, realize he's not for me anymore. In a way, his new affair is the best thing that happened to me. I have a whole new life ahead of me without him. If I love again, it will be with someone monogamous. I finally know who I am and what I want."

This woman worked to integrate both her husband's previous affair and his new affair into her stages of love, crisis, relationship, and intimate separateness. She was ready to live, now, in significant separateness to build a new self. She told me that she was spending a lot of time in the woods at a retreat center. "Talk about a journey into 'separateness,'" she chuckled. "That's the journey I'm on. It's definitely the way I've found to deal with this. No more intimacy for a while, lots of separateness."

Knowing that I love poetry and literature, she brought me a piece of paper with words from a writer she had discovered, a writer I had never heard of, Etty Hillesum (1914–1943). She said I could keep this copy of the words, and she said it was her own sentiment right now, "what I'm working toward, this feeling of giving myself over to solitude, nature, and detachment."

> . . . near that flowing stream, I poured out all my tenderness, all the tenderness one cannot express for a man even when one loves him very, very much. . . . I poured it all out into the great, all-embracing spring night. I stood on the little bridge and looked across the water; I melted into the landscape and offered all my tenderness up to the sky and the stars and the water and to the little bridge. And that was the best moment of the day. I felt this was the only way of transforming all the many and deep and tender feelings one carries; to entrust them to nature, to let them stream out under the open spring sky and to realize that there is no other way of letting them go.

I was moved by this and so glad she gave it to me. I read it many ways, some of them obvious—about finding peace and intimacy in nature—and some of them specifically about sexuality. Sex is nature and nature is sex. Few things are more primal than sex and, thus, for our healthy living, few things need both more intimacy and *more psychological separateness* within our growing, evolving psyches than sexuality.

The Hillesum quotation also took me back to myself. In my own healing from post-traumatic sexual confusion, I remember spending a great deal of time in nature, exploring the spirituality of natural life. It is one of the reasons I became a student of biology, human nature, and the link between nature and spirituality. Given the power of nature in our lives—its mountain streams, misty pathways, and green meadows—any one of us who is suffering from sexual issues can find, in the natural world, what scientists now call "nature therapy." All of us can find some measure of deep separateness and healing among the birds and the flowers and the open sky. There, in nature, our feelings of betrayal and hurt can find euphoric connection in nature, and a detachment of ourselves from the rest of the world can occur—a detachment in which we gain the strength to become reimmersed later, in love, re-trusting of attachment with what is natural to us, the heart of love that beats seemingly at the center of all that is true and good.

Chapter 8

Busting Through the Myths of Marriage

LACK OF EMOTIONAL FULFILLMENT NEED NOT BE THE END OF A MARRIAGE

BOTH WOMEN AND MEN CAN BE LED ASTRAY BY GENDER STEREOTYPES

Thomas, thirty-nine, and Andrew, thirty-seven, had been married for eleven years, though the marriage did not become legal until the laws were changed in our state in 2011. Prior to their partnering in 2000, each had been in a relationship, but not one, as Thomas said, "that satisfied me to the core like my marriage to Andrew." When I asked Thomas why he had come to see me without Andrew, he said, "Andrew doesn't believe in counseling, but I do. I know our marriage needs help. We've developed a number of blocks to intimacy. I figured if I could get to know you, see that you understood gay men's relationships, I could convince Andrew you weren't his worst nightmare."

Thomas described a relationship in which both of them wanted more intimacy but didn't know how to achieve it. Even though I had only Thomas's point of view, I could see that he and his partner were locked in power struggle.

Among most gay and lesbian couples, the basic issues of intimacy and separateness are similar to those faced by heterosexual couples. Certain cultural aspects of the relationship are different, and certain traumas have been experienced uniquely by LGBT individuals and couples, but problems of intimate separateness are universal. As Thomas talked further, I learned that Andrew wanted more time together, more daily and hourly connection, and he blamed Thomas for being a workaholic. But Thomas wanted more "comfort and stability, less drama. . . . Andrew overreacts to everything!" Thomas reported. "He's constantly talking about everything that is wrong, how badly I'm doing at loving him, and how badly he's doing. He'll admit he's wrong, he'll blame himself—it's not like he just blames me—but he also won't shut up about it all. We just end up fighting or withdrawing to our own corners. We haven't had sex in six months. We're hardly friends anymore."

Fortunately, after three sessions with Thomas alone, Andrew agreed to come in. As I worked with this couple, I discovered patterns in their intimacy-separateness history involving mother-son and father-son relationships that had caused trauma in each man, as well as developmental trauma they experienced as gay boys and young men (each of them had been significantly abused in public for their sexual orientation in respective places of origin, urban Georgia and rural Florida). The two men were now locked in enmeshment/abandonment cycles that kept them in the Stage 3 Power Struggle.

A primary way this power struggle manifested was that Andrew "monologued" rather than "dialogued." This is a situation in which one of the partners in a marriage does nearly all the talking. It is dangerous to both healthy intimacy and healthy separateness; it throws off the rhythm of a healthy, collaborative relationship. For many couples, especially if a partner is more naturally verbal and/or extroverted than the other, it is quite normal for him or her to talk more. But when the verbalization becomes a monologue (one that involves many minutes or more of talking without engaging the interlocutor in questions or conversation), there is often evidence of a personality disorder in the person and/or a deep issue with the person's ability to be both intimate and separate.

In Andrew's case, I realized gradually that I was working with a monologuer who used words as defense mechanisms. While he professed to wanting more love and attention, he was scared of it. By monologuing, he could maintain distance from intimacy and control his partner's affection (it also turned out that most of his friends complained, as did Thomas, about his "never shutting up"). When I asked Andrew about his previous relationships, he talked about a partner, Harry, who was "nothing like Thomas. Harry paid attention to me, loved to listen to me, not Thomas." Thomas had known Harry socially, and he concurred with his partner's assessment: "Harry was and still is the best listener in the world." Andrew had felt rewarded more constantly by Harry's passive personality; Harry was a mild receptacle of Andrew's words, and nodded and smiled, making Andrew feel good. In Thomas, however, he had a very different partner, one whose more interactive (less passive) personality caused significant anxiety in Andrew. Yet, Andrew loved Thomas and had married Thomas for the person Thomas was. This couple had been together for a long time.

For this relationship to survive, I felt that Andrew needed help to discover that Thomas's personality might be a better fit for Andrew than someone who just passively and constantly let him monologue. As counseling continued, we worked together to dig into what he liked about Thomas and the intimacy Thomas was actually able to provide—intimacy that was different from Harry's. Unfortunately, however, counseling was not successful in prolonging this marriage. Within a year, the marriage ended and the couple went their own ways. It was Thomas who asked for the divorce. Andrew left counseling before Thomas, saying, "I don't think I want to change. I don't think I should have to." Thomas called him a "narcissist," and that was that.

In my last visit with Thomas, Thomas said to me, "I learned a lot, and Andrew did, too, but I think we were just too far gone. I wish we had seen the signs of trouble about five years before. But we'll both be okay, we'll move on." When I saw Thomas recently, he seemed happily placed in a new relationship, yet he had feelings for Andrew that he felt he would never have for anyone else. When times with Andrew had been good, he had felt a wonder of intimacy unique to their love.

Seeing the Signs of Trouble Early

One of the greatest difficulties a marriage counselor encounters is the sense of being "too late." A couple comes into therapy after the relationship is too far down the road. The couple has seen the signs of trouble too late (or has admitted them too late) to save the marriage. To help you or someone you love to avoid being too late, I've created this Essential Questions Survey, which has two parts.

Essential Questions Survey 10, Is Our Relationship in Trouble? Part I: Early Stages

This part of the survey explores marital resilience for couples without children and/or who have been married (basically cohabiting) for fewer than seven years.

1. Does your partner or do you say, "I'm not into getting married?" Yes ___. No ___. If your partner says this and it's okay with you, then no harm done. But if one person says this, and it feels like a knife wound to the other, the relationship may need immediate help.

2. Does one partner say, "I don't want children" or, on the other hand, "I want children very soon"? Disagreement on whether and when to have children can be primal drivers of marital and relationship difficulty if the disagreement goes on for quite a while.

3. Is one of you constantly angry and/or anxious, and/or depressed? If so, your relationship or marriage can be in significant distress.

4. Are you having too little sex for one or both of you to feel satisfied and/or having sex that is not mutually satisfying? If so, your relationship could be suffering stressors that the sexual difficulty is masking. As soon as possible, sexuality may need to be discussed and resolved either between the two of you or with a sex therapist or other therapist.

5. Are one or both of you thinking about or keeping "on the hook" one or more other potential lovers? If so, that partner may not be as fully committed to this primary love relationship as needed for it to survive and thrive.

6. Are one or both of your sets of parents divorced? Studies show that children whose parents have divorced are more likely to choose the divorce option in their own love relationships. If you sense difficulties in your relationship and come from a history of divorce, this history will hopefully inspire you to get help a bit more quickly than you might have otherwise.

7. Are one or both of you choosing work or another task over the relationship? This is a matter of balance. If you are both working very hard away from the relationship but you make sure to have date nights, phone-talk time, sexual time, and nice ritual times together, you may be living with a good balance of work and love; but if one or both of you constantly cancels date nights, and you don't make up that lost relationship time in some other way, your relationship could be headed for termination. Especially in the first seven years of a relationship (and especially before children are born), constant relational interaction (frequent physical, sexual, and emotional intimacy) is essential.

Essential Questions Survey 10,
Is Our Relationship in Trouble?
Part II: Later Stages

This part of the survey explores marital resilience for couples married with children and/or married or together for more than seven years.

1. Do we both say (or do one or both of us feel) that "We no longer love each other"? If even one person believes one or both of you no longer love the other, marital help will be needed immediately.

2. Do we both (or does one of us) feel that "We've grown apart"? If even one of the partners feels the two of you have grown apart or "are on different tracks now," or "don't see eye to eye anymore," the relationship could be in serious trouble.

3. Are one or both of you constantly angry, anxious, or depressed? If so, and especially if the irritability, anxiety, and/or depression has lasted for more than two months, the individual clinical condition may need assistance right away; relationship repair may also be immediately needed. The relationship may have been in crisis and stress mode for some time.

4. Has one or more major crisis attacked your relationship in ways that have pulled you apart? If the breadwinning partner has lost a job, a partner cannot have children, a child has died, or major stresses are attacking the marriage from many quarters, ending the relationship can come to seem like a natural way of relieving the individual's stress. Counseling can help bring everything into perspective so that the marriage is not "blamed" for the marital stress.

5. Are you having sex as much as both of you wish to and in ways relatively satisfying to you both? If there are significant issues in a sex life and the relationship is in Stages 1 through 6 of love, the chances of marriage failure are higher than if your sex lives have dissipated or become misaligned in the second six stages (Stages 7–12). Especially if you are fifty or younger, significant distress in sex life can be a harbinger of marital failure.

6. Do you practice intimacy rituals with mutual enjoyment? Date nights, phone talks during the day or week if traveling, times every day to talk about the kids, asking one another questions about feelings and thoughts, resolving conflicts in healthy ways—if these things are not happening in your marriage, the marriage may need immediate assistance.

7. Are you enjoying separate interests as well as common interests, and separate friends as well as common friends? Intimacy between two people generally does not survive if it is not balanced by intimacy with other people, other interests, other areas of focus.

In both of these surveys, if you are experiencing only one out of seven signs of distress, your marriage is probably not significantly damaged. The marriage or relationship could be going through a transition phase, as could one of you be going through a particularly stressful time. If you see three out of seven signs of distress, you may have significant cause for concern. And if you see four or more signs of distress, you will most likely need to study and assist your marriage immediately.

A Balanced Approach to the Signs of Trouble

For at least two years, Thomas and Andrew had experienced at least four of the seven signs of trouble in their marriage. And they had let the problems slide for too long. If they had reacted to the signs earlier, they may have been able to discover the balance between "merging" (romance, closeness) and "separating" (self-identity, mutual respect)— a balance that proves to partners, every day, that love is strong enough to survive and thrive through all adversity.

When lovers feel this balance, they experience something akin to twin electrical currents running through the relationship. They will probably call one of those electrical currents something like "still being in love" or "being even more in love with him or her now than ever before." And they will refer to the other electrical current as "love sure is hard work," and "sometimes I just want to quit it." It is normal for a marriage to exist somewhere between feelings of romance and—yes— suffering.

Keeping Romance Alive

Take a moment to feel inspired by the romantic part of your relation-ship. Remember how you met your lover, what you felt, what she or he felt. Recall the early attachment, the merging of your selves into one self. "Lovers sense in each other that which always exists . . . as they embrace, they promise each other eternity," wrote the romantic poet Rainer Maria Rilke in his second of the *Duino Elegies*. You and your partner felt this eternity and made its promise to one another through your laughter, touching, eye gazing, sharing, sexual immersion in one another, and talks about the future as if your love would last forever. Remember all of that. Journal about it. Bring it to the surface.

"When I see your face, there's not a thing I would change, cause just the way you are, you're so amazing," pop icon Bruno Mars sings in "Just the Way You Are." This was part of the grace of romance—that it felt like each of you was utterly nonjudgmental early on. In fact, judgment would have been blasphemy; who the other person was—his or her identity—was everything needed during early romance. The poet Rumi says, "I don't care about marvelous sights. I only want to be in your presence." Feel what that was like. Bring it forward in your journal, thoughts, meditations, prayers. For love to remain balanced, for intimate separateness to last, romance needs to keep existing in your relationship.

"When I got off the plane in LAX," a friend recalls, "and saw him standing there, I fell immediately in love with him. There was something about his shyness that touched my soul."

Another friend said, "Grace and I knew each other in high school and didn't like each other at first, but then one day we were at a football game because some friends dragged us there, and we got seated next to each other and kind of made fun of the game together, and that's when it happened: we just kind of fell in love right then. And we both like football now, too. Life is very strange. I think Grace likes it more than I do now."

Remember your own first moments together, remember the moment you knew you fell in love. Journal about it. Talk about it.

A client recalled, "We were at a rally on Martin Luther King Day, and I was manning the Gay and Lesbian Activists Alliance table when she came up to me and asked if I was going to march to the courthouse. Before you know it, we were marching together, chatting, spending the day together, and I remember our elbows touched and I felt something. Laura's been my partner for thirteen years now, and it began that day when we first touched elbows on the street."

Everyone who has fallen in love—absolutely everyone—has implanted a memory of the first time their two psyches, bodies, and souls merged. We need to keep looking back at those memories to keep romance alive. At social gatherings, when people ask us about "how we met," they are instinctively helping us keep romance alive. We must always remember the imprinted memories of falling in love; this experience of "falling" into a complete merging of self with self is so universal—and necessary—to the pro-social human psyche and its stable pair-bonds that millions of songs are written about it. We each have our own song.

Increasing Marital Intelligence:
Keeping the Other Half Alive

But to just have romance is not to have love. The cult of romance in America is mythic—and it is also a cult of despair. As mentioned earlier, the other electrical current running through real love is not euphoric romance but, rather, actual suffering. For two merged souls to learn how to exist *equally well and in close proximity,* they must survive the external sufferings (in life, work, child-raising, etc.), as well as the "suffering" of having to detach from early attachment, to separate and exist as detached, independent, separate selves in partnership. Deep intimacy is short lived if two merged bodies and souls can't thrive together through stress. Kahlil Gibran wrote in *The Prophet* that pain is the "breaking of the shell that encloses your understanding." Without the pain of loving, we would not understand enough about ourselves or others to grow as lovers. Putting this another way, poet Naomi Shihab Nye says, "Before you know kindness as the deepest thing inside you, you must know sorrow as the other deepest thing."

Early romance and merging created a vessel for an immense kindness in both lovers, a kindness they didn't know was inside each of them until they came together as soul mates. But that immense kindness is incomplete and cannot last (in fact, it can turn to hate or indifference quickly) if the lovers do not see beyond the myth of romance and accomplish the safe pulling apart that, although it feels like suffering, will turn into mature kindness. Thus, real love is anchored on the foundation of romance's chemistry and merging (oneness), but the house's walls and roof are constructed by how smartly we suffer together as a couple over a lifetime. As Marcel Proust wrote, "We are healed of our suffering only by experiencing it in full."

Andrew wanted to be healed of his life's sufferings by defending against them in monologues. Being with Thomas challenged him to experience his suffering in full, but he could not do it. Thomas, for his part, decided to move away from love for a while, and he suffered and he grew. Doris Lessing wisely suggested, "Learn to trust your own judgment, learn inner independence, learn to trust that time will sort good from bad—including your own bad." Trust happens in stages; we learn how to love ever more deeply with each experience, by negotiating as two independent beings for an equal place in a cycle of love that we can trust, not because we've mastered its mythologies of romance but because others who are further along in the stages of love have mastered it. We can observe and model these people.

Intimate separateness, the balance of romance and suffering, of merging and independence, is humbling. If you are not utterly humble right now in your relationship, get help to become so. When we are intimate with one another in the first stages of love, especially during our romantic time, we are not yet fully aware of our humbling limitations in the big world—limitations that will need a map for sorting through. Gradually, though, it is essential we realize we are being humbled by love. Gradually, we come to look less toward horizons and more to inward depths.

"The true value of a human being," Albert Einstein said, "is determined primarily by the measure and the sense in which he has attained liberation from the self." As he grew older he became more aware of the Eastern concept of detachment and saw it as crucial to human growth and love. And the poet Rilke found it in this phrasing: "Is it not time to free ourselves from the beloved even as, trembling, we endure the loving?" As we separate from the myths of romance ("free ourselves from the beloved"), we gain a deep freedom to be who we are in the presence of our lover and we gain support of our lover's own journey of freedom, liberation, and intimate detached self; all the while, we are trembling with intimacy.

As we move toward the end of this book, take some time to celebrate your relationship's twin tracks of merging and separating, of enmeshing and disentangling, of embracing joyfully and of freeing yourself from one another with equal passion. Track how the sufferings in your relationship—the crises, the battles, the struggles, and the make-up sex—forge new agreements and new experiments in love; and how equalizing your separate domains yields interpersonal respect, so that you live the real journey of love that human beings have been mastering for millennia.

Removing Two Dangerous Myths
from Millennial Relationships

To fully protect love in our marriages, we may need help from our society and its social practices and theories in ways most of us have not yet fully realized. There are two myths of marriage that often destroy the ability of couples to sustain long-lasting love, enjoy both joy and suffering, and balance intimacy and separateness. I do not believe we can move forward as a culture into a future that is protective of safe, long-lasting marriage unless couples grapple with these two myths and make conscious choices about them. One of the myths embodies the "romance" undercurrent of love as we have just described it, and the other captures the "suffering" undercurrent. Myths are popular beliefs or legends that we might want to believe, but they are not necessarily true. These myths can influence us as couples far more than we realize, and so we must separate ourselves from them. In fact, the people I've featured in this book have all grappled with these myths:

- Lack of emotional fulfillment is a good reason to get a divorce. Put another way, divorcing because one or both people feel a lack of emotional closeness (feel that they have "fallen out of love with one another") is an advance in human freedom.

- As a residue of patriarchal oppression of women and repression of men's emotions, males create the majority of marriage and family problems in America.

Myth 1: Emotional Fulfillment and Divorce

Divorce is an option for every couple, and it's often necessary to free the body, heart, and soul from a painful situation. That said, divorce's prevalence in the new millennium, especially in the United States, affects attachment security in profound ways. It does so, as we noted in the book's Introduction, in approximately one out of every two marriages, often occurring at between four and seven years of marriage. Meanwhile, divorce is also increasing in couples who have been married for ten or more years. In 1990, fewer than one in ten people over fifty got a divorce. By 2009, the number was one in four. University of Washington marriage researcher Pepper Schwartz, pondering this new elder-divorce phenomenon, recently answered the question, "Why are so many more people in their sixties divorcing?" with the observation, "We live so much longer now. Half a century ago, an unhappy couple in their mid-sixties might have stayed together because they thought it wasn't worth divorcing if they had only a few years left to live. Now, sixty-five-year-olds can easily envision at least twenty more active years—and they don't want them to be loveless, or full of frustration or disappointment." It is difficult to argue with this logic.

I will not do so. Rather, I will make a different point. "Loveless," "frustration," and "disappointment" with love are feelings and terms that fall under the category of "lack of emotional fulfillment." While some couples at any age divorce because of abuse in the marriage, addiction, or other dangers, most people divorce because one or both are not experiencing *emotional fulfillment*. This term and condition needs our focus and understanding.

In our American (and, overall, Western) model of contemporary marriage, "emotional fulfillment" has become paramount. If one person feels its lack for a long time, that person asks for or unilaterally pursues a divorce. Unfulfilled and emotionally dissatisfied, feeling constantly rejected and abandoned or enmeshed and impinged, one or both partners seek freedom. Especially for the first few months, and even a year after the divorce, the sense of joy and freedom is paramount for most people who divorce. The cruelty of a court or custody proceeding can darken that joy, but for a while, at least one of the couple tends to feel significant liberation.

Does it last? Studies have recently shown that the majority of divorced individuals are no happier one year after their divorce. This is especially true of individuals who have children; it's less true of elders whose children are grown, and it's even less true of couples who have not had children. These statistics have stimulated me to place into various categories people who look toward divorce for emotional fulfillment. As a counselor, I immediately look at these questions:

1. Does the couple have children?
2. Are the children grown (at least late adolescent)?

Every reason for divorce has validity, and every divorce can be a sacred occurrence in the lifetime of a marriage. That is a given. At the same time, over the last five or so decades, we have put heavy pressure on individuals in marriages to make sure those marriages possess *emotional fulfillment of both parties*. We constantly—both unconsciously and consciously—measure our marriage's success by whether we are feeling emotionally fulfilled by that marriage and/or (most likely) by the other person. American couples especially seem to see emotional fulfillment as the bedrock of attachment security. I want to challenge this bedrock assumption with you, especially if you have children in your home.

THE WISDOM OF SEPARATENESS

I believe the whole idea of talking about feelings may be overrated to begin with for both males and females. A number of fascinating research findings call into question the long-held assumption that it's unhealthy to keep your feelings to yourself. . . . For instance, in Tel Aviv, researchers studied people who had had heart attacks to track the long-term outcomes for those who minimized or denied the traumatic effect of this medical event. They found that those who tended to think about, worry about, and talk about their heart attacks had a poorer outcome than those who chose to ignore or deny. Only 7 percent of the more stoic group developed posttraumatic stress disorder seven months after the heart attack, com-

pared with 19 percent of the more reactive group. Other studies of different traumatic events have had similar outcomes. Research finds like these suggest that in some cases repression and avoidance are healthy coping tactics—and that overly processing negative events can actually increase emotional stress in many people.
—Scott Haltzman, MD, author of *The Secrets of Happily Married Men* and *The Secrets of Happily Married Women*

Intimacy and the Deceptive Muse

I want to argue for a moment, from an evolutionary standpoint, that emotional fulfillment is not the top priority of a loving marriage that has children in the home. In looking at this with you, I am assuming that we are not talking now about marriages that are dangerous—that is, not the 10 percent or so of marriages in which survival requires leaving the partner.

As I study marriage over my lifetime, I believe that we have unconsciously and systematically made "romantic feelings of intimacy and emotional satisfaction" the dominating standard for marital success. We feel that, if we go more than a few months not feeling fully emotionally fulfilled, our marriage is in trouble. In believing this, we doom millions of marriages because "constant emotional satisfaction" is an impossible standard: it does not fit human nature. Marriages were never set up in human evolution to be constantly emotionally fulfilling, nor for the experience of emotional fulfillment to be the top priority of human love.

It is from this context that I introduce the term "deceptive muse." The cult of romance—and its later manifestation inside a marriage ("I need to be constantly emotionally fulfilled by my partner!")—is a muse for much poetry and is also source of a great deal of joy—but it is deceptive, too, for lifelong intimacy because it promises something appropriate for early attachment that is not necessarily appropriate for later attachment. As a marriage and family counselor, I make sure to express my bias about this deceptive muse to new couple clients in the first session if they have children. I say, "Because you have children in the home, my job will be to try to help you stay married. Science-based and evidence-based research over the last two decades indicates to me that, for couples with children, lack of emotional fulfillment is not enough reason to risk the substantial trauma of divorce (and its years of aftermath) in children's and adults' lives."

Sometimes the couple leaves my office right then; but most of the time, they stay. Sometimes one or both partners will say, "But I heard in the press somewhere that, actually, divorce is not bad for kids—it's good for a lot of kids, in fact." This leads to a good dialogue about all the research, some of which does show that for some children of constantly fighting parents, divorce can be helpful longitudinally (in the long term). Simultaneously, I remind these clients that the vast majority of longitudinal research shows the difficulties children face when they are raised outside of marriage and/or after a divorce: more sexual, physical, and emotional abuse during the remainder of childhood; more adjustment and attachment issues later; lower self-esteem and self-confidence; marital difficulties later in life.

One of the primary drivers of difficulty for children of divorce was recently expressed by the psychiatrist Ned Holstein, who is the director of the National Parents Organization. His organization studies how children fare after divorce, and their research confirms that a primary reason many children suffer after divorce is that, in the vast majority of cases, the divorces involve alienation of the child or children from one parent. This causes significant psychological and neurological trauma. That is, either Mom or Dad is tossed, to a great extent, out of the child's life, and that trauma becomes life defining.

Many couples I have counseled have seen the distress that their children's friends (whose parents have separated, are currently divorcing, or are divorced) are under; they've seen the greater chance of failure at school, social isolation, depression, panic attacks, anorexia/bulimia, violence, self-cutting, and victimization of nearly every kind. Ultimately, the point I make with them is not that divorce is bad or wrong. In fact, I am very frank with clients that if they decide to divorce, I will help them all the way. My point is that "lack of emotional fulfillment" is not enough reason to break apart a family unless it goes on for so many years that chronic depression has set in. And with appropriate help, it does not need to. As couples work together or separately in the intimate-separateness paradigm, a great deal of emotional fulfillment immediately begins to occur, expectations of marriage go through changes, expectations of one another change, new stages of life evolve in thrilling new ways, and frameworks for real marriage expand to include decades of stability. Part of what changes involves the deceptive muse—couples go through a shift in how they perceive emotional satisfaction.

Somewhat like a broken record (and some of my clients have teased me about my constant use of this example and research), I talk to clients about the arranged marriages I observed in two of the countries in which I have lived and worked, India and Turkey. As we discuss this "other way" of doing marriage—a way practiced by much of the world's population—we observe that two people *who did not even fall in love at all in the beginning of their partnership* (i.e., had no romantic attachment in the beginning), have stayed married for life by practicing intimate separateness. They live and love intimately, and they live and love in psychological separateness, balancing both their attachment and their detachment, while expressly avoiding the traumas of enmeshment/abandonment whenever possible—and specifically avoiding the deceptive muse.

The couple I mentioned in Chapter 6, Sevda and Tarik, had an arranged marriage. Though they looked toward the ideas and imagery of the Western world for much of their personal fulfillment (both having been educated in the West), they enjoyed a context for marriage in which something more severe than temporary emotional unhappiness would be needed to break them apart. They love the West, but they have not bought into the Western idea of emotional fulfillment as the dominant marker in a marriage.

I hope you will ponder this in regard to your marriage, with your counselor, and in your community discussions. If you are feeling a lack of emotional fulfillment in your marriage right now, I hope you will know that it is something you can gain distance from and ponder aloud in your present stage of life. If you still feel in your heart even a small spark of love for your partner, and if your partner has even a small spark remaining for you, and if you are feeling a lack of emotional fulfillment, you may be locked in only Stage 3 of your relationship. There is much more joy awaiting both of you.

A Case Study

Jagdish, 37, had slept with another woman during his wife's two pregnancies (I met him when she was six months pregnant with their second child). He was highly dependent on sexual intimacy for experiencing emotional intimacy. His wife withheld this as she went inward during her pregnancy, and he became anxious and depressed. He self-medicated his depression by seeking sex outside his marriage. On the day he introduced himself to me, he was in significant distress, feeling guilty and ashamed, and yet he realized he needed more emotionality and sexuality from his pregnant wife than she could give him during this time.

My immediate work with Jagdish involved helping him desist from the sexual (thus emotional) contact outside his marriage. Because his wife "goes away when she gets pregnant" (his words), and because she was not interested in therapy, but was significantly angry with him, I became an emotional mentor to the man, as did the men in the men's group he joined. As I and the group worked with him on a number of his issues, I helped him understand the link between sexual fulfillment and emotional fulfillment. We looked at the causes of that link in nature (striving to understand what might be happening in the centers of his brain that release the reward chemical dopamine), nurture (his father was nonmonogamous and a "womanizer," in Jagdish's words), and culture (the south Indian village-to-city culture he was raised in back home, in which there was inherent chauvinism around women and sexuality).

Those understandings elicited conversations regarding his "lack of emotional fulfillment" in his marriage. As we talked, he said he loved his wife and felt that she was "very strong" and he was "weak" for doing what he was doing. Using his language of "strong" and "weak," I helped him delve into a frame for his psyche that could transcend his present behavior. Here is some of our dialogue.

Me: Being strong and not being weak are important to you and to every man, right?

Jagdish: Yeah.

Me: You use these words "strong" and "weak" a lot.

Jagdish: Uh, huh.

Me: Do I get it—that you feel weak when you feel like Hillary isn't sexually and emotionally connected to you, and you go try to get sex elsewhere to feel emotionally stronger?

Jagdish: I guess so. I feel like I'm falling apart, I guess. I get kind of depressed, I think. Sex makes me feel better.

Me (filling in blanks for him, as he was a very difficult client to work with verbally): You get the butterflies in your stomach and your heart beats faster. You get nervous.

Jagdish: Yeah.

Me: And your pattern is that you go call a female friend or prostitute and set up sex with her?

Jagdish: Yeah.

Me: So, do you see the link between emotional fulfillment and sexual fulfillment for you? Do you see how they're connected?

Jagdish: I do. Yeah. I'm weak. At least in this area I'm really weak.

Me: So, what will you do to stay emotionally stronger? What change will you make?

Jagdish: I've decided I'll, um, you know . . . jerk off more instead of calling someone.

Me: When you have this feeling of nervousness in your stomach, you'll masturbate?

Jagdish: Yeah.

Me: When you feel emotionally unfulfilled and abandoned by Hillary, you'll masturbate?

Jagdish: Yes.

Me: Will you ask Hillary to help you?

Jagdish: Should I do that? I want to. It is embarrassing to me . . . culturally and otherwise . . . but I want to. I want to have that intimacy with her.

Me: Will you ask her? Do you think you should?

Jagdish: Yes. I do.

Me: You'll ask her to have sex with you through helping you masturbate? Being emotionally intimate that way?

Jagdish: Yeah. Is that good?

Me: What do you think? (A long silence.)

Jagdish: I wish I was so strong I didn't even need sex, but yeah, I think that's good. I want to do that. I love her. I love her. I don't want to hurt her.

I had referred Jagdish to a psychologist who could determine whether he had a sex addiction, since I am not qualified to diagnose that. The diagnosis for sex addiction had come back negative, so I suggested that, as he worked on various other ways to be emotionally intimate, he add this one—to connect with Hillary through masturbation. This was a compromise—it united his internal connection between sexual gratification and emotional fulfillment with the hope that he could connect with Hillary through mutual masturbation rather than stepping out of his marriage for oral sex or coitus. Hillary's post-pregnancy health problems appeared to require at least another year of lack of intercourse, and she was not inclined at this point to consider oral sex as an option. (Mainly because of her anger toward Jagdish, she wanted to remain as separate from him as possible.) But there was still a spark in both these people, and some alternative innovation was required to help them. In the end, Jagdish did ask Hillary to help him masturbate. To do that, he had to see through some of his own associations of sex and emotions with "strong" and "weak."

This client's (and this couple's) case was multilayered and did not resolve without significant stress. They separated, lived apart, then reconciled when the children were four and five years old. In our work together, I was constantly saying to this man, "Emotional fulfillment, even of the sexual kind, is just not as important as character, protecting your children's mother, being strong. It is not enough reason to destroy your marriage. You must find other options, even if they involve no coitus." All in all, I was working with him to find a middle ground, even in sexuality, between intimacy and separateness.

If Not for Emotional Fulfillment, Why Are We Married?

As I work with clients on exposing the emotional-fulfillment myth, one or both people quite logically ask, "Okay, so if you're saying emotional fulfillment should not be the primary reason for being married, what is?" I have a responsive list in mind but I withhold it until the client makes a list reflecting his or her own thoughts, ideas, values, and instincts. I ask the individual to bring that list back the next week. Jagdish chose not to make this list—he found journaling didn't work for him, and he resisted homework—but many clients have created lists. Here are a few responses from lists over the last fifteen years that answer this question: "What are the primary reasons for being married, besides emotional fulfillment?"

- Take care of our kids, keep them safe, that's why we're married, I guess. I hate to admit it. I don't want to let Mark off the hook for not opening up to me emotionally, but yes, right now, our kids have to be our primary focus.

- Make sure our kids are happy even if we're not happy. I worry that if we stay together just for the kids, they'll be even more traumatized, but when I take my own need for emotional fulfillment out of it, like you suggest, I think it's true that the kids will be happier if we stay together.

- Pool our economic resources so we can build a nest egg for the future. Our kids are grown and we could divorce without the hassle of custody, but if we do divorce, it's going to be a financial nightmare. We have to weigh emotions on one hand and economics on the other. We might need to just live separately now, but stay legally married.

- Make sacrifices for each other, even when it hurts or feels bad. My kids are seven, nine, and eleven. My husband has had an affair and we're trying to patch things up. I feel like I've made every possible sacrifice and now just want to be happy, but there's always another sacrifice to be made, I guess.

- Be safe with someone who has enough shared values to bond us together. Bob is not very emotional. He's not even very sexual. He's just not very intimate. But he's a good man. I sometimes forget how much that matters. He has good character. He's safe and we have raised good kids together. There are worse things than a passionless man.

- Whenever I feel that Anna is too cold and unforgiving, I have to remember that God's plan put me with her for a reason. I have to keep remembering that. I have to figure out why God put us together.

- Love our children so much I'll sacrifice nearly anything for their safety and health, even my happiness. I don't think what Gurian is saying is going to sway me; I think I have to get a divorce, but I'm thinking about it a little longer again. The point he's making is that I have to make every sacrifice possible for my kids *before* I make a final decision. That word "sacrifice" is something I forgot until now.

- Learning to assert myself better than I do. It takes time, I guess. My problem is that I am too accommodating. I do everything for everyone else—Pete, the kids, my folks, my friends, everyone—but then I hate myself, I hate everyone,

I hate him. I'm in this unhappy marriage for a reason, and I
have to figure that reason out.

- Learning to accommodate someone better than I do. Being
  married gives me a chance to work on myself even if I'm
  unhappy sometimes. I'm too emotionally closed down and
  selfish. I work hard and I'm good at the traditional stuff, but
  I just can't listen to Gwen all the time. She drives me crazy.
  It's mean of me. I know it is. I hope I can change.

- Have companionship. I get so into my own feelings and
  emotions and dramas I sometimes forget real life. If my
  marriage is going to be a friendship, I have to expect a few
  years now and then of crap and bad stuff and pain. There's
  no law in the world that says I have to be happy all the
  time.

- Enjoy the good parts, like the sex and the family time
  together. He's good at sex, I'll give him that. He keeps me
  coming back for more of that. And he's good with the kids.
  He's a good father. That's important. Can I put up with how
  often he criticizes me, though? I don't know. I just don't
  know.

- Focus on making the family work and making the house
  a home and just live with how distracted she is. When we
  got married, she made all sorts of promises. Now, all she
  does is work. I'm the stay-at-home dad, something I never
  thought I'd be, and she's the alpha dog, and I try to be okay
  with it, but when she makes me feel like I'm worth nothing
  compared to her, I just want to end the marriage right then.
  At least the kids need me, though. That's good.

- I've lived for ten years with a cold man, and I just can't do
  it anymore. If he doesn't change within one year, I'm done.

I'll take the kids and I'll try to be nice about it, but there's no reason I should put off my happiness for a guy who has to have everything so neat (I'm a born slob and love it), a guy who settles (I don't want to settle). All this stuff is "emotional fulfillment" stuff and I get that, so I will give it one more year, but that's it. That's final.

Each list and each conversation about emotional fulfillment is different, yet there are some patterns to the conversations, the lists, the journaling, and the thinking processes of clients on this subject. The patterns that seem most hidden at first, and that bring great help during the process of marital repair (and/or slower movement toward divorce), often involve making a comparison between "attachment security" as a top priority and "emotional fulfillment" as a top priority. In that context, there is often a need to deepen the couple's conversation around not just intimacy but also separateness. Here's an example.

A Solution to Attachment
Insecurity: Live Separately

A client's parents were sick of one another. The mother, in her seventies, had become ill with an undetermined nerve problem that made her bedridden. When she got psychiatric help, her doctor said, "You are overwhelmed by depression. We need to help you deal with your marriage, or you may have to be hospitalized not just for this nerve problem but also for mental problems." Her husband, seeing her unhappiness, moved out of the house and into an apartment. The couple had been married forty-eight years but, in his wife's words, "We've never really been intimate." She wanted that intimacy, she said. She wouldn't settle, she said. Divorce was needed. But when the couple consulted lawyers, they discovered that they would both take severe financial hits if they divorced.

And something else happened, too.

Once they lived separately, they got along better. She was treated for depression, and her mental condition improved considerably.

Gradually, the nerve issue disappeared. In counseling, she verbal-ized a surprise: over the last year of living apart, she realized that at seventy-eight she did not want a new intimate partnership. She wanted solitude, her girlfriends, her children and grandchildren, and, once a week or so, a dinner out with her husband of five decades. Not more intimacy, but more separateness brought gifts of becoming at peace with her own identity, emotional and mental improvement, and *attachment security* with her husband. She stayed married to her husband, they found more happiness than they had before, and now, many years later, the husband has passed away, and she continues to live independently at eighty-four.

Self, identity, and mental and physical health were all at stake here, and attachment security had declined so significantly that divorce seemed necessary. Yet, because this woman was of a generation that was not primed to immediately divorce for lack of emotional fulfill-ment, she took the long view and ended up glad she had not divorced. Via increased separateness—living apart—she avoided familial, per-sonal, legal, and economic complications of divorce. Later, as she helped her husband die—he battled cancer for two years—she felt a new kind of emotional fulfillment that completed her journey with the man she had lived with most of her life. The long view of marriage helped this woman to feel a deep emotional satisfaction about her life she could not have found without becoming separate (psychologically, emotionally, physically) from her noncommunicative husband.

If you are contemplating divorce for reasons of lack of emotional fulfillment, I hope you will use this book as a guide to making a *separ-ateness challenge* for yourself: get help in setting up a situation whereby you and your partner will become separate (to a much greater extent than you are now) for at least one year. If economics require you to live in the same house, set up separate bedrooms and live relatively apart. If economics allow you to live in separate domiciles, take advantage of that opportunity.

Throughout this process, get help from counselors and mentors to navigate the separation toward its most necessary end for your fam-ily; that end may well be divorce, but give yourself at least a year (and more if needed) to get counseling that helps you move beyond "lack of emotional fulfillment" or "falling out of love" as the cause of the divorce. Try to discover a deeper, more pressing cause for a divorce. If you do not immediately see a deeper cause than "We are not emotionally fulfilling one another," I can promise you that enmeshment/abandonment cycles, dangerous merging, and other issues described in this book will lie hidden inside your next relationship. Those issues will most likely need to be dealt with in therapy and in your life if you don't deal with them now.

Obviously, if you find that there is a dangerous cause of marital distress—an addiction that is not curable, anger or aggression that cannot be managed differently, infidelity that cannot be regulated—your divorce will still feel less regretful to you years later because you will be divorcing after having studied issues that go beyond emotional fulfillment. On the other hand, if you find, after a few months or years of separateness, that there really are no reasons to divorce beyond lack of emotional fulfillment and the enmeshment/abandonment cycle implicit in it, you may well find your way back to one another, renew your wedding vows or ritualize your new marriage in some other way, and discover a path to emotional fulfillment out of the separation that you could not see before.

Elizabeth Bernstein, a *Wall Street Journal* reporter, tells a story of this latter occurrence. Lise and Emil Stoessel, of Charlottesville, Virginia, found themselves emotionally unfulfilled after their kids had grown. They had grown apart after nearly thirty years of marriage. Lise told her husband, "I am not fun, you are not fun. We are in each other's way." The marriage seemed over. But as the couple talked and looked at all the consequences of divorce, Lise realized the separation option. Emil was a contractor and had an attachment to the house as a place he was constantly fixing up and improving, and Lise wanted something smaller, less work. The couple had the economic ability to get a separate domicile for Lise, and she moved into that place with a sense of new adventure.

Emil expressed the practical (and, thus, emotional) satisfactions of this arrangement immediately. "I . . . have my house to myself and (don't) have to worry about making it look a certain way or what she would like or wouldn't like. I can expand, unfold, feel free." Lise echoed this new freedom.

The couple has been happily married another six years, as of 2014. Bernstein reports, "They have dinner at her house on Monday and Tuesday, spend Wednesday evening alone, and sleep over at one or the other home Thursday through Sunday. They also go for regular long walks and have date nights out at restaurants." The couple told Bernstein that the separation arrangement saved their marriage. "We don't try to impose anything on each other; we live without all the baggage," Emil said. "Our time together is much more intentional," Lise says, "And there's not the constant annoyance of being alone together."

The wonder of intimacy was rediscovered in this couple by the wonder of separateness.

• • •

Moving "lack of emotional fulfillment" down the priority list for divorce is not about disrespecting the unhappiness, pain, or sadness of being emotionally unfulfilled by a partner at any given time. It is more about standing back from the feelings to integrate them into a larger context for human love. If, after we stand back for one to three years (if we have children in the home), we still see a lifetime of unhappiness ahead of us, divorce will almost undoubtedly ensue—but at least we will have tried doing what, statistically, most married people in the world do who fall in love *after* they have been married a while: we will take a view of marriage in which we value emotional fulfillment somewhat, but don't raise it up as the single most important asset of a happy marriage. In order to keep emotional fulfillment a personal priority but not the heaviest pressure on our marriage, we will likely need to try physical or other kinds of separateness; and we will need to join groups of other women and men who can become emotional confidants and friends—fulfilling us emotionally so that our partner does not have to do more of that work than she or he can.

Myth 2: Gender Stereotypes and Power Issues

When my daughter Davita was twenty years old, she came back home from college for an Easter visit and reported women's rights discussions she had been having in her college classes and among her friends. In one discussion, one of her friends said, "I should be able to go to a frat house in the sexiest clothing I want to dress in, get drunk if I want, flirt, kiss, all that, but then if I decide not to have sex, I shouldn't have to have sex." Everyone in the room agreed with this, but then Davita asked, "Okay, but if sex occurs, don't you have some responsibility in that situation, too?"

Her friend said no.

Davita asked, "Really? Is all the responsibility on the guy to know what you're doing and what you do and don't want, even when you dress the way you dress, show off your boobs, get drunk, flirt with him, grind with him, and all that?"

Her friend said, "You mean, like, if I get raped, is it my fault? No way! Let the *guy* adapt to me. I get to be just who I am."

Davita pressed, "Yes, rape is rape. Of course. But what I'm talking about is, you're dressed in a way that says 'Fuck me,' so that's the signal you're sending, and you're in a frat house with a bunch of horny guys who invited you there to see if they could get laid, and you're drunk and pulling at his clothes. What's *your* responsibility in the relationship? I mean, you're part of the whole thing, too, right? Why is everything the guy's responsibility?"

Davita reported to me: "The whole room went ballistic. My friends talked about feminism and gender stereotypes and male dominance, and we got into a huge argument. The guys in the room didn't even get to say anything, and finally I just gave up and went and did my homework. There was no way these girls were gonna see that playing the victim card is so friggin' immature and stupid. And there was no way they could see that life's more complicated than 'men run everything.'"

As Davita and I discussed this, she reflected on the fact that she may have harmed her friendship with at least one of her female housemates. My heart went out to her, but I was also proud of my daughter for trying to study, with depth, a situation that most young women and men face at some point today: the complexity of hormones, booze, and intimacy in a high-risk, sometimes dangerous environment. While her friends didn't fully understand the point Davita was trying to make, her mother, Gail, who is a rape crisis counselor, and I appreciated it. We felt that her cognizance of what was really happening in the natural, visceral experience of male and female in the frat situation would help her in life.

Meanwhile, there was more here for Davita in all this than a discussion about rape. She had a steady boyfriend who did not fit the "female victimization at the hands of masculine stereotypes" kind of discussion. An International Studies major, she was studying oppression of females around the world; she saw a great deal of patriarchy and oppression of women worldwide, but she saw American women differently.

Over dinner one night, she said to her mother and me, "It's terrible what's going on in Africa and India and Saudi Arabia to women. It's atrocious! But these American girls in college who claim they're oppressed by men—that's just bizarre. They're not being raped in villages in Africa or kept out of school or beaten by boyfriends because they're girls. They're not oppressed by a patriarchy or gender stereotypes. Hell, these girls run everything, especially their relationships."

This latter was hyperbole, and she knew it, but she was trying to make a point recently hinted at by feminist Cheryl Sandberg in her business book, *Lean In.* Only around 25 percent of American women call themselves feminists today—and even fewer young women Davita's age accept the moniker. Why? Davita answered this question by bringing up the French psychiatrist Frantz Fanon, whom she was studying in one of her classes. While he mainly studied colonialism in Africa, she said, his studies have been used to understand oppression in many settings. Davita noted that many early and present-day feminists developed feminist theory regarding marriage and male/female relationships from oppression and colonialism models like Fanon's, arguing that women are inherently oppressed in marriages and workplaces because they are "colonized" or even "enslaved" by men. As I listened to Davita, I remembered back to being college age; we were all, women and men, feminists who saw things Fanon's way. But now, as Davita was indicating, could this view really still hold? Were American women colonized by American men?

Davita further analyzed Fanon (I've condensed a long discussion) in a way that connects directly to the questions of power struggle and intimate separateness. Her reading of Fanon was: if females are to become liberated from systemic male oppression, they must, individually and en masse, engage in constant power struggle against (1) men; and (2) male-driven social imagery that colonizes, puts down, marginalizes, oppresses, or traps women in gender stereotypes. Quoting Simone de Beauvoir's *The Second Sex* and Mary Wollstonecraft's *A Vindication of the Rights of Woman,* Davita understood how Fanon's and other early twentieth-century research became absorbed into feminist research and thus became the normative vision of male/female relationships in academic dialogue to this day.

As we talked, I asked her the million-dollar question: "So, Davita, are you a feminist?" She responded, "For women around the world who are suffering, I'm a feminist, but not as an American woman in a relationship with a man in the United States. The patriarchy, gender stereotypes, and oppression of women are not really what's going on in my relationship." This took us back to Sandberg's statistic. While the feminist frame for relationships is the easiest and simplest for the media and culture to handle, it is not resonating with most couples anymore, young or old, nor even most women.

Yet, many women (and thus, men) who are facing issues in love have bought into the feminist frame of male versus female often without realizing it. Its argument attacks marriage with a dangerous pseudoscience of oppression—dangerous because there is always a victim and a villain in the oppression frame, even if no oppression is taking place. By my best guess (it is only a guess based on twenty-five years of research; it is not a solid fact because I don't know how, in fact, it can be studied clearly), just over 10 percent of American couples are dominated by oppressive, patriarchal male dominance. Addictions, mental illnesses (especially depression), physical illnesses, personality disorders, anxiety disorders, and many other difficulties plague another 10 to 15 percent of marriages. This leaves a large portion of distressed marriages—millions of them—in the darkness as to what is distressing them.

In most of these marriages, I believe, a lack of intimacy-separateness balance (including significant enmeshment/abandonment cycles) is a primary cause of distress, not lack of women's empowerment at the hands of patriarchal gender stereotypes. For most marriages, then, the myth of victim and a villain is a dangerous one, with another deceptive myth often leading the woman to blame men as 1) least capable of emotional fulfillment and 2) the cause of the couple's problems. Blaming one half of a marriage en masse for failure is setting up future generations to have difficulty seeing the truth about marriage; that is, when the genders are perceived as being at war with one another, real love is a struggle that cannot be won.

Here's an example: I was recently asked by a reporter to talk about the case of a woman in her thirties who was, in the reporter's words, "afraid to eat much in front of men she was dating because they would think she was fat and judge her. This woman had been raised in the gender stereotypes and patriarchal social imagery of skinny women, so she was scared to be herself in front of men, scared to even eat a good meal." The reporter wanted me to confirm that patriarchal attitudes, gender oppression, and gender stereotypes were the cause of this woman's behavior. The reporter continued, "Feminist theorist Susan Bordo has said that women are trained in a complex set of ways to become 'perfect bodies.' When women deviate from what is considered perfect, they are often seen as unfeminine or even less valuable by either sex. Nicole has a massive fear of eating in front of men and usually acts as though she's not hungry. She says one of her oft-repeated refrains—'No thanks, I'm not hungry'—stems from her fear that men might see her as greedy or overindulgent with food. This is part and parcel of her belief that she should lose weight in order for men to consider her desirable."

As I responded to this, I told the reporter I doubted that men or women were forcing gender stereotypes on this woman. Most likely she had an eating disorder, which affected her neurology. As we discussed this possibility, I asked the reporter if she felt that America was a patriarchal country in which a woman's personality disorder or other disorder could be caused by men. She said, "Yes, men's images run our world. If women are going to get what they need, they have to battle the power of those images every day."

As she and I talked, Davita's comments echoed in my mind. In that moment it was clear to me how important it has become for most couples today to step away from gender politics in order to be whole. If the young woman who was not eating in front of men was convinced by her culture that her behavior was caused by men/the patriarchy, and that gender stereotypes had been forced on her, she would live an unhappy life and never get real help. In believing she was a victim of male villainous social constructs, she was following a myth, one that all of us, including the media, needed to recognize as incomplete.

In reality, women (and men) face significant personal and marital distresses—personal developmental stresses; stresses around house-work, child-raising, sex, intimacy, enmeshment, abandonment, divorce, child alienation, brain disorders, personality disorders, and violence—but there is no scientific proof in America to show that most of these stem from "the patriarchy." While many popular interpretations involve female oppression by males, this thinking actually locks many couples unnecessarily in Stage 3, the power struggle, long enough for love to fail. The victim and villain view requires, by its very nature, a power struggle.

As you take on your own marriage's power struggles, look closely at the extent to which popular myths and claims of female oppression are promulgated by friends, the media, academics, counselors or therapists, and the legal system. If you encounter a therapist or friend who is pushing you toward an oppression interpretation of your marriage, be cautious; become a love-scientist and really study what is happening. If it's the right assessment, then face that reality. But if not, don't allow it to destroy your chance for real personal growth.

If, for instance, you are going to a therapist who is trained in patriarchal and gender stereotypes theory, she or he may blame the man for the relationship's troubles (whether consciously or unconsciously). You are most likely dealing with a well-meaning and competent therapist who has bought into the psychology of oppression taught in graduate school or elsewhere in the culture.

Protecting Women and Men in Marriage

Most men are not misogynists. Most men (and, in truth, most women, I believe) are trying to move past Stage 3, Power Struggle. When I say to men in a workshop, "Okay, guys, if you want your marriage to last, you need to marry a reasonable woman, and do everything she says," most men say, "Yes, I have." Women and men both chuckle. To women, I say, "But remember, this means you have to be reasonable!" This brings more chuckles and grins, and we have a good time with it.

Beneath the good time, though, is a truth: most men are willing to follow their partner's lead on marital and familial issues—as long as that lead is *reasonable*. To men, "reasonable" means a good deal of intimacy but also a good deal of separateness. When men feel they are treated reasonably and there is respect for *their* emotional systems, they tend to follow. Despite myths to the contrary, most males are protective and caring—and they continue to be so throughout their lives. I hope that you will talk about this in your marriage or partnership. Together, work past the myth of male victimization of females in modern marriage. Together, see men for who they are: pro-social, protective, generous, hopeful, thrilling, fun—and often prone to a bit more emotional separateness than, perhaps, their partner might be, but as adaptable as they can be for the sake of love.

YOUR INSIGHTS

In my and Frank's journey of increasing our emotional and marital intelligence, I've learned to figure out what my "song" is and my "loops" are. Being conscious of these—raising them up beyond emotional rumination and into marital intelligence—has helped me to avoid the trap of ruminating so much that I create crisis.

In terms of good tools, journaling has been a big deal, because I can see the song and the loops repeating themselves. Counseling has been a part of my life for years as well, and can help a lot. Communicating about the loops with my partner has been a big deal, too. Accepting them as a part of who I am and how my marriage works—that has been huge, too.

My song is: I need more of his love if I am going to feel happy; if I don't get that love the way I think I want it, I will be sad and anxious.

The repeating refrain or chorus in my song is "Why aren't you giving me the love I want when I want it?"

I don't sing this song or this refrain all the time, but when I get stressed, I ruminate too much about every small thing, I become anxious, and I sing it really loud. He tries his best to help me, but at some point his strong marital intelligence kicks in—he tells me to stop over-thinking and gives me a hug and says, "You're looping again. You know I love you. I adore you. Let's go for a walk." He suggests something like that and he listens for a while then he's done.

I used to hate that. I used to think that thinking about and talking about all my deep dark sad unloved feelings was what would save our marriage. I didn't know there was a word for what I was doing, "ruminating" or "hyper-ruminating" and "hyper-intimacy." I thought good emotional intelligence and good marital intelligence meant talking about feelings a lot.

I still like it, but with Frank, I've learned to like how he listens to my song for a while, then he's done. This helps me not to go back and forth on a daily basis between feeling like I am worthy of love and then unworthy of love. It seems strange now, but I used to blame Frank for my own looping, but now that I'm focusing more on separateness and on the dangers of rumination, I am able to get the distance I need on myself to see how calming and safe love really can be.

—Marianne, 42, married fourteen years, mother of two

Protecting Marriage in Therapeutic Settings

Society has degraded males over the last fifty years, and we have lost, in the process, some of our ability to have long-lasting marriages. In saying this I am not denying our patriarchal past, nor the existence of patriarchy in many parts of the world; nor am I denying male chauvinism and male mistakes in marriage and life. Yet, too, males have some very important wisdom about love, and a primary way we have lost that wisdom is by buying into therapeutic solutions to marital issues in which male marital intelligence is less respected than female. Females had been oppressed in marriage previously, so it was logical for the psychology profession to lift up female marital intelligence and lower the male counterpart. But now, in the new millennium, it might be better to reignite the fire of male marital intelligence in ways that can complement female.

If we move forward into a post-feminist world in which we respect female and male ways of emotional intelligence, we will gain new tools that both strengthen marriage and ensure gender equality.

YOUR WISDOM

Go into the relationship and continue it with the attitude that you will always give more than you need to. If each person gives more than they need to, then each feels like every day is a gift. Once you start keeping tabs on how much you GET, selfishness ruins it.

If there is something you love having done for you, do that for your partner. Without asking, you will soon have them doing the same thing for you.

Respect and support your loved one for who he or she is. Expect the same from him or her. Accept him for who he is and don't try or expect him to change to fit your needs (if you find yourself hoping he will change, then he is probably not the right person for you!); and believe him when he shows who he is — if he shows honor in his actions, then he is likely an honorable person, and vice versa. Show who you truly are as well. Listen to him with an open mind and heart.

I think about my long-term relationships throughout my life, and the ones that succeeded were those where each of us made the other person's life better in some way. We provided something that each other needed—humor, emotional support, physical support, acceptance, etc. And that support was mutual, not one-sided or lopsided. And it was fluid—it changed and morphed easily over time.

Don't expect the other person to change to fit your needs. Compromise is one thing (and a good thing), but we can't change our values, personalities, etc.

Don't hit below the belt—keep communications respectful. If an argument gets heated, take time to cool off before talking more, because once you say something, you can never take it back. Consider that cooling-down period an investment in constructive, respectful communication with the one you love.

I have harbored resentment toward my ex for words said and deeds done. It only prolonged the agony. And I made excuses for bad behavior, thinking things would get better, when I was really receiving strong messages that this was not the man for me.

And then I made the mistake for resenting him for being who he is. Not fair for either of us! If I could do one thing for people younger than me, it would be to help them realize the person they love (even when they are breaking up with him or her) is not an ogre—resentment usually hurts everyone: kids, the ex, and, ironically, yourself. Love, love, and love . . . these are better for everyone. Get distance on what has happened as soon as possible and see that it exists in your life so you can grow from it. No lover you've had exists in your life so you can cling to them through resentment and pretend the world will be a better place because of your anger. It won't. It is only better from love.

—Darlene, 66, married ten years, divorced five
years, then married twenty-four years

The Wonder of Intimacy

"A good relationship has a pattern like a dance," Anne Morrow Lindbergh wrote over a hundred years ago. "It is built on some of the same rules. The partners do not need to hold on tightly, because they move confidently in the same pattern, intricate but gay and swift and free, like a country dance of Mozart's. To touch heavily would be to arrest the pattern and freeze the movement, to check the endlessly changing beauty of its unfolding."

Anne Morrow Lindbergh's poetic language has influenced the work of psychologist Harriet Lerner (*The Dance of Anger, The Dance of Connection, The Dance of Intimacy*). Lerner and others have likened a couple's love to a dance in which we give and take as we move together across a dance floor—not being so close as to overwhelm one another, not so far away as to let someone else cut in.

Loving a partner in a way that is basically free of enmeshment, abandonment, dangerous merging, and harmful cultural myths is this kind of dance. One of the ways we can know we are performing this dance (and will be able to keep dancing for decades) is in examining what happens in that dance. In all paired dancing, the couple moves together to the music, whether it be a waltz, a country dance, rock 'n' roll, or hip-hop. The latter two are less formal, but the couple intuitively picks up the rhythm and moves together seamlessly. If you go to a bar and watch the couples dancing, you'll see these patterns, a comfortable blend of their individual beauty and their balanced relationship of distance and closeness.

When you find this beautiful dance in your marriage, hold on to it. Enjoy it. If you feel dissatisfied, step back and remember this: it took you years—decades, really—to find this pattern, and those dance steps can be found again. The dance will have its moments of awkwardness—you may step on each other's feet at times—but the music will call you back onto the dance floor and reward you with the feeling of coming home.

We asked earlier, "Why do we marry?" We marry, ultimately, not

just for ourselves but also for the world. We dance together to experience joy, and from that joy we do good for the world. Our marriage
radiates joy, support, kindness, challenge, and love into that world. It
has always been this way; marriage will remain a useful human institu-
tion as long as the world has people in it. As we set down the rules for
our particular dance of love, we can turn our attention outward; we are
renewed as a couple and grow outward to heal and enliven the world.

After twenty-nine years of marriage, I can say that this becomes
the ultimate joy of marriage: to join together as two lights that help
illuminate our children, our home, our neighborhood, our friends,
our workplaces, ourselves, and our world. We two lights remain two
independent lights dancing in an embrace in the night, so powerful
together that we appear to our children and others as one light, a single
wonderful light that has the ability, if we will keep sharing our wisdom
and our stories, to teach others how to love.

Epilogue

Intimate separateness is not the source of early romance's power—the source of that power is pure, close, constantly touching, eye-gazing, sexual-organ-arousing intimacy. Separateness is useful for those first few months of ecstatic love for one reason only: to increase our desperation to return to one another and merge together again in the early morning or the dark night; gaze at one another over lunch; caress the other's shoulder in the hallway, see if the brief time in an elevator can accomplish utter connection. "Separateness" is not the key to romance early in our love relationships, though it can be an aphrodisiac.

But healthy separateness is the key to love after romance and after the power struggle. While "keeping the romance going" is certainly important for a couple who has been married for twenty or thirty years, and while some struggle will always accompany love at any stage, few can argue that marriage lasts because of romance or struggle. When they speak about their lives, couples who have been together a long time tend to integrate "romance" and "struggle" into other equally and more important aspects of love. Whether or not they say the words "stages" or "separateness," they are talking about a kind of evolution in which they learned a balance of intimacy and separateness, attachment and detachment, passion and peace with who the other person is, and who they themselves are.

Without intimacy we cannot bond, but without separateness we cannot learn how to love in the long term. Through the ongoing experience of being neither too far away from your partner psychologically for too long nor being too close to your partner psychologically for too long, you develop true and real love. The great finding of couples like those you met in this book is that they last—beyond the four-year itch, the seven-year itch, the ten-year itch, the empty nest, the crises and the difficulties, beyond the fears and terrors of love, the trembling of soul and self, the fears everyone has at some point over the decades that we might not be lovable, are not loved, or don't know how to love. In our present-day world and culture, in which love is no longer forced to last, the sheer length of time our particular marriage lasts ends up being strong proof that we are lovable, we are loved, and we know how to love.

My hope in writing this book is to feed the dreams you have for a healthy, long-lasting love. The dream of love I hope you take from this book will be one in which you want to travel so deeply into the science and spirit of separateness, as well as intimacy, that you say, "Ah, here, too, is a secret to long-lasting love. Now I finally understand the yin and the yang of love."

We have to spread the word about this one person, one couple, one study group at a time. I hope you will do that. I hope you will bring this work into your reading groups and community dialogues. Let's change the way we love for the better.

Appendix I

PERSONALITY MAPPING

Here are some of the survey instruments available to you. This is not an exhaustive list by any means. If you prefer other instruments, please use them online or in book form. I hope you and your partner will complete one or more of these surveys.

The Big Five Trait Taxonomy

In the 1970s, Paul Costa and Robert McCrae (at the National Institutes of Health), Warren Norman (at the University of Michigan), and Lewis Goldberg (at the University of Oregon) discovered that most established human personality traits (established by the time people marry) can be boiled down to five broad dimensions of personality, regardless of language or culture. They came to this conclusion separately by asking hundreds of questions of many thousands of people, then using a statistical process called "factor analysis" to collate the data.

If you are a bit of a science geek, you might enjoy reading O. P. John and S. Srivastava's essay "The Big Five Trait Taxonomy: History, Measurement, and Theoretical Perspectives," in *Handbook of Personality: Theory and Research*, edited by L. A. Pervin and O. P. John (New York: Guilford, 1999). But whether or not science is your thing, please learn more about yourself and your partner by going to websites that specialize in the "Big Five Personality Types." At these sites, you can take the surveys and assess your and your partner's core personalities, then talk together about the results. Some of your power struggle may dissipate immediately.

Myers-Briggs Type Indicator

Carl Jung's work in personality typologies influenced Isabel Briggs Myers in the early part of the twentieth century to develop the Myers-Briggs Type Indicator (MBTI). You can go online and type in "Myers Briggs," then find numerous sites at which to take different tests. There are sixteen types, eight preferences, and other tools available. When you complete the tests, you'll obtain at least a four-letter type formula; www.myersbriggs.org is just one of the websites that can get you started quickly. Do these tests, collate your results, then talk together about the results. You may have powerful insights about your power struggles.

Minnesota Multiphasic Personality Inventory

The Minnesota Multiphasic Personality inventory (MMPI) is used by the Department of Defense, CIA, and other organizations, as well as countless businesses and corporations. Therapists and counselors also rely on it to help assess client personalities and mental health issues. Dr. Auke Tellegen (University of Minnesota) and Dr. Yossef Ben-Porath (Kent State University) have developed some of the latest versions of the MMPI. Do as much of this as you have time and inclination. Talk about the results with your partner and therapist. Powerful insights about your power struggles should ensue, as well as organically generated practical strategies for moving beyond power struggle in your own marriage.

Jungian Archetypes

The Hero Within, by Carol Pearson, can be used by both women and men to compare archetypal personality traits and the different situations that bring out different parts of a person's personality. There are also numerous books for women and men separately that can help, such as *Women Who Run with the Wolves* by Clarissa Pinkola Estes and *King, Warrior, Magician, Lover* by Robert Moore and Douglas Gillette. You can also utilize my three early Jungian works: *The Prince and the King*, *The Invisible Presence*, and *Love's Journey*.

Eneagrams

Eneagrams have been popular with some of my clients in the last decade. Go to any website that provides the research or go to the books themselves and take the tests. You will end up saying things like, "I'm a 2, 6, 9 and my partner is a 3, 6, 8." The comparison will reveal many of the things you fight about or have conflicts over now—many, you'll notice, are related to your personality types. This will help you develop healthy separateness and dissipate some of your power struggle.

Nurture the Nature Learning Style Profile

This tool is published in the softcover edition of my book *Nurture the Nature*. It has been used by couples to see the different ways in which they respond to everyday life. After taking the test, one partner will often notice that she or he approaches communication one way and her or his spouse another, and friction emerges because of unrealistic expectations of sameness.

Helen Fisher's Love Styles

See if you are predominantly a Negotiator, a Director, or other among the personality styles that people bring to love. Helen Fisher and her colleagues completed a decade-long longitudinal study of couples and found four basic love styles. Knowing where you fit can help inspire your journey out of power struggle. To learn more and take the tests, immerse yourself in the work of Helen Fisher. It is multicultural and very helpful.

Brain Sex

This online gender test can be taken by both women and men to enhance their understanding of how their own place on the gender spectrum impacts their personalities and relationships. Even if you took my survey in Chapter 3, I still suggest you take the Brain Sex quiz online (type in "Brain Sex Gender Quiz" on Google and you will go to the latest site for the test). It takes only a few minutes, but it can be immensely revealing.

Appendix II

1. A Balance of Intimacy and Separateness Creates a Happy Marriage

2. Marriages Suffer When We Become and Remain Too Close

3. Understanding How Women and Men Love Differently Can Help Build Lifelong Intimacy

4. Navigating the Twelve Stages of Intimacy Can Save Marriages

5. Five Practical Strategies Can End Your Power Struggles

6. To Be Happy in Marriage, We Each Need Our Own Domains

7. Every Crisis, Including Infidelity, Can Teach Us About Love

8. Lack of Emotional Fulfillment Need Not Be the End of a Marriage

9. Both Women and Men Can Be Led Astray by Gender Stereotypes

Acknowledgments

Attachment theorists and brain researchers have been particularly helpful to this book's theory and practice. Thank you to John Bowlby, Ruben Gur, Daniel Amen, Tracey Shors, and Shelley Taylor for producing the primary research that makes the intimate-separateness theory useful and practical.

Thank you, Christiane Northrup, for changing the way women think about relationships throughout the life span, and similarly Jed Diamond, for helping integrate the science of andropause into men's lives. Michael Roizen's *RealAge*, Roizen and Mehmet Oz's *You* books, Andrew Weil's *Healthy Aging*, and Daniel Amen's *Unleashing the Power of the Female Brain* provide insights and practical strategies for continuing to explore intimate separateness in all stages of life, including the latter stages.

Nancy Snyderman, MD, has been generous in sharing with me her insights. As medical reporter for *NBC News* and the *Today* show, she has traveled the world interviewing and observing leading-edge medical and human research.

For specific insights, conversations, and correspondence regarding the subject of this book, thanks go to Nancy Snyderman, MD; Daniel Amen, MD; Michael Thompson, PhD; Jed Diamond, PhD; John Ratey, MD; JoAnn Deak, PhD; Louann Brizendine, MD; Adie Goldberg, LCSW; Harold Koplewicz, MD; Phon Hudkins, PhD; Tracey Shors, PhD; Gregg Jantz, PhD; Joanna Ellington, PhD, Rabbi Jacob Izakson and Rabbi Henry Glazer; Reverend William Houff, PhD; Pastor Tim Wright; Lloyd Halpern, MD; Marny Tobin, RN; Tom Tobin,

MD; Pam Brown, MA; and Jeannie Corkill, MSW. Your research and insights inspire me to keep pushing the envelope.

Thank you also to the women and men who have responded to my surveys and joined my focus groups. Your stories, questions, and challenges have made possible my own thinking and service. To my clients I extend my profound gratitude. By letting me serve you, you have taught me more than you know. I have altered your stories and formed composites in this book in order, always, to protect your privacy and confidentiality. I know that my work would lack wisdom and depth without your work.

To our circle of friends who let me borrow them constantly for research, reading, brainstorming, and fact-checking, many thanks; you know who you are, but in case you don't, you'll know soon because I'll be calling on you again! Thank you also to "the six couples" for your help throughout these many years of marriage: Carmen and Lloyd Halpern, Lesley and Murray Huppin, Helene and Paul Paroff, Sue and Mark Silver, Susan and Ira Armstadter, and Dale Severance and Fabian Napolsky.

To all those who have aided us in the Gurian Institute's wisdom-of-practice research over the last seventeen years, thank you for your time and wisdom. We could not conduct our research without your help. Kathy Stevens, our former executive director, passed away just before this book was written; her words and thoughts appear in these pages. Many others in the Gurian Institute continue her legacy, including Dakota Hoyt, Janet Allison, and all our team members.

To my literary agent, Bonnie Solow, and the wonderful people at Atria and Simon & Schuster, especially Donna Loffredo and Judith Curr: thank you for your confidence and wisdom. It is a joy to be on your team. Thank you also to Sarah Durand for starting this book on its publishing path and Greer Hendricks for nurturing it.

To Gail and our daughters, Gabrielle and Davita, I extend the kind of gratitude that can barely be expressed in words. Thank you for guiding my work in your generous and powerful ways. We grow together, one book at a time!

Notes and References

INTRODUCTION: THE SURPRISING SECRET OF LOVE

D. J. Macunovich, *Re-visiting the Easterlin Hypothesis: Marriage in the U.S. 1968–2010* (Discussion Paper Series, 2011). Institute for the Study of Labor. Retrieved from http://papers.ssrn.com/sol3/papers.cfm?abstract_id=1906189.

John Gottman and Nan Silver, *The Seven Principles for Making a Marriage Work* (New York: Harmony, 2000).

Helen Fisher, *Anatomy of Love* (New York: Ballantine, 2000).

Helen Fisher, "The Brain, How We Fall in Love, and How We Stay Together: An Interview with Helen Fisher," *Family Therapy Magazine,* May–June 2011. See also Brett J. Atkinson, "Reconditioning Emotional Habits," *Family Therapy Magazine,* May–June 2011.

D. P. Schmitt, "Sociosexuality from Argentina to Zimbabwe: A 48-Nation Study of Sex, Culture, and Strategies of Human Mating," *Behavioral and Brain Sciences* 28 (2005): 247–74.

A. M. Slaughter, "Why Women Still Can't Have It All," *The Atlantic* 310 (July/August 2012): 84–102.

J. T. Spence and R. L. Helmreich, *Masculinity and Femininity: Their Psychological Dimensions, Correlates and Antecedents* (Austin, TX: University of Texas Press, 1978).

P. England and J. Bearak, "Women's Education and Their Likelihood of Marriage: A Historical Reversal," *Fact Sheet Prepared for The Council on Contemporary Families,* retrieved from http://www.contemporaryfamilies.org/marriage-partnership-divorce/fact-sheet-marriage-and-education.html.

A. Feingold, "Gender Differences in Mate Selection Preferences: A Test of the Parental Investment Model," *Psychological Bulletin* 112 (1992): 125–39.

M. M. Sweeney, "Two Decades of Family Change: The Shifting Economic Foundations of Marriage," *American Sociological Review* 67 (2002): 132–47.

M. M. Sweeney and M. Cancian, "The Changing Importance of White Women's Economic Prospects for Assortative Mating," *Journal of Marriage and Family* 66 (2004): 1015–28.

R. Trivers, "Parental Investment and Sexual Selection," in *Sexual Selection and the Descent of Man: 1871–1971,* ed. B. Campbell, 136–79 (Chicago, IL: Aldine, 1972).

R. K. Unger, "Toward a Redefinition of Sex and Gender," *American Psychologist* 34 (1979): 1085–94.

U.S. Census Bureau (2012), *Estimated Median Age at First Marriage, by Sex* (Table MS-2), retrieved from www.census.gov/population/socdemo/hh-fam/ms2.xls.

J. Ratey, *A User's Guide to the Brain* (New York: Pantheon, 2001).

Margaret Mead is quoted in John Gottman and Nan Silver, *The Seven Principles for Making a Marriage Work* (New York: Harmony, 2000).

CHAPTER 1: THE INTIMATE SEPARATENESS PARADIGM

Allan Schore, quoted in John Bowlby, *A Secure Base* (Basic Books: New York, 1988).

D. W. Winnicott, *Human Nature* (New York: Schocken, 1988).

Daniel Stern, *The Motherhood Constellation* (Basic Books: New York, 1995).

Louise J. Kaplan, *Oneness and Separateness* (Touchstone: New York, 1978).

Martin Lynch, "Attachment, Autonomy, and Emotional Reliance: A Multilevel Model," *Journal of Counseling and Development* 91 (July 2013): 301–12.

The Gurian Institute, Stacey Behring, and Adie Goldberg, *It's a Baby Boy!* and *It's a Baby Girl!* (San Francisco: Jossey-Bass/John Wiley, 2009).

John Gottman and Nan Silver, *The Seven Principles for Making a Marriage Work* (New York: Harmony, 2000).

Helen Fisher, *Anatomy of Love* (New York: Ballantine, 2000).

Pierre Teilhard de Chardin, *The Phenomenon of Man* (New York: Harper Perennial Modern Classics, 2008).

David Buss, *The Evolution of Desire* (New York: Basic, 2003).

Thomas E. Schlaepfer et al., "Structural Differences in the Cerebral Cortex of Healthy Female and Male Subjects: A Magnetic Resonance Imaging Study," *Psychiatry Research: Neuroimaging* 61, no. 3 (September 29, 1995): 129–35.

Tracey J. Shors, "Significant Life Events and the Shape of Memories to Come: A Hypothesis," *Neurobiology of Learning and Memory* 85, no. 2 (March 2006): 103–15; available at http://www.rci.rutgers.edu/~shors.

M. de Lacoste et al., "Sex Differences in the Fetal Human Corpus Callosum," *Human Neurobiology* 5, no. 2 (1986): 93–96.

L. A. Kilpatrick et al., "Sex-Related Differences in Amygdala Functional Connectivity During Resting Conditions," *NeuroImage* 30, no. 2 (April 1, 2006): 452–61; available at http://today.uci.edu/news/release_detail.asp?key=1458.

S. Hamann et al., "Men and Women Differ in Amygdala Response to Visual Sexual Stimuli," *Nature Neuroscience* 7, no. 4 (April 2004): 411–16.

William Killgore et al., "Sex-Specific Developmental Changes in Amygdala Responses to Affective Faces," *NeuroReport* 12, no. 2 (February 12, 2001): 427–33.

W. D. Killgore and D. A. Yurgelun-Todd, "Sex-Related Developmental Differences in the Lateralized Activation of the Prefrontal Cortex and Amygdala During Perception of Facial Affect," *Perceptual and Motor Skills* 99, no. 2 (October 2004): 371–91.

CHAPTER 2: BECOMING THE SCIENTIST OF YOUR OWN MARRIAGE

Helen Fisher's very readable brain-based book, *Anatomy of Love* (New York: Ballantine, 2000), joins with David Buss's *The Evolution of Desire* (New York: Basic, 2003) to provide a strong foundation for some of the key ideas of this chapter.

L. A. Martin, H. Neighbors, and D. Griffith, "The Experience of Symptoms of Depression in Men vs. Women," *JAMA Psychiatry* 70, no. 10 (2013): 1100–106.

B. L. Hankin and L. Y. Abramson, "Development of Gender Differences in Depression: An Elaborated Cognitive Vulnerability–Transactional Stress Theory," *Psychological Bulletin* 127 (2001): 773–96.

J. S. Hyde, A. H. Mezulis, and L. Y. Abramson, "The ABCs of Depression: Integrating Affective, Biological, and Cognitive Models to Explain the Emergence of the Gender Difference in Depression," *Psychological Review* 115 (2008): 291–313.

Michael Liebowitz is quoted in Helen Fisher's *Anatomy of Love.*

James Masterson's work is central to our understanding of the neurobiology of personality, as well as the way our personalities form bonds with objects (others) in relation to internal needs. Some of his most compelling works are *The Personality Disorders Through the Lens of Attachment Theory and the Neurobiologic Development of the Self* (Phoenix, AZ: Zeig, Tucker & Theisen, 2005); *The Search for the Real Self: Unmasking the Personality Disorders of Our Age* (New York: Simon & Schuster, 1988); and *The Narcissistic and Borderline Disorders* (New York: Brunner/Mazel, 1981).

For detail on the medical and psychological effects of menopause and andropause on intimacy, see Christiane Northrup, *The Wisdom of Menopause,* rev. ed. (New York: Bantam, 2012) and Jed Diamond, *Surviving Male Menopause* (Naperville, IL: Sourcebooks, 2000). See also J. S. Moser, S. B. Most, and R. F. Simons, "Increasing Negative Emotions by Reappraisal Enhances Subsequent Cognitive Control: A Combined Behavioral and Electrophysiological Study," *Cognitive, Affective, and Behavioral Neuroscience* 10 (2010): 195–207.

I. Salomon, E. Hart, and E. Winter, "Oxytocin Decreases Accuracy in the Perception for Social Deception," *Psychological Science,* published online November 13, 2013.

T. F. Heatherton, "Neuroscience of Self and Self-Regulation," *Annual Review of Psychology* 62 (2011): 363–90.

M. Hines, "Prenatal Gonadal Hormones and Sex Differences in Human Behavior," *Psychological Bulletin* 92 (1982): 56–80.

M. Hines and R. J. Green, "Human Hormonal and Neural Correlates of Sex-typed Behaviors," in *American Psychiatric Press Review of Psychiatry,* ed. A. Tasman and S. M. Goldfinger, 10: 536–55 (Arlington, VA: American Psychiatric Association, 1991).

A. C. Huston, "Sex Typing," in *Handbook of Child Psychology,* 4th ed., ed. P. H. Mussen (series ed.) and E. M. Hetherington (vol. ed.), 4:387–467 (New York: John Wiley, 1983).

J. S. Hyde, "How Large Are Gender Differences in Aggression? A Developmental Meta-Analysis," *Developmental Psychology* 20 (1984): 722–36.

J. S. Hyde, "The Gender Similarities Hypothesis," *American Psychologist* 60 (2005): 581–92.

Yehuda Amichai, *Open Closed Open,* trans. Chana Bloch (New York: Mariner, 2006).

Yehuda Amichai, *Selected Poetry,* trans. Chana Bloch and Stephen Mitchell (Los Angeles: University of California Press, 1994).

John Bowlby, *A Secure Base* (New York: Basic, 1988).

The Katha Upanishad, Surya Das, and Krishnamurti quotes were handed to me without source citing, but I believe they are relatively accurate.

St. John of the Cross, quoted in Aldous Huxley's classic *The Perennial Philosophy (New York:* HarperPerennial, 2009).

Rabbi Glazer, phone interview, July 2013.

Ibn-Arabi, quoted in Swami Abhayanada's *History of Mysticism* (London: Atma, 2010).

CHAPTER 3: RELATIONSHIP WISDOM FROM BOTH WOMEN AND MEN

This chapter is the outgrowth of more than twenty-five years spent integrating science-based studies into my work with women and men. Here are just some of the studies that ground this work. I have divided many of them into subject areas for you. You'll recognize some of the topic areas in direct relation to the points I make in this chapter; others I am including so that, if you are someone who likes to read the science yourself, you will have a number of places to go.

By my count, there are more than a thousand studies worldwide that reflect various aspects of male/female difference.

Scientific Studies on Gender Differences

Daniel Amen has generously provided the brain scans in this chapter. Two of his books on this subject include *Unleashing the Power of the Female Brain* (New York: Bantam, 2013) and *Sex on the Brain* (New York: Bantam, 2005). Another seminal book is Simon Baron-Cohen, *The Essential Difference* (New York: Basic, 2003). These are just three of the many very fine books that reveal and summarize gender-brain research. Many others are noted in the Bibliography.

Further research studies include:

Arthur Wunderlich et al., "Brain Activation During Human Navigation: Gender-Different Neural Networks as Substrate of Performance," *Nature Neuroscience* 3, no. 4 (April 2000): 404–408.

Ruben Gur et al., "An fMRI Study of Sex Differences in Regional Activation to a Verbal and Spatial Task," *Brain and Language* 74, no. 2 (September 2000): 157–70.

N. Sandstrom et al., "Males and Females Use Different Distal Cues in a Virtual Environment Navigation Task," *Cognitive Brain Research* 6, no. 4 (April 1998): 351–60.

M. Eals and I. Silverman, "The Hunter-Gatherer Theory of Spatial Sex Differences: Proximate Factors Mediating the Female Advantage in Recall of Object Arrays," *Ethology and Sociobiology* 15, no. 2 (March 1994): 95–105.

I. Silverman and M. Eals, "Sex Differences in Spatial Abilities: Evolutionary Theory and Data," in *The Adapted Mind: Evolutionary Psychology and the Generation of Culture*, ed. J. Barkow, L. Cosmides, and J. Tooby, 487–503 (New York: Oxford University Press: 1992).

D. Saucier et al., "Are Sex Differences in Navigation Caused by Sexually Dimorphic Strategies or by Differences in the Ability to Use the Strategies?" *Behavioral Neuroscience* 116, no. 3 (June 2002): 403–10.

Gray and White Matter Processing
Ruben Gur et al., "Sex Differences Found in Proportions of Gray and White Matter in the Brain: Links to Differences in Cognitive Performance Seen," study, University of Pennsylvania Medical Center, May 18, 1999, available at http://www.sciencedaily.com/releases/1999/05/990518072823.htm.

Maria Elena Cordero et al., "Sexual Dimorphism in Number and Proportion of Neurons in the Human Median Raphe Nucleus," *Developmental Brain Research* 124, nos. 1–2 (November 2000): 43–52.

Marian Diamond, "Male and Female Brains," lecture for Women's Forum West Annual Meeting, San Francisco, California, 2003.

R. C. Gur et al., "Sex Differences in Brain Gray and White Matter in Healthy Young Adults," *Journal of Neuroscience* 19, no. 10 (May 15, 1999): 4065–72.

Beatrice and John Whiting's research is reported in Helen Fisher's *Anatomy of Love* (New York: Ballantine, 2000).

Brain Chemistry: Our Neurochemicals and Hormones
H. E. Albers et al., "Hormonal Basis of Social Conflict and Communication," in *Hormones, Brain, and Behavior*, ed. D. W. Pfaff, A. P. Arnold, A. M. Etgen, et al., 1: 393–433 (New York: Academic, 2002).

Lynda Liu, "Keep Testosterone in Balance: The Positive and Negative Effects of the Male Hormone," *WebMD*, January 2005.

K. Christiansen, "Behavioral Effects of Androgen in Men and Women," *Journal of Endocrinology* 170, no. 1 (July 2001): 39–48.

J. C. Compaan et al., "Vasopressin and the Individual Differentiation in Aggression in Male House Mice," *Annals of the New York Academy of Sciences* 652 (June 1992): 458–59.

K. Alexanderson, "An Assessment Protocol for Gender Analysis of Medical Literature," *Women and Health* 29, no. 2 (1999): 81–98.

For More on Men and the Biochemical Cycles
Gabrielle Lichterman, "Men's Room: The Male Hormone Cycle," available online at http://www.hormonology.info/malehormonecycle.htm.

Deborah Blum, *Sex on the Brain: The Biological Differences Between Men and Women* (New York: Penguin, 1998).

S. M. van Anders and K. L. Goldey, "Testosterone and Partnering Are Linked via Relationship Status for Women" and "Relationship Orientation for Men," *Hormones and Behavior* 58 (2010): 820–26.

S. M. van Anders, K. L. Goldey, and P. X. Kuo, "The Steroid/Peptide Theory of Social Bonds: Integrating Testosterone and Peptide Responses for Classifying Social Behavioral Contexts," *Psychoneuroendocrinology* 36 (2011): 1265–75.

S. M. van Anders and N. V. Watson, "Testosterone Levels in Women and Men Who Are Single, in Long-Distance Relationships, or Same-City Relationships," *Hormones and Behavior* 51 (2007): 286–91.

W. Wood and A. H. Eagly, "A Cross-Cultural Analysis of the Behavior of Women and Men: Implications for the Origins of Sex Differences," *Psychological Bulletin* 128 (2002): 699–727.

Verbal Communication Differences

Bennett A. Shaywitz et al., "Sex Differences in the Functional Organization of the Brain for Language," *Nature* 373 (February 16, 1995): 607–609.

J. D. Bremner et al., "Gender Differences in Cognitive and Neural Correlates in Remembrance of Emotional Words," *Psychopharmacology Bulletin* 35, no. 3 (Summer 2001): 55–78.

Michael Phillips et al., "Temporal Lobe Activation Demonstrates Sex-Based Differences During Passive Listening," *Radiology* 220, no. 1 (July 2001): 202–207.

Frank Schneider et al., "Gender Differences in Regional Cerebral Activity During Sadness," *Human Brain Mapping* 9, no. 4 (April 2000): 226–38.

R. Salomone, *Same, Different, Equal* (New Haven, CT: Yale University Press, 2003).

Elizabeth Sowell et al., "Development of Cortical and Subcortical Brain Structures in Childhood and Adolescence: A Structural MRI Study," *Developmental Medicine and Child Neurology* 44, no. 1 (January 2002): 4–16.

Elizabeth Sowell et al., "Mapping Cortical Change Across the Human Life Span," *Nature Neuroscience* 6, no. 3 (March 2003): 309–15.

Nonverbal Communication

J. A. Hall, *Nonverbal Sex Differences: Communication Accuracy and Expressive Style* (Baltimore: Johns Hopkins University Press, 1984).

J. A. Hall et al., "Status Roles and Recall of Nonverbal Cues," *Journal of Nonverbal Behavior* 25, no. 2 (2001): 79–100.

T. G. Horgan, *Thinking More Versus Less About Interpreting Nonverbal Behavior: A Gender Difference in Decoding Style*, unpublished doctoral dissertation, Northeastern University, 2001.

R. F. McGivern et al., "Gender Differences in Incidental Learning and Visual Recognition Memory: Support for a Sex Difference in Unconscious Environmental Awareness," *Personality and Individual Differences* 25, no. 2 (August 1998): 223–32.

D. McGuinness and J. Symonds, "Sex Differences in Choice Behaviour: The Object-Person Dimension," *Perception* 6, no. 6 (1977): 691–94.

S. J. McKelvie, "Sex Differences in Memory for Faces," *Journal of Psychology* 107 (1981): 109–25.

S. J. McKelvie, L. Standing, D. St. Jean, and J. Law, "Gender Differences in Recognition Memory for Faces and Cars: Evidence for the Interest Hypothesis," *Bulletin of the Psychonomic Society* 31, no. 5 (September 1993): 447–48.

S. Nowicki Jr. and M. P. Duke, "Nonverbal Receptivity: The Diagnostic Analysis of Nonverbal Accuracy (DANVA)," in *Interpersonal Sensitivity: Theory and Measurement*, ed. J. A. Hall and F. J. Bernieri, 183–98 (Mahwah, NJ: Lawrence Erlbaum, 2001).

P. A. Powers, J. L. Andriks, and E. F. Loftus, "Eyewitness Accounts of Females and Males," *Journal of Applied Psychology* 64, no. 3 (June 1979): 339–47.

L. Seidlitz and E. Diener, "Sex Differences in the Recall of Affective Experiences," *Journal of Personality and Social Psychology* 74, no. 1 (January 1998): 262–71.

P. N. Shapiro and S. Penrod, "Meta-Analysis of Facial Identification Studies," *Psychological Bulletin* 100, no. 2 (September 1986): 139–56.

J. A. Hall and D. Matsumoto, "Gender Differences in Judgments of Multiple Emotions from Facial Expressions," *Emotion* 4, no. 2 (June 2004): 201–206.

Hara Estroff Marano, "The Opposite Sex: The New Sex Scorecard," *Psychology Today* (July–August 2003): 38–44.

E. B. McClure et al., "A Developmental Examination of Gender Differences in Brain Engagement During Evaluation of Threat," *Biological Psychiatry* 55, no. 11 (June 1, 2004): 1047–55.

J. F. Thayer and B. H. Johnsen, "Sex Differences in Judgement of Facial Affect: A Multivariate Analysis of Recognition Errors," *Scandinavian Journal of Psychology* 41, no. 3 (September 2000): 243–46.

Memory Differences

D. A. Casiere and N. L. Ashton, "Eyewitness Accuracy and Gender," *Perceptual and Motor Skills* 83, no. 3 part 1 (December 1996): 914.

P. J. Davis, "Gender Differences in Autobiographical Memory for Childhood Emotional Experiences," *Journal of Personality and Social Psychology* 76, no. 3 (March 1999): 498–510.

R. W. Doherty, "The Emotional Contagion Scale: A Measure of Individual Differences," *Journal of Nonverbal Behavior* 21, no. 2 (Summer 1997): 131–54.

Terrence G. Horgan et al., "Gender Differences in Memory for the Appearance of Others," *Personality and Social Psychology Bulletin* 30, no. 2 (February 2004): 185–96.

A. Herlitz, L. G. Nilsson, and L. Backman, "Gender Differences in Episodic Memory," *Memory and Cognition* 25, no. 6 (November 1997): 801–11.

D. J. Herrmann, M. Crawford, and M. Holdsworth, "Gender-Linked Differences in Everyday Memory Performance," *British Journal of Psychology* 83, part 2 (May 1992): 221–31.

Gender and Body Image

S. E. Cross and L. Madson, "Models of the Self: Self-Construals and Gender," *Psychological Bulletin* 122, no. 1 (July 1997): 5–37.

D. M. Driscoll, J. R. Kelly, and W. L. Henderson, "Can Perceivers Identify Likelihood to Sexually Harass?" *Sex Roles* 38, nos. 7–8 (April 1998): 557–88.

S. Gabriel and W. L. Gardner, "Are There 'His' and 'Hers' Types of Interdependence? The Implications of Gender Differences in Collective Versus Relational Interdependence for Affect, Behavior, and Cognition," *Journal of Personality and Social Psychology* 77, no. 3 (September 1999): 642–55.

M. B. Harris, R. J. Harris, and S. Bochner, "Fat, Four-Eyed, and Female: Stereotypes of Obesity, Glasses, and Gender," *Journal of Applied Social Psychology* 12, no. 6 (December 1982): 503–16.

L. A. Jackson, L. A. Sullivan, and J. S. Hymes, "Gender, Gender Role, and Physical Appearance," *Journal of Psychology* 121, no. 1 (January 1987): 51–56.

S. Jobson and J. S. Watson, "Sex and Age Differences in Choice Behaviour: The Object-Person Dimension," *Perception* 13, no. 6 (February 1984): 719–24.

Gender and Grief

K. J. Doka and T. Martin, *Grieving Beyond Gender* (New York: Routledge, 2012).

T. Martin and K. J. Doka, *Men Don't Cry, Women Do: Transcending Gender Stereotypes of Grief* (Philadelphia: Taylor & Francis, 1999).

P. Rosenblatt, R. Walsh, and D. Jackson, *Grief and Mourning in Cross-Cultural Perspective* (Washington, DC: HRAF Press, 1976).

A. Wolfelt, "Gender Roles and Grief: Why Men's Grief Is Naturally Complicated," *Thanatos* 15, no. 30 (1990): 20–24.

John Gottman and Nan Silver, *The Seven Principles for Making a Marriage Work* (New York: Harmony, 2000).

Men, Competition, Aggression, Cooperation

M. Van Vugt, D. De Cremer, and D. P. Janssen, "Gender Differences in Cooperation and Competition: The Male-Warrior Hypothesis," *Psychological Science* 18, no. 1 (January 2007): 19–23.

J. Van Honk and D. J. Schutter, "Testosterone Reduces Conscious Detection of Signals Serving Social Correction," *Psychological Science* 18, no. 8 (August 2007): 663–67.

Shelley E. Taylor, *The Tending Instinct* (New York: Times/Henry Holt, 2002).

Judith E. Owen Blakemore, Steve R. Baumgardner, and Allen H. Keniston, "Male and Female Nurturing: Perceptions of Style and Competence," *Sex Roles* 18, nos. 7–8 (April 1988): 449–59.

Women, Oxytocin, Trust, and Bonding

J. A. Amico and B. E. Finley, "Breast Stimulation in Cycling Women, Pregnant Women and a Woman with Induced Lactation: Pattern of Release of Oxytocin, Prolactin and Luteinizing Hormone," *Clinical Endocrinology* 25 (1986): 97–106.

J. A. Bartz, J. Zaki, N. Bolger, and K. N. Ochsner, "Social Effects of Oxytocin in Humans: Context and Person Matter," *Trends in Cognitive Sciences* 15 (2011): 301–309.

M. Belot, V. Bhaskar, and J. van de Ven, "Can Observers Predict Trustworthiness?" *Review of Economics and Statistics* 94 (2012): 246–59.

C. F. Bond and B. M. DePaulo, "Accuracy of Deception Judgments," *Personality and Social Psychology Review* 10 (2006): 214–34.

M. S. Carmichael et al., "Plasma Oxytocin Increases in the Human Sexual Response," *Journal of Clinical Endocrinology and Metabolism* 64 (1987): 27–31.

M. S. Carmichael et al., "Relationship Among Cardiovascular, Muscular, and Oxytocin Responses During Human Sexual Activity," *Archives of Sexual Behavior* 23 (1994): 59–79.

S. D. Dandeneau et al., "Cutting Stress Off at the Pass: Reducing Vigilance and Responsiveness to Social Threat by Manipulating Attention," *Journal of Personality and Social Psychology* 93 (2007): 651–66.

M. Davis and P. J. Whalen, "The Amygdala: Vigilance and Emotion," *Molecular Psychiatry* 6 (2001): 13–34.

C. H. Declerck, C. Boone, and T. Kiyonari, "Oxytocin and Cooperation Under Conditions of Uncertainty: The Modulating Role of Incentives and Social Information," *Hormones and Behavior* 57 (2010): 368–74.

C. K. De Dreu et al., "The Neuropeptide Oxytocin Regulates Parochial Altruism in Intergroup Conflict Among Humans," *Science* 328 (2010): 1408–11.

B. M. DePaulo and W. L. Morris, "Discerning Lies from Truths: Behavioural Cues to

Deception and the Indirect Pathway of Intuition," in *The Detection of Deception in Forensic Contexts*, ed. P. A. Granhag and L. A. Strömwall, 15–40 (Cambridge, UK: Cambridge University Press, 2004).

G. Domes et al., "Oxytocin Attenuates Amygdala Responses to Emotional Faces Regardless of Valence," *Biological Psychiatry* 62 (2007): 1187–90.

S. Evans, S. S. Shergill, and B. B. Averbeck, "Oxytocin Decreases Aversion to Angry Faces in an Associative Learning Task," *Neuropsychopharmacology* 35 (2010): 2502–509.

M. Gamer, B. Zurowski, and C. Büchel, "Different Amygdala Subregions Mediate Valence-Related and Attentional Effects of Oxytocin in Humans," *Proceedings of the National Academy of Sciences of the USA*, 107 (2010): 9400–405.

K. M. Grewen et al., "Effects of Partner Support on Resting Oxytocin, Cortisol, Norepinephrine, and Blood Pressure Before and After Warm Partner Contact," *Psychosomatic Medicine* 67 (2005): 531–38.

S. E. Groppe et al., "Oxytocin Influences Processing of Socially Relevant Cues in the Ventral Tegmental Area of the Human Brain," *Biological Psychiatry* 13 (2013): 172–79.

M. Heinrichs et al., "Social Support and Oxytocin Interact to Suppress Cortisol and Subjective Responses to Psychosocial Stress," *Biological Psychiatry* 54 (2003): 1389–98.

P. Kirsch et al., "Oxytocin Modulates Neural Circuitry for Social Cognition and Fear in Humans," *Journal of Neuroscience* 25 (2005): 11489–93.

M. Kosfeld et al., "Oxytocin Increases Trust in Humans," *Nature* 435 (2005): 673–76.

K. C. Light, K. M. Grewen, and J. A. Amico, "More Frequent Partner Hugs and Higher Oxytocin Levels Are Linked to Lower Blood Pressure and Heart Rate in Premenopausal Women," *Biological Psychology* 69 (2005): 5–21.

A. Meyer-Lindenberg et al., "Oxytocin and Vasopressin in the Human Brain: Social Neuropeptides for Translational Medicine," *Nature Reviews Neuroscience* 12 (2011): 524–38.

M. Mikolajczak et al., "Oxytocin Makes People Trusting, Not Gullible," *Psychological Science* 21 (2010): 1072–74.

G. J. Norman et al., "Selective Influences of Oxytocin on the Evaluative Processing of Social Stimuli," *Journal of Psychopharmacology* 25 (2011): 1313–19.

L. A. Parr et al., "Intranasal Oxytocin Selectively Attenuates Rhesus Monkeys' Attention to Negative Facial Expressions," *Psychoneuroendocrinology* 38 (2013): 1748–56.

P. Petrovic et al., "Oxytocin Attenuates Affective Evaluations of Conditioned Faces and Amygdala Activity," *Journal of Neuroscience* 28 (2008): 6607–15.

A. Radke, K. Roelofs, and E. R. de Bruijn, "Acting on Anger: Social Anxiety Modulates Approach-Avoidance Tendencies After Oxytocin Administration," *Psychological Science* 24 (2013): 1573–78.

A. Salonia et al., "Menstrual Cycle-Related Changes in Plasma Oxytocin Are Relevant to Normal Sexual Function in Healthy Women," *Hormonal Behavior* 47 (2005): 164–69.

I. Schneiderman et al., "Oxytocin during the Initial Stages of Romantic Attachment: Relations to Couples' Interactive Reciprocity," *Psychoneuroendocrinology* 37 (2012): 1277–85.

C. T. Snowden and T. E. Ziegler, "Reproductive Hormones," chapter 14, 3rd ed., of *Handbook of Psychophysiology*, ed. John Cacioppo, Louis G. Tassinary, and Gary G. Berntson, 319–46 (Cambridge, UK: Cambridge University Press, 2007).

Men and Family

P. B. Gray et al., "Marriage and Fatherhood Are Associated with Lower Testosterone in Males," *Evolution and Human Behavior* 23, no. 3 (May 2002): 193–201.

"Daddy's Brains," *Parent Magazine,* January 2006.

Brian Braiker, "Just Don't Call Me Mr. Mom," *Newsweek,* October 8, 2007.

Stephen Johnson, *The Sacred Path* (Los Angeles: Sacred Path, 2012).

S. A. Berenbaum and A. M. Beltz, "Sexual Differentiation of Human Behavior: Effects of Prenatal and Pubertal Organizational Hormones," *Frontiers in Neuroendocrinology* 32 (2011): 183–200.

S. A. Berenbaum, J. E. O. Blakemore, and A. M. Beltz, "A Role for Biology in Gender-Related Behavior," *Sex Roles* 64 (2011): 804–25.

M. Daly and M. Wilson, *Sex, Evolution and Behavior,* 2nd ed. (Belmont, CA: Wadsworth, 1983).

C. Darwin, *The Descent of Man, and Selection in Relation to Sex* (London: John Murray, 1871).

C. Davatzikos and S. M. Resnick, "Sex Differences in Anatomic Measures of Interhemispheric Connectivity: Correlations with Cognition in Women but Not Men," *Cerebral Cortex* 8 (1998): 635–40.

K. Deaux, "From Individual Differences to Social Categories: Analysis of a Decade's Research on Gender," *American Psychologist* 39 (1984): 105–16.

A. H. Eagly, "Gender and Social Influence: A Social Psychological Analysis," *American Psychologist* 38 (1983): 971–81.

A. H. Eagly, "The His and Hers of Prosocial Behavior: An Examination of the Social Psychology of Gender," *American Psychologist* 64 (2009): 644–58.

More Clinical Studies Regarding Gender Differences that Affect Intimacy

A. H. Eagly and L. L. Carli, "Sex of Researchers and Sextyped Communications as Determinants of Sex Differences in Influenceability: A Meta-Analysis of Social Influence Studies," *Psychological Bulletin* 90 (1981): 1–20.

C. R. Harris, "Menstrual Cycle and Facial Preferences Reconsidered," *Sex Roles* 64 (2011): 669–81.

C. R. Harris, M. Jenkins, and D. Glaser, "Gender Differences in Risk Assessment: Why Do Women Take Fewer Risks Than Men?" *Judgment and Decision Making* 1 (2006): 48–63.

M. Hausmann et al., "Interactive Effects of Sex Hormones and Gender Stereotypes on Cognitive Sex Differences—A Psychobiosocial Approach," *Psychoneuroendocrinology* 34 (2009): 389–401.

J. James et al., "Sexspecific Pathways to Early Puberty, Sexual Debut, and Sexual Risk Taking: Tests of an Integrated Evolutionary–Developmental Model," *Developmental Psychology* 48 (2012): 687–702.

J. Kagan, "Acquisition and Significance of Sex Typing and Sex Role Identity," in *Review of Child Development Research,* ed. M. Hoffman and L. Hoffman, 1: 137–68 (New York: Russell Sage Foundation, 1964).

D. K. Kenrick, J. K. Maner, and N. P. Li, "Evolutionary Social Psychology," in *The Handbook of Evolutionary Psychology,* ed. D. M. Buss, 803–27 (Hoboken, NJ: John Wiley, 2005).

M. M. Kimball, "Television and Sex-role Attitudes," in *The Impact of Television: A Natural Experiment in Three Communities,* ed. T. M. Williams, 265–301 (Orlando, FL: Academic, 1986).

C. Leaper, "Gender Development during Childhood," in *Oxford Handbook of Developmental Psychology,* ed. P. D. Zelazo, 327–77 (New York: Oxford University Press, 2013).

R. Lickliter and H. Honeycutt, "Developmental Dynamics: Toward a Biologically Plausible Evolutionary Psychology," *Psychological Bulletin* 129 (2003): 819–35.

E. E. Maccoby, *The Two Sexes: Growing up Apart, Coming Together* (Cambridge, MA: Belknap Press, 1998).

E. E. Maccoby and C. N. Jacklin, *The Psychology of Sex Differences* (Stanford, CA: Stanford University Press, 1974).

C. L. Martin, D. N. Ruble, and J. Szkrybalo, "Cognitive Theories of Early Gender Development," *Psychological Bulletin* 128 (2002): 903–33.

A. Mazur and A. Booth, "Testosterone and Dominance in Men," *Behavioral and Brain Sciences* 21 (1998): 353–63.

S. M. McHale, A. C. Crouter, and S. D. Whiteman, "The Family Contexts of Gender Development in Childhood and Adolescence," *Social Development* 12 (2003): 125–48.

A. N. Meltzoff, "'Like Me': A Foundation for Social Cognition," *Developmental Science* 10 (2007): 126–34.

W. Mischel, "A Social Learning View of Sex Differences in Behavior," in *The Development of Sex Differences,* ed. E. E. Maccoby, 56–81 (Stanford, CA: Stanford University Press, 1966).

J. Money and A. A. Ehrhardt, *Man and Woman, Boy and Girl: Differentiation and Dimorphism of Gender Identity from Conception to Maturity* (Baltimore: Johns Hopkins University Press, 1972).

R. Plomin, *Genetics and Experience: The Interplay between Nature and Nurture* (Thousand Oaks, CA: Sage, 1994).

E. M. Pomerantz and D. N. Ruble, "The Role of Maternal Control in the Development of Sex Differences in Child Self-Evaluative Factors," *Child Development* 69 (1998): 458–78.

P. J. Richerson and R. Boyd, *Not by Genes Alone: How Culture Transformed Human Evolution* (Chicago: University of Chicago Press, 2005).

D. N. Ruble and C. L. Martin, "Gender Development," in *Handbook of Child Psychology,* 5th ed., ed. W. Damon and N. Eisenberg, 3: 933–1016 (Hoboken, NJ: John Wiley, 1998).

B. B. Sherwin, "A Comparative Analysis of the Role of Androgen in Human Male and Female Sexual Behavior: Behavioral Specificity, Critical Thresholds, and Sensitivity," *Psychobiology* 16 (1988): 416–25.

N. Signorielli, "Television's Gender-Role Images and Contribution to Stereotyping: Past, Present, Future," in *Handbook of Children and the Media,* 2nd ed., ed. D. G. Singer and J. L. Singer, 321–39 (Thousand Oaks, CA: Sage, 2012).

S. D. Simpkins, J. A. Fredricks, and J. S. Eccles, "Charting the Eccles' Expectancy-Value Model From Mothers' Beliefs in Childhood to Youths' Activities in Adolescence," *Developmental Psychology* 48 (2012): 1019–32.

S. E. Taylor et al., "Biobehavioral Responses to Stress in Females: Tend-and-Befriend, Not Fight-or-Flight," *Psychological Review* 107 (2000): 411–29.

J. Tooby and L. Cosmides, "Psychological Foundations of Culture," in *The Adapted Mind*, ed. J. Barkow, L. Cosmides, and J. Tooby, 19–136 (New York: Oxford University Press, 1992).

D. Voyer, S. Voyer, and M. P. Bryden, "Magnitude of Sex Differences in Spatial Abilities: A Meta-Analysis and Consideration of Critical Variables," *Psychological Bulletin* 117 (1995): 250–70.

N. Weisstein, *Kinder, Kirche, Kuche as Scientific Law: Psychology Constructs the Female* (Boston: New England Press, 1968).

J. E. Williams and D. L. Best, *Measuring Sex Stereotypes: A Thirty-Nation Study* (Beverly Hills, CA: Sage, 1982).

E. O. Wilson, *Sociobiology: The New Synthesis* (Cambridge, MA: Harvard University Press, 1975).

M. G. Witt and W. Wood, "Self-regulation of Gendered Behavior in Everyday Life," *Sex Roles* 62 (2010): 635–46.

W. Wood, "Meta-Analytic Review of Sex Differences in Group Performance," *Psychological Bulletin* 102 (1987): 53–71.

W. Wood and A. H. Eagly, "Gender Identity," in *Handbook of Individual Differences in Social Behavior*, ed. M. R. Leary and R. H. Hoyle, 109–25 (New York: Guilford, 2009).

W. Wood and A. H. Eagly, "Gender," in *Handbook of Social Psychology*, 5th ed., ed. S. T. Fiske, D. T. Gilbert, and G. Lindzey, 629–67 (Hoboken, NJ: John Wiley, 2010).

W. Wood and A. H. Eagly, "Biosocial Construction of Sex Differences and Similarities in Behavior," in *Advances in Experimental Social Psychology*, ed. J. M. Olson and M. P. Zanna, 46: 55–123 (London: Elsevier, 2012).

V. Yzerbyt and S. Demoulin, "Intergroup Relations," in *Handbook of Social Psychology*, ed. S. Fiske, D. Gilbert, and G. Lindzey, 2: 1024–83 (Hoboken, NJ: John Wiley, 2010).

D. H. Lawrence, *The Selected Poems* (New York: Penguin,1989).

CHAPTER 4: LIVING ALL TWELVE STAGES OF LOVE SUCCESSFULLY

I could not have developed the twelve-stages model without the research I've noted in the Notes to the previous chapter. From a scientific study of male/female dynamics has come a wealth of insight into the staging of those dynamics. I thank all the primary researchers for their work.

Jeff Hedge, DO, is founding partner of Inland Psychiatry and Psychology in Spokane, Washington.

John Bradshaw, *Bradshaw On: The Family* (Dearfield Beach, FL: Health Communications, 1988).

For a detailed look at the connection between parent-child attachment and stages of relationship and growth, please also see my *Love's Journey* (Boston: Shambhala, 1993) and *Nurture the Nature* (San Francisco: Jossey-Bass/John Wiley, 2007).

Sue Carter, "The Love Hormones," *Family Therapy Magazine*, May–June 2012. This article includes endnotes of some of the most compelling primary studies available regarding the brain research referred to in this chapter.

Maryanne Vandervelde, author of *Parallel Play*, quoted in Michael Gurian, *The Wonder of Aging* (New York: Atria, 2013).

Amir Levine and Rachel Heller, *Attached* (New York: Tarcher/Penguin, 2010).

J. Ratey, *A User's Guide to the Brain* (New York: Pantheon, 2001).

CHAPTER 5: ENDING POWER STRUGGLE IN YOUR RELATIONSHIP

Susan Rosenthal, PhD, and Daniel Eckstein, PhD, in "Two Couples' Problem-Solving Activities: The 1-Hour Conference and a Six-Step Dialectical Method," *The Family Journal* 21, no. 3 (July 2013): 352–46.

Scott Haltzman with Theresa Foy Digeronimo, *The Secrets of Happily Married Men* (San Francisco: Jossey-Bass/John Wiley, 2006).

Gregory L. Jantz with Ann McMurray, *Overcoming Anxiety, Worry, and Fear* (Grand Rapids, MI: Revell, 2011).

Jed Diamond, *Male Menopause* (Naperville, IL: Sourcebooks, 1997).

Deborah Sichel and Jean Watson Driscoll, *Women's Moods* (New York: Harper, 2010).

Louann Brizendine, *The Male Brain* (New York: Three Rivers, 2010).

P. H. Mehta and J. Beer, "Neural Mechanisms of the Testosterone–Aggression Relation: The Role of Orbitofrontal Cortex," *Journal of Cognitive Neuroscience* 22 (2010): 2357–68.

M. T. Notman and C. C. Nadelson, "A Review of Gender Differences in Brain and Behavior," in *Issues in Psychiatry. Women and Men: New Perspectives on Gender Differences*, ed. M. T. Notman and C. C. Nadelson, 23–34 (Arlington, VA: American Psychiatric Association, 1991).

K. A. Pfannkuche, A. Bouma, and T. G. G. Groothuis, "Does Testosterone Affect Lateralization of Brain and Behaviour? A Meta-Analysis in Humans and Other Animal Species," *Philosophical Transactions of the Royal Society B*, 364 (2009): 929–42.

A. H. Eagly and M. Crowley, "Gender and Helping Behavior: A Meta-Analytic Review of the Social Psychological Literature," *Psychological Bulletin* 100 (1986): 283–308.

N. Eisenberg and R. Lennon, "Sex Differences in Empathy and Related Capacities," *Psychological Bulletin* 94 (1983): 100–31.

N. Ellemers and S. A. Haslam, "Social Identity Theory," in *Handbook of Theories in Social Psychology*, ed. P. van Lange, A. Kruglanski, and E. T. Higgins, 2: 379–98 (London: Sage, 2012).

N. M. Else-Quest et al., "Gender Differences in Temperament: A Meta-Analysis," *Psychological Bulletin* 132 (2012): 33–72.

A. Feingold, "Gender Differences in Effects of Physical Attractiveness on Romantic Attraction: A Comparison Across Five Research Paradigms," *Journal of Personality and Social Psychology* 59 (1990): 981–93.

A. Feingold, "Gender Differences in Personality: A Meta-Analysis," *Psychological Bulletin* 116 (1994): 429–56.

S. E. Fisher, "Tangled Webs: Tracing the Connections Between Genes and Cognition," *Cognition* 101 (2006): 270–97.

J. D. Higley and Steve Suomi are featured in Helen Fisher's *Anatomy of Love* (New York: Ballantine, 2000).

Srijan Sen, Margit Burmeister, and Debashis Ghosh, "Meta-Analysis of the Association Between a Serotonin Transporter Promoter Polymorphism (5-HTTLPR) and Anxiety-Related Personality Traits," *American Journal of Medical Genetics* 127B, no. 1 (2004): 85–89.

J. A. Schinka, R. M. Busch, and N. Robichaux-Keene, "A Meta-Analysis of the Association Between the Serotonin Transporter Gene Polymorphism (5-HTTLPR) and Trait Anxiety," *Molecular Psychiatry* 9, no. 2 (2004): 197–92.

K. Kendler et al., "The Interaction of Stressful Life Events and a Serotonin Transporter Polymorphism in the Prediction of Episodes of Major Depression: A Replication," *Archives of General Psychiatry* 62, no. 5 (2005): 529–35.

N. Risch et al., "Interaction Between the Serotonin Transporter Gene (5-HTTLPR), Stressful Life Events, and Risk of Depression: A Meta-Analysis," *Journal of the American Medical Association* 301, no. 23 (2009): 2462–71.

Helen Fisher's *Why Him? Why Her?: Finding Real Love by Understanding Your Personality Type* (New York: Holt, 2010) is just one of many useful volumes on personality types. See also the Appendix for more resources.

John Welwood, *Perfect Love, Imperfect Heart* (New York: Trumpeter, 2007).

CHAPTER 6: PRACTICING INTIMATE SEPARATNESS FOR LIFE

A classic text in this study is Janice Kiecolt-Glaser and Ron Glaser, *Handbook of Stress and Immunity* (Waltham, MA: Academic Press, 1994). A more recent project appears in Bruce McEwen, "The Brain Under Stress," http://developingchild.harvard.edu/resources/multimedia/lectures_and_presentations/mcewen-lecture/. McEwen, PhD, who is Alfred E. Mirsky Professor and head of the Harold and Margaret Milliken Hatch Laboratory of Neuroendocrinology at the Rockefeller University, spoke at Harvard University on September 27, 2011, as part of the center's Distinguished Scholars Lecture Series.

Steve Cole, PhD, is a professor of medicine and psychiatry and biobehavioral sciences at the UCLA School of Medicine. His work researches the biological pathways by which social environments influence gene expression by viral, cancer, and immune cell genomes. See his "Social Regulation of Human Gene Expression," *Current Directions in Psychological Science* 18, no. 3 (2009): 132–37.

Tracey Shors, PhD, is Professor, Department of Psychology and Center for Collaborative Neuroscience, Rutgers University. She has been generous in sharing the neurogenetics research with me. A number of her authored and coauthored articles on the subject are available at www.traceyshors.com.

For a number of years, Phon Hudkins, at the Human Ethology Exchange in Washington, DC, has been a source of information regarding stress in American relationships and marriage. He is constantly informing my research, and I want to thank him for his passion.

Gwendolyn Wood and Tracey J. Shors, "Stress Facilitates Classical Conditioning in Males, but Impairs Classical Conditioning in Females Through Activational Effects of Ovarian Hormones," *Proceedings of the National Academy of Sciences* 95, no. 7 (March 31, 1998): 4066–71.

Tracey J. Shors, "Stress and Sex Effects on Associative Learning: For Better or for Worse," *Neuroscientist* 4, no. 5 (September 1998): 353–64.

Tracey J. Shors and George Miesegaes, "Testosterone *in Utero* and at Birth Dictates How Stressful Experience Will Affect Learning in Adulthood," *Proceedings of the National Academy of Sciences* 99, no. 21 (October 15, 2002): 13955–60.

Lauren A. Weiss et al., "Sex-Specific Genetic Architecture of Whole Blood Serotonin Levels," *American Journal of Human Genetics* 76, no. 1 (January 2005): 33–41.

Rossana Arletti et al., "Oxytocin Involvement in Male and Female Sexual Behavior," *Annals of the New York Academy of Sciences* 652, no. 1 (June 1992): 180–93.

Andrea Decapua and Diana Boxer, "Bragging, Boasting and Bravado: Male Banter in a Brokerage House," *Women and Language* 22, no. 1 (Spring 1999): 5–11.

A. H. Eagly, P. W. Eastwick, and M. Johannesen-Schmidt, "Possible Selves in Marital Roles: The Impact of the Anticipated Division of Labor on the Mate Preferences of Women and Men," *Personality and Social Psychology Bulletin* 35 (2009): 403–14.

A. H. Eagly et al., "Feminism and Psychology: Analysis of a Half-century of Research," *American Psychologist* 67 (2012): 211–230.

A. H. Eagly and B. T. Johnson, "Gender and Leadership Style: A Meta-Analysis," *Psychological Bulletin* 108 (1990): 233–56.

A. H. Eagly and V. J. Steffen, "Gender and Aggressive Behavior: A Meta-Analytic Review of the Social Psychological Literature," *Psychological Bulletin* 100 (1986): 309–30.

A. H. Eagly and W. Wood, "The Origins of Sex Differences in Human Behavior: Evolved Dispositions versus Social Roles," *American Psychologist* 54 (1999): 408–23.

Dan McKinney, who is featured twice in this chapter, is an educational consultant and friend of the Gurian Institute.

CHAPTER 7: THE POWERFUL LESSONS OF AFFAIRS AND INFIDELITY

Michael Gurian, *The Invisible Presence* (originally published as *Mothers, Sons, and Lovers*) (Boston: Shambhala, 2010).

Scott Haltzman, *The Secrets of Surviving Infidelity* (Baltimore: Johns Hopkins University Press, 2013).

Omri Gillith, "What's Love Got to Do with It," *Observer* (Association for Psychological Science) 23, no. 6 (July–August 2010): 23.

For original source material and for more depth regarding sexuality facts, see the National Survey of Sexual Health and Behavior at Indiana University. I have used the 2010 version (www.nationalsexstudy.indiana.edu). Sexual health and behavior statistics are fluid, and one of the best ways to see their evolution is to go to the Indiana University website and browse through the postings and links. I thank the team at Indiana University for bringing together this information in such a compact and powerful way. Their work allows me to draw some of the conclusions I make in this chapter.

See also Louann Brizendine, *The Female Brain* (New York: Three Rivers, 2007).

Ogi Ogas and Sai Gaddam, "The Online World of Female Desire," *Wall Street Journal*, April 30–May 1, 2011.

See also T. D. Conley et al., "Women, Men, and the Bedroom," *Current Directions in Psychological Science* 20, no. 5 (October 2011): 296–300.

Regarding the genetics of monogamy, see H. Walum et al., "Genetic Variation in the Vasopressin Receptor 1a Gene (AVPR1A) Associates with Pair-Bonding Behavior in Humans," *Proceedings of the National Academy of Sciences* 105, no. 37 (September 16, 2008): 14153–56.

J. Lammers et al., "Power Increases Infidelity Among Men and Women," *Psychological Science* 22, no. 9 (April 13, 2011): 1191–97. This article includes endnotes that provide further scientific studies regarding monogamy.

You will find additional information regarding the monogamy gene in Louann Brizendine, *The Female Brain* (New York: Three Rivers, 2007); Helen Fisher, *Anatomy of Love* (New York: Ballantine, 2000); David Buss, *Dangerous Passions* (New York: Free Press, 2011), and *The Evolution of Desire* (New York: Basic, 2003).

J. E. O. Blakemore, S. A. Berenbaum, and L. S. Liben, *Gender Development* (New York: Psychology Press, 2009).

R. Bleier, "Gender Ideology and the Brain: Sex Differences Research," in *Issues in Psychiatry: Women and Men: New Perspectives on Gender Differences,* ed. M. T. Notman and C. C. Nadelson, 63–73 (Arlington, VA: American Psychiatric Association, 1991).

A. Booth et al., "Testosterone and Social Behavior," *Social Forces* 85 (2006): 167–91.

U. Bronfenbrenner and P. A. Morris, "The Bioecological Model of Human Development," in *Handbook of Child Psychology,* 6th ed., ed. R. M. Lerner and W. Damon, 1: 793–828 (Hoboken, NJ: John Wiley, 2006).

D. M. Buss, "Sex Differences in Human Mate Preferences: Evolutionary Hypotheses Tested in 37 Cultures," *Behavioral and Brain Sciences* 12 (1989): 1–49.

D. M. Buss and D. P. Schmitt, "Evolutionary Psychology and Feminism," *Sex Roles* 64 (2011): 768–87.

D. M. Buss et al., "A Half Century of Mate Preferences: The Cultural Evolution of Values," *Journal of Marriage and Family* 63 (2001): 491–503.

K. Bussey and A. Bandura, "Self-Regulatory Mechanisms Governing Gender Development," *Child Development* 63 (1992): 1236–50.

J. P. Byrnes, D. C. Miller, and W. D. Schafer, "Gender Differences in Risk Taking: A Meta-Analysis," *Psychological Bulletin* 125 (1999): 367–83.

A. Campbell, "The Study of Sex Differences: Feminism and Biology," *Zeitschrift für Psychologie [Journal of Psychology]* 220 (2012): 137–43.

B. J. Carothers and H. T. Reis, "Men and Women Are from Earth: Examining the Latent Structure of Gender," *Journal of Personality and Social Psychology* 104 (2013): 385–407.

K. H. Chou et al., "Sex-linked White Matter Microstructure of the Social and Analytic Brain," *NeuroImage* 54 (2011): 725–33.

R. D. Clark and E. Hatfield, "Gender Differences in Receptivity to Sexual Offers," *Journal of Psychology and Human Sexuality* 2 (1989): 39–55.

M. L. Collaer and H. Hines, "Human Behavioral Sex Differences: A Role for Gonadal Hormones During Early Development?" *Psychological Bulletin* 118 (1995): 55–107.

J. C. Confer et al., "Evolutionary Psychology: Controversies, Questions, Prospects, and Limitations," *American Psychologist* 65 (2010): 110–26.

T. D. Conley, "Perceived Proposer Personality Characteristics and Gender Differences in Acceptance of Casual Sex Offers," *Journal of Personality and Social Psychology* 100 (2011): 309–29.

U. S. Anderson et al., "I Only Have Eyes for You: Ovulation Redirects Attention (But Not Memory) to Attractive Men," *Journal of Experimental Social Psychology* 46 (2010): 804–808.

S. B. Bullivant et al., "Women's Sexual Experience During the Menstrual Cycle: Identification of the Sexual Phase by Noninvasive Measurement of Luteinizing Hormone," *Journal of Sex Research* 41 (2004): 82–93.

A. B. Cohen et al., "Social versus Individual Motivation: Implications for Normative Definitions of Religious Orientation," *Personality and Social Psychology Review* 9 (2005): 48–61.

L. M. DeBruine, B. C. Jones, and D. I. Perrett, "Women's Attractiveness Judgments of Self-Resembling Faces Change Across the Menstrual Cycle," *Hormones and Behavior* 47 (2005): 379–83.

K. M. Durante et al., "Ovulation, Female Competition, and Product Choice: Hormonal Influences on Consumer Behavior," *Journal of Consumer Research* 37 (2011): 921–34.

K. M. Durante et al., "Ovulation Leads Women to Perceive Sexy Cads as Good Dads," *Journal of Personality and Social Psychology* 103 (2012): 292–305.

K. M. Durante, N. P. Li, and M. G. Haselton, "Changes in Women's Choice of Dress Across the Ovulatory Cycle: Naturalistic and Laboratory Task-Based Evidence," *Personality and Social Psychology Bulletin* 34 (2008): 1451–60.

P. W. Eastwick and E. J. Finkel, "The Evolutionary Armistice: Attachment Bonds Moderate the Function of Ovulatory Cycle Adaptations," *Personality and Social Psychology Bulletin* 38 (2012): 174–84.

S. W. Gangestad, R. Thornhill, and C. E. Garver, "Changes in Women's Sexual Interests and Their Partner's Mate-Retention Tactics Across the Menstrual Cycle: Evidence for Shifting Conflicts of Interest," *Proceedings of the Royal Society B: Biological Sciences* 269 (2002): 975–82.

D. M. Buss et al., "Adaptations to Ovulation," in *The Handbook of Evolutionary Psychology*, ed. D. M. Buss, 344–71 (Hoboken, NJ: John Wiley, 2005).

C. E. Garver-Apgar et al., "Major Histocompatibility Complex Alleles, Sexual Responsivity, and Unfaithfulness in Romantic Couples," *Psychological Science* 17 (2006): 830–35.

M. G. Haselton and S. W. Gangestad, "Conditional Expression of Women's Desires and Men's Mate Guarding Across the Ovulatory Cycle," *Hormones and Behavior* 49 (2006): 509–18.

M. G. Haselton and K. Gildersleeve, "Can Men Detect Ovulation?" *Current Directions in Psychological Science* 20 (2011): 87–92.

M. G. Haselton et al., "Ovulatory Shifts in Human Female Ornamentation," *Hormones and Behavior* 51 (2007): 40–45.

R. Kurzban, A. Dukes, and J. Weeden, "Sex, Drugs, and Moral Goals: Reproductive Strategies and Views About Recreational Drugs," *Proceedings of the Royal Society B: Biological Sciences* 277 (2010): 3501–508.

Y. J. Li et al., "Mating Competitors Increase Religious Beliefs," *Journal of Experimental Social Psychology* 46 (2009): 428–31.

M. E. McCullough et al., "The Varieties of Religious Development in Adulthood: A Longitudinal Investigation of Religion and Rational Choice," *Journal of Personality and Social Psychology* 89 (2005): 78–89.

C. D. Navarrete et al., "Race Bias Tracks Conception Risk Across the Menstrual Cycle," *Psychological Science* 20 (2009): 661–65.

E. G. Pillsworth and M. G. Haselton, "Male Sexual Attractiveness Predicts Differential Ovulatory Shifts in Female Extra-Pair Attraction and Male Mate Retention," *Evolution and Human Behavior* 27 (2006): 247–58.

E. G. Pillsworth, M. G. Haselton, and D. M. Buss, "Ovulatory Shifts in Female Sexual Desire," *Journal of Sex Research* 41 (2004): 55–65.

R. Thornhill and S. W. Gangestad, *The Evolutionary Biology of Human Female Sexuality* (New York: Oxford University Press, 2008).

J. Weeden, A. B. Cohen, and D. T. Kenrick, "Religious Participation and Reproductive Strategies," *Evolution and Human Behavior* 29 (2008): 327–34.

Daniel Goleman, *Emotional Intelligence* (New York: Bantam, 1995).

Louann Brizendine, *The Female Brain* (New York: Three Rivers, 2007).

Louann Brizendine, *The Male Brain* (New York: Three Rivers, 2010).

Alan Watts, *The Wisdom of Insecurity* (New York: Vintage, 2011).

Joanna Ellington, *Slippery When Wet* (Spokane: Dr. E Publishing, LLC, 2014).

Robert Johnson is the author of, among other powerful works, the three volumes *He, She, We.*

The Etty Hillesum quote was handed to me by my client, without a citation; however, I believe the Etty Hillesum she referred to was the anti-Nazi activist—like Anne Frank—who wrote diaries such as *An Interrupted Life,* published in 1999 by Persephone Books.

CHAPTER 8: BUSTING THROUGH THE MYTHS OF MARRIAGE

A. R. Orage, *On Love and Psychological Exercises* (Newburyport, MA: Red Wheel Weiser, 1998).

I began working on translations of Rumi from Turkish when Gail and I lived in Ankara from 1986 to 1988. Translating Rumi has been a spiritual experience for me, as have been my attempts to translate Rilke from the German. However, because I am an amateur, not a professional translator, I know that my translations are more projections of meaning than literal translation.

For professional translations of Rumi, I especially recommend Coleman Barks's beautiful volume *The Essential Rumi.* For translations of Rainer Maria Rilke, the Barrow and Macy volumes, such as *Rilke's Book of Hours,* are very powerful.

Rumi can also be found in Robert Bly et al., *Rag and Bone Shop of the Heart* (New York: Harper Perennial, 1990). This collection with commentary by Robert Bly, James Hillman, and Michael Meade is a powerful addition to any man's library on love. It is for men what Marilyn Sewell's anthology *Cries of the Spirit* (Boston: Beacon, 2000) is for some women. I highly recommend both as books to read together.

Kahlil Gibran, *The Prophet* (New York: Knopf, 2011).

Nye is quoted in Roger Housden's poetry anthology *Risking Everything* (New York: Harmony, 2003).

Anita Barrows and Joanna Marie Macy have translated *Sonnets to Orpheus, The Duino Elegies,* and many other volumes. Translations by Stephen Mitchell of the same Rilke books give yet another translator's perspective.

Pepper Schwartz is quoted in Ellen Bernstein's *Wall Street Journal* column "The Loneliness of the Empty Nest," July 1, 2013.

See John Gottman and Nan Silver, *The Seven Principles for Making a Marriage Work* (New York: Harmony, 2000).

Bibliography

Amen, Daniel. *Change Your Brain, Change Your Life.* New York: Bantam, 2010.

———. *Sex on the Brain.* New York: Bantam, 2005.

———. *Unleashing the Power of the Female Brain.* New York: Bantam. 2013.

Amichai, Yehuda. *Open Closed Open.* Trans. Chana Bloch. New York: Mariner, 2006.

———. *Selected Poetry.* Trans. Chana Bloch and Stephen Mitchell. Los Angeles: University of California Press, 1994.

Arnot, Robert. *The Biology of Success.* Boston: Little, Brown, 2001.

Barks, Coleman, and John Moyne. *The Essential Rumi.* New York: Harper One, 2004.

Baron-Cohen, Simon. *The Essential Difference.* New York: Basic, 2003.

Barrows, Anita, and Joanna Marie Macy. *Rilke's Book of Hours.* New York: Riverhead, 2005.

Bear, Mark, Barry Connors, and Michael Paradiso. *Neuroscience.* Baltimore: Williams & Wilkins, 1996.

Bennett, Amanda. *The Cost of Hope.* New York: Random House, 2012.

Blum, Deborah. *Sex on the Brain.* New York: Penguin, 1998.

Boston Women's Health Collective. *Our Bodies, Ourselves.* New York: Touchstone, 2005.

Bowlby, John. *A Secure Base.* New York: Basic, 1988.

Bradshaw, John. *Bradshaw On: The Family.* Dearfield Beach, FL: Health Communications, 1988.

Brizendine, Louann. *The Female Brain.* New York: Three Rivers, 2007.

———. *The Male Brain.* New York: Three Rivers, 2010.

Buss, David. *Dangerous Passions.* New York: Free Press, 2011.

———. *The Evolution of Desire.* New York: Basic, 2003.

Carter, Rita. *Mapping the Mind.* Los Angeles: University of California Press, 1998.

Deak, JoAnn. *Girls Will Be Girls.* New York: Hyperion, 2003.

Diamond, Jared. *Guns, Germs, and Steel.* New York: W. W. Norton, 1997.

———. *The Third Chimpanzee.* New York: Harper Perennial, 1992.

Diamond, Jed. *Mr. Mean.* New York: Vox Novus, 2010.

———. *Surviving Male Menopause.* Naperville, IL: Sourcebooks, 2000.

Eisner, Mark, ed. and trans. *The Essential Neruda: Selected Poems.* San Francisco: City Lights, 2004.

Ellington, J.E. *Slippery When Wet.* Spokane: Dr. E Publishing, LLC, 2014.

Faludi, S. *Stiffed: The Betrayal of the American Man.* New York: Harper Perennial, 2000.

Farrell, W. *The Myth of Male Power.* New York: Berkley, 2001.

Fisher, Helen. *Anatomy of Love.* New York: Ballantine, 2000.

Flinders, Carol. *The Values of Belonging.* San Francisco: Harper San Francisco, 2002.

Friedan, B. *The Second Stage.* Cambridge, MA: Harvard University Press, 1981/1998.

Gilmore, David. *Manhood in the Making.* New Haven, CT: Yale University Press, 1990.

Golden, T. R. *Swallowed by a Snake.* Gaithersburg, MD: G H Publishing, 2000.

Goleman, Daniel. *Emotional Intelligence.* New York: Bantam, 1995.

Gottman, John, and Nan Silver. *The Seven Principles for Making a Marriage Work.* New York: Harmony, 2000.

Gurian, J. P., and J. Gurian. *The Dependency Tendency.* New York: Rowman & Littlefield, 1983.

Gurian, M. *The Wonder of Aging.* New York: Atria, 2013.

Gurian, Michael. *The Invisible Presence.* Boston: Shambhala, 2010.

———. *Leadership and the Sexes.* San Francisco: Jossey-Bass/John Wiley, 2008.

———. *Love's Journey.* Boston: Shambhala, 1993.

———. *Nurture the Nature.* San Francisco: Jossey-Bass/John Wiley, 2007.

———. *What Could He Be Thinking?* New York: St. Martin's, 2004.

Haltzman, Scott, with Theresa Foy Digeronimo. *The Secrets of Happily Married Men.* San Francisco: Jossey-Bass/John Wiley, 2006.

Haltzmann, Scott. *The Secret of Surviving Infidelity.* Baltimore: Johns Hopkins University Press, 2013.

Harris, Judith R. *The Nurture Assumption.* New York: Free Press, 1998.

Jantz, Gregory L., with Ann McMurray. *Overcoming Anxiety, Worry, and Fear.* Grand Rapids, MI: Revell, 2011.

Jessel, David, and Anne Moir. *Brain Sex.* New York: Dell, 1989.

Johnson, Stephen. *The Sacred Path.* Los Angeles: Sacred Path, 2012.

Kandel, Eric, James Schwartz, and Thomas Jessell. *Essentials of Neural Science and Behavior.* Norwalk, CT: Appleton & Lange, 1995.

Kaplan, Louise J. *Oneness and Separateness.* New York: Touchstone, 1978.

Kinnell, Galway. *A New Selected Poems.* New York: Mariner, 2001.

Ladinsky, Daniel. *Love Poems from God.* New York: Penguin Compass, 2002.

Legato, Marianne. *Why Men Die First.* New York: Macmillan, 2008.

Moir, Anne, and David Jessel. *Brain Sex.* New York: Laurel, 1990.

Moir, Anne, and Bill Moir. *Why Men Don't Iron.* New York: Citadel, 1999.

Newberg, Andrew, et al. *Why God Won't Go Away.* New York: Ballantine, 2002.

Northrup, Christiane. *The Wisdom of Menopause.* New York: Bantam, 2012.

Oliver, Mary. *New and Selected Poems,* vols. 1 and 2. Boston: Beacon, 2005/2007.

Payne, Ruby. *A Framework for Understanding Poverty.* Highlands, TX: AhaProcess, 2000.

Ratey, John, and Eric Hagerman. *Spark: The Revolutionary New Science of Exercise and the Brain.* New York: Little, Brown, 2008.

Real, Terrence. *I Don't Want to Talk About It.* New York: Fireside, 1997.

Rhoads, Steven E. *Taking Sex Differences Seriously.* San Francisco: Encounter, 2004.

Robbins, John. *Healthy at 100.* New York: Ballantine, 2006.

Roizen, Michael, and Mehmet Oz. *You.* New York: Free Press, 2007.

Roizen, Michael, and Mary Jo Putney. *RealAge.* New York: William Morrow, 1999.

Sewell, Marilyn. *Cries of the Spirit.* Boston: Beacon, 2000.

Siegel, Daniel J. *The Developing Mind.* New York: Guilford, 1999.

Snyderman, Nancy. *Medical Myths That Can Kill You.* New York: Three Rivers, 2009.

Stern, Daniel. *The Motherhood Constellation.* New York: Basic, 1995.

Swami, Abhayanada. *A History of Mysticism.* San Francisco: Watkins, 2002.

Sykes, Bryan. *Adam's Curse.* New York: W. W. Norton, 2003.

Tannen, Deborah. *You Just Don't Understand: Women and Men in Conversation.* New York: Morrow, 1991.

Taylor, Shelley E. *The Tending Instinct.* New York: Times/Henry Holt, 2002.

Thompson, Michael. *Homesick and Happy.* New York: Ballantine, 2012.

Thornhill, R., and S. W. Gangestad. *The Evolutionary Biology of Human Female Sexuality.* New York: Oxford University Press, 2008.

Welwood, John. *Perfect Love, Imperfect Heart.* New York: Trumpeter, 2007.

Winnicott, D. W. *Human Nature.* New York: Schocken, 1988.

Woody, Jane DiVita. *How Can We Talk About That?* San Francisco: Jossey-Bass, 2002.

Wright, Tim. *Searching for Tom Sawyer.* Phoenix: Tim Wright Ministry Press, 2013

Index

ABOUT THE AUTHOR

Michael Gurian is a marriage and family counselor in his twenty-fifth year of private practice and is a *New York Times* bestselling author of twenty-eight books, with more than one million copies in print. The Gurian Institute, which he cofounded in 1996, conducts research internationally, launches pilot programs, and trains professionals. Michael has been called "the people's philosopher" for his ability to bring together people's ordinary lives and scientific ideas.

Gurian provides between twenty and thirty keynotes a year at conferences and provides consulting to community agencies, schools, corporations, physicians, hospitals, and faith communities. He has provided training at NASA, Google, Cisco Systems, Boeing, Frito-Lay/Pepsico, World Presidents Organization, and many organizations, as well as the US Departments of Treasury and Corrections and many other government agencies.

Michael previously taught at Gonzaga University, Eastern Washington University, and Ankara University. His more recent academic speaking engagements include Harvard University, Johns Hopkins University, Stanford University, Morehouse College, the University of Colorado, the University of Missouri–Kansas City, and UCLA. His multicultural philosophy reflects the diverse cultures (European, Asian, Middle Eastern, and American) in which he has lived, worked, and studied.

Gurian's work has been featured multiple times in nearly all the major media, including the *New York Times*, the *Washington Post, USA Today, Newsweek, Time, Psychology Today, AARP Magazine, People, Reader's Digest,* the *Wall Street Journal, Forbes Magazine, Parenting, Good Housekeeping, Family Therapy Magazine, Redbook*, and many others. Gurian has also made multiple appearances on *Today, Good Morning America, CNN, PBS, National Public Radio*, and many others.

Gurian lives in Spokane, Washington, with his wife, Gail, a family therapist in private practice. The couple has two grown daughters, Gabrielle and Davita.

ABOUT THE GURIAN INSTITUTE

The Gurian Institute, founded in 1996, provides professional development, training services, and pilot programs. All of the institute's work is science based, research driven, and practice oriented. The institute has trainers throughout the world. The institute also provides products such as DVDs, books, workbooks, newsletters, and a user-friendly website at www.gurian-institute.com.

The Gurian Institute Corporate Division provides training and consulting in gender diversity for businesses, corporations, and government agencies. This work has inspired the book *Leadership and the Sexes*, which looks at both women and men in our workforce from a gender-science perspective. For more about this work, see www.genderleadership.com.

Michael's personal website is www.michaelgurian.com.